THE COMPLETE MANUAL OF
WOODFINISHING

THE AUTHOR

Photo by A. J. Gigg

THE COMPLETE MANUAL

OF

WOOD FINISHING

FREDERICK OUGHTON

Fellow of the Royal Society of Arts

STOBART & SON LTD
LONDON

FOR EVE

Published 1982 (Hardcover) and 1986 (First paperback edition)
Reprinted 1987

ISBN 0 85442 030 4

Stobart & Son Ltd 67–73 Worship Street London EC2A 2EL

Printed in Great Britain by A. Wheaton & Co. Ltd, Exeter

CONTENTS

1

The Evolution of

Surface Finishes

URNITURE design and surface finish are inseparably linked. Early furniture was built on the very basic principle of fastening planked lengths together, and it was only after the twelfth century that beds, chairs and cupboards were embellished with stereotyped systems of carved pattern. One form of decoration was used in the thirteenth century. In 1245 Henry III 'ordered that the posts in his chamber at Ludgershall should be painted the colour of marble, and ten years later that the pillars and arches of the hall in Guildford Castle should be marbled (marbrai)' (L. F. Salzman FSA: *Building in England*, Clarendon, 1952). Forms of marbling were done in the seventeenth century and continued well into the nineteenth century, and were used principally on tables and commodes.

From the fifteenth century, in the royal and ducal courts in Paris, Burgundy, southern Germany and in the commercial centre at Flanders, decorative panelling became common. During this same period the Flemish introduced linenfold carving, a representation of linen in vertical folds used on chests, presses, panelling and chimneypieces. It was in this period that decorative carving drew its inspiration from architecture and tracery, using oak, elm, walnut, fruitwood and cypress. Until 1700 Spain trod a somewhat different path, influenced by Moorish art. But it had not always been so. In the fifteenth century there was a Flemish influence at work, created by the Dutch woodcarvers. It disappeared following the political alliance between the countries, probably as a result of the carved work of the Mudéjares, the Moors who remained after the fall of Granada in 1492 and renounced Islam. They were talented workers in wood, particularly in the small-scale inlay of geometric patterns. After 1700 changes occurred with the introduction of various types of bargueño, a chest containing many small drawers and decorated externally with inlaid ornament of ivory and precious metals worked by silversmiths and known as plateresque embellishment.

The Renaissance in Italy caused a decline of the European Gothic influence. Surface decoration of chests utilised such materials as parchment, and patrons favoured gilded and painted gesso, much of it executed by professional artists. Gesso, much used in the medieval period, was made with parchment size and whiting, and used for carved decoration. One of the best examples from the period is the Coronation Chair of 1300, now in Westminster Abbey, displaying a wide variety of incised pattern. In Italy walnut was used extensively, where it was carved and polished by a special process to resemble bronze. The surface decorators also excelled at intarsia in which pieces of contrasting woods were inset in geometric patterns or used for the composition of pictorial subjects. The technique spread rapidly from Italy to Holland, where it was applied during a grotesque and bulbous phase of design, doing little enough to enhance it.

The late sixteenth century in Germany witnessed forms of surface decoration which utilised precious materials, including ivory and silver. At Eger in Bohemia a new industry was established, and it produced decorative panels composed of a vast number of woods, including cedar and boxwood. Marquetry revived, this time with the addition of mother-of-pearl, and it was used principally to decorate cabinets which also depicted scenes from contemporary life and mythology. In the seventeenth century red tortoiseshell and ebony were used to achieve an even greater flamboyance, but in the age of the baroque it was surpassed by the introduction of *pietre dure* (Italian, 'hard stones'), a method of mosaic using lapis lazuli, jasper, sardonyx, agate and many other polished stones. The centre of this new industry was Florence, where the tradition of using marquetry to portray floral motifs originated. A factory, started in 1588 by the Grand Duke Ferdinand, continued to operate in the Uffizi until well into the nineteenth century. Table-tops and cabinet panels had a dazzling polychromatic brilliance and found wealthy buyers not only throughout Europe but much wider afield. The Robert Adam cabinet, now in the Victoria and Albert Museum, incorporates a panel made by Baccio Cappelli, a leading craftsman in the Uffizi between 1621 and 1670.

Rome itself had a gilded baroque taste, favouring furniture which was populated, some say infested, with shining tritons, putti and nudes. This extravagant passion progressed to the point where it was practically impossible to detect any purely natural material beneath the visual and physical weight of the surface encrustation. Entire rooms in the palaces of state were decorated not for the purposes of normal occupation or even stiff formal occasions but as huge showcases for monumental pieces of glittering and largely impractical furniture. Visual eccentricity included at least one palace in Genoa, where a tiny gilded throne was placed against a wall occupied by a mass of carved and gilded floriation, like a nighmarish petrified jungle.

In Holland a lighter touch appeared in the art of surface finish, due in no small part to the arrival of woods from the Oriental trade routes, including padouk, kingwood and acacia. These and others provided the craftsmen with new opportunities, not only in the imparting of polished surfaces but also in parquetry, marquetry and inlay. While there was now a new passion for geometrical patterns the traditional strain remained strong and interpreted in wood many of the great masterpieces of the Dutch school of flower painting. Even so, the furniture decorators eschewed the design opulence of the rest of Europe, and their work was in comparison more simple and comparatively austere.

The Dutch were responsible for introducing the innovation of Oriental lacquer late in the seventeenth century. Screens and decorated boards were brought back by traders, the boards being incorporated in otherwise conventional furniture, often without any design considerations. It was the high cost of such sought after items that created a demand, not only in the Netherlands but also elsewhere, and this, in turn, inspired German and Italian entrepreneurs to explore the secrets of lacquer making and application. Cabinets, cupboards and harpsichord cases began to appear, decorated with Continental lacquer. By 1687 the workshops in Berlin, Paris and Venice were engaged in what we would nowadays call mass production with an inevitable lowering of quality. It seemed improbable that Continental craftsmen would be able to emulate the Far Eastern art, which had roots going back to the fourth and third centuries BC. Genuine lacquer called for thirty to thirty-five processes before painting and gilding could be applied. Some of the Continental workshops which lacked facilities started to send furniture to the lacquer shops of China for treatment. In the early eighteenth century, however, the French family of artist-craftsmen, Martin, left their trade of coach painting and developed a form of lacquering to such an extent that by 1748 they had three Paris factories and became famous for the process known as *Vernis Martin*. Some of their finest endeavours were commissioned by La Pompadour for her palace at Bellevue, and substantial orders came from the royal courts of Russia, Portugal and Spain.

From 1660 the influence continued to emanate from France, and is perhaps best exemplified in the Louis XVII cabinet with its carved ebony veneer, but by 1640 the persistent marquetry once again spread through the industry from other parts of Europe with a predominance of the Italian influence. In the design motifs the Saracenic and Arabian arabesque was dominant, expressed in pewter and silver inlays, and polished stone mosaic, and *pietra dure* with its Florentine ancestry. The visual appearance of the Louis XIV period may to our eyes be almost overpowering in its ostentatious opulence, and this is due in part to the introduction of boulle, named after its so-called inventor, André-Charles Boulle (1642–1732). Born in Paris, he was of Swiss origin, the son of a carpenter, and he reached the position of being the foremost cabinet-maker of his day. His work was typified by inlays in tortoiseshell, pewter and brass, but he was also earlier known for the marquetry in which he worked floral designs in imitation of the Antwerp painters. The year 1685 was particularly significant, for it marked the appearance of many examples of his work in which he covered large pieces of furniture with foliage, metal arabesques and red and brown tortoiseshell set in borders of ebony. His gilded ormolu mounts, developed originally to protect the surfaces, gradually took on the role of decoration until they became objects of magnificence in their own right.

Painted furniture created its own demand between 1700 and 1765, but after 1791 the Paris workshops produced ordinary furniture in much larger quantities than before. At least part of the reason for the increased demand was the result of improvements in public housing. Surface finishes were now less individualistic, amounting invariably to nothing more than gilding and polishing, though veneer held its place from 1720, principally because it was a cheap way of covering inferior carcase timbers to give the impression of tulipwood, kingwood and purplewood. Veneer was used by the sheet rather than in ribbons and strips, utilising the grain direction to achieve a solid-wood effect. After 1740 marquetry once more asserted itself, sometimes entirely covering all surface areas. The meticulous attention paid to surface decoration at this time is suggested by reference to Havard's *Dictionnaire de l'Ameublement*, in which it is said that as many as forty native and fifty-seven exotic woods might be used to decorate a typical piece of furniture. The total cost of the piece could be at least £30,000 in terms of modern currency.

The quest for novelty in surface finish caused the French to supplement the range of finishes by introducing such materials as porcelain plaques and tablets, painted glass panels and flakes of mother-of-pearl, all of which enjoyed relatively brief periods of popularity. At one time it was proposed to use the wings of thousands of tropical butterflies as pattern components. The consignment was to be imported at great expense from the East, but there is no record of this grand, if somewhat sick, project ever reaching a successful conclusion. Quite possibly the butterfly wings were reduced to dust while still on the high seas.

Oriental lacquer and gilded wood continued to predominate in Italy where the masters were Piffetti and Bonzanigo. Petro Piffetti (1700–1777) exercised a huge talent for working in ivory, ebony and bronze and an excellence in the art of veneer, using a great number of Oriental woods, hardstones, steel and mother-of-pearl, creating an amalgam of materials which were exemplified in the still extant Tiepolo Room of the Palazzo Clerici in Milan. The furniture of his period resembles sculpture, patterned with painted floral garlands in bright red, green and white, overpainted with a varnish to enrich the toning. A cheaper but still striking imitation of the Piffetti technique was achieved by Enrico Hugford, Abbot of Vallombroso, who used scaglio pastes, made from powered selenite composition, to imitate the *pietra dure* effect.

In contrast to Pifetti, Guiseppe Maria Bonzanigo (1740–1820) designed and built furniture in the neo-classical idiom with painted and gilded surfaces, exploiting a light-coloured spectrum and often adapting the Louis XVI style.

Pietra dure still held its place as a decorative surface finish, no doubt inspired by the workshops and their output. Some time before the late sixteenth century the Grand Duke of Tuscany started workshops in Florence, known as the Opificio delle Pietra Dure, all labour being directed to both raised and flat decoration. A great deal of the output was sent to France, and trade was extremely prosperous, but all the larger examples remained in Italy, many of them becoming features of palace state rooms.

The French taste for rococo found variations elsewhere. In the Rhineland there was a predominance of Belgian and French styling, but in Vienna the light-hearted Italian and Paris tones were evident. Relatively few of the nobility could afford the luxury of this fashionable and highly decorated furniture, much of it enhanced with panels made in Mainz, where a large industry devoted its energies to inlaying large cupboards and cabinets with marquetry.

In 1770 and onwards there occurred a new marriage between lacquer, marquetry and ormolu which found its use in the decoration of the flat and the curved surfaces of classical forms in French furniture. Other countries drew for inspiration on architectural forms. In Germany the parquetry trade exploited geometric designs based on the cube and the rectangle. Its leading exponent was Jean-Francois Oeben (1720–1763), a pupil of the Boulle firm, while his successor, Jean-Henri Riesener (1734–1806), introduced trellis motifs in marquetry. Riesener, cabinet-maker at the Court of Louis XVI, was German, and he served an apprenticeship under Oeben, taking over the workshops on the death of Oeben and marrying the widow. By 1774 he was made Cabinet-maker to the Crown, and his furniture was installed in the royal palaces at Versailles, Fontainbleau, Trianon and Marly. His marquetry remains very individualistic, combining many different woods to portray birds, flowers, emblems and arabesques. It was his habit to veneer the insides of drawers and even the hidden surfaces were covered with marquetry designs. Riesener's fortunes went into a decline when his furniture was priced so highly that he gradually lost all noble patronage.

By 1800 the surface decoration of furniture in France began to fall, due to the impoverishment of the moneyed classes after the Revolution. Veneer, ormolu and marquetry became lost visual pleasures. By 1814 funiture design shifted towards Imperial Rome, but it was drably uniform and relied almost entirely upon plain mahogany veneer for decorative effect. By 1810 some surface finishers were attempting to lighten the dull atmosphere by using such woods as burr-yew, beech, ash and elm. Very little of this furniture was in the luxury class, and the workshops which introduced such innovations eventually closed down for lack of patronage.

Outside France carved side-tables and chairs were invariably gilded on all surfaces, though the Neopolitan furniture of the 1780s was both painted and gilded. In Milan Guiseppe Maglioni introduced a system of using as many as eighty-five different woods to decorate a single piece of furniture but without following the customary trade practice of using stains and dyes to achieve colour contrasts. His marquetry embodied grotesques with bold patterns in great profusion, and incorporated entire landscapes and figures. Unlike many craftsmen, Maglioni signed many of his pieces.

Creating a summary of the immigration of styles through the many periods and influences is understandably difficult, as Herbert Cescinsky found when he wrote his *English Furniture of the Eighteenth Century* (Sadler, 1909). 'This history of the manufactures of a country refuses to conform to periods bounded by centuries, or the duration of the reigns of monarchs, and I have therefore styled the period of the furniture made in England between 1685 and 1800 by the general title of "eighteenth century". The first date is that of the Revocation of the Edict of Nantes which exiled over 40,000 French families, who landed on these shores bringing with them the arts and industries of their own country. From 1685 to 1689 when William the Stadtholder ascended the throne of England, and from thence onwards, the design of English furniture was influenced to a marked and permanent degree. The resulting effect is exceedingly complicated. Certain forms can be traced directly to France and Italy, others have originated from these two countries, or from Spain and Portugal, but filtered through Holland and Flanders, becoming strongly tinged with details of the Dutch and Flemish Renaissance. In the Low Countries, the scene for many years of fierce strife between the Dutch, the Spanish, and the French, with Spain supreme from 1555 to 1584, it was inevitable that the influence of Spain to a major degree, and Portugal to a lesser one, should have left an indelible imprint on the furniture of Holland, this being in turn transmitted to England by the Dutch workmen who followed William

III to this country. We have therefore to trace not only the effect of the direct introduction of French, Italian and Spanish forms on English furniture of this period, but also the same transmuted through Dutch and Flemish hands.'

One of the natural incongruities of the history and the development of wood finishing is that most of the niceties of surface enhancement were imported into England, which played the role of the catalyst rather than that of the originator. Before the period to which Cescinsky refers in his great work, the scene was perhaps very primitive. After 1540 the oak panel and frame method of furniture construction did little enough to beautify the appearance of the material itself, and it was some time before joinery as we know it was practised to any great extent, reliance being placed almost entirely on the simple mortise and tenon joint, which followed the original nailing and pegging, a common cause of splitting when unseasoned wood was used. In the fifteenth-century the start of surface decoration was heralded by the arrival of linenfold carving. Finer examples, culled very often from the predominant Antwerp school, were sometimes darkened and then waxed. But it was the trade of the cofferer which attracted the patronage of the wealthy. It was his business to cover furniture with painted parchment, treated animal skins, damask and silken fabrics.

It was Henry VIII's enthusiastic interest in what we have come to call the Classical Revival, and the importation of Italian craftsmen, which resulted, in the early sixteenth century, in a veritable flood of Romayne work. This was the incorporation in furniture of carved small profile-heads in medallions, sometimes combined with Tudor roses, gothic tracery and linenfold. The phase lasted until the Reformation and for the century which followed 1530 the surface decoration of English furniture was dominated by certain trends in the Protestant areas of Germany and the Low Countries. The painting and covering of surface areas was in decline to be replaced by a richness of ornamental carving on which oil and wax finishes which were used to reach the characteristically deep sheen and the darkening of the light-coloured oak. All this was in direct contrast to English furniture prior to the fifteenth century, when many pieces were brightly and even garishly painted, the purpose being to protect the often inferior wood rather than as a means of artistic expression.

In 1660, when Charles II was restored to the throne, a new injection of ideas occurred with the arrival in England of master craftsmen from Holland, some of them French by nationality. They brought with them a typical ebullience and brilliance of execution. The monarch's desire for luxury and his often reckless attitude towards state spending was to lead, however indirectly, to innovations in housing. Dwellings were now brick-built with large sash windows and airy rooms with ample light, their walls and ceilings being painted in bright and bold colours. This volte-face in domestic environment caused a wholesale banishing of the old and traditional heavy oak furniture to be replaced by much lighter furniture, veneered and often embellished with hand-painted scenes from the countryside and the hunting field, and enriched with marquetry and parquetry in laburnum, olive and walnut. There was also a reappearance of the Chinese lacquer brought originally to England by the merchantmen of the East India Company.

At this time the craft of surface finishing was surrounded by secrecy, and it was encouraged by the Continental craftsmen who naturally wished to safeguard their livelihood, but there was at least one attempt to encourage the amateur to practise lacquering, known in its English version as japanning. It appeared in the form of an illustrated book by John Stalker and George Parker under the title *A Treatise of Japanning* and it was first published in 1688. What the authors could not know was that their instructional tome moved right outside the amateur sphere to directly inspire a whole new industry in which japanning gave employment to a large number of people. Japanning uses a ground of white, yellow, blue, green, black or red. A tough film is laid with multiple coats of varnish made from shellac and spirit. This is polished with tripoli powder made from rottenstone or broken-down siliceous limestone. The decoration is applied, either painted or else inlaid in metallic shapes. The tradesmen of the time were vastly encouraged, for they had only recently forced Parliament to impose exorbitant tariffs on imported lacquer, as a result of which the English lacquer, or japanning, trade was now achieving prosperity. What more natural than to directly imitate the Oriental designs while using a home-grown process?

From 1702 the technique of polishing the popular walnut reached perfection, and it continued to 1714 and the reign of Queen Anne. Surface finishing now had a new importance, and it was brought to a fresh prominence by the introduction of new types of furniture, such as the bookcase, actually recorded in the first instance in Samuel Pepys' diary in July 1666. Apart from surface finish there was also decoration proper, seen to the greatest advantage in 'grandfather' or long case clocks and the table, or portable, timepieces which were produced up to 1704, when many of Thomas Tompion's long-cases were covered with a profusion of marquetry. Tompion (1639–1713), said to be the greatest clock-maker of all times and all countries, was not himself a cabinet-maker, of course, and it now seems likely that the most outstanding cases made to accommodate his mechanisms were manufactured in work-shops near his premises in Water Lane, Fleet Street, London, in turn setting the style for the French master, Antoine Foulet, who flourished in 1749 in Paris and produced the Louis XV marquetry long-case, later to become the French leader in clock-case design.

Clock cases had for some years provided cabinet-makers with opportunities for virtuoso performances as far as design and surface finish were concerned. Early cases were made of oak and a veneer of walnut, olive wood, laburnum, kingwood and ebony, and some decoration was gilded metal or even gold. By the time Edward East was made Chief Clockmaker and Keeper of the Privy Clocks in 1662 the ebony veneer was common, and there was a fashion for walnut inlaid with herring-bone lines and a cross-banded border. But by the early eighteenth century the age of the highly ornate case was at an end, to be replaced by conventional walnut veneer and minor banding inlay.

Despite the increase of interest in the natural beauty of walnut and other woods, the more traditional gilded decoration held persistent sway to remain predominant well into the Georgian period, 1714–1830. In this golden age of English furniture the main reason for the resurgence of taste can be attributed to the enlightenment of the clients who patronised the individual craftsmen. Nobility could not claim to have come of age until they had completed the Grand Tour and studied classical antiquities. By the time they had been educated and indulged in the delights of travel they could not avoid developing a certain taste, however elitist it might seem to our eyes. They knew what they wanted, and they found the craftsmen who could guide them and meet their demands. By this time a wide array of fine woods was available for the realisation of their dreams. In the three new phases of baroque, neo-classical and rococo many woods were pressed into service, and yet one, mahogany, remained predominant. After 1725 and the suspension of import duties large quantities of this king of woods began to reach England. Even the previously favoured walnut went out of fashion because it was believed that mahogany was more durable and workable with the additional advantage of yielding such attractive figuring as fiddleback, curls, feathers and mottle when cut as a veneer. It could also be used in heavy plank form for table-tops and cupboards. It required less staining than other woods because it had a naturally rich red appearance which could be coaxed into being with uncomplicated wax polishing. In the meantime the boom in mahogany furniture was fed by the consignments which continued to arrive from America, the West Indies, San Domingo, Jamaica and, best of all, from Honduras and Cuba.

At this time English furniture was of pleasant size and dimension, it fell into an eminently splendid liaison with its environment, and now, for the first time in many years, the surface finish was in accord with design. This was due in part to the influence of William Kent (1685–1748) and his patron, the Earl of Burlington, who was having an affair with the Palladian style of architecture and eventually seduced Kent into following the almost overbearing largeness and sad vulgarity of the baroque in which the furniture surfaces were covered with grotesques, shells and leonine masks. It was one of the Earl's fundamental weaknesses that he wanted too much of everything in full evidence, though he did show a contrast in his somewhat more austere taste in architecture. Some of Kent's commissioned furniture was so encrusted and laden down with decoration that very little of the base mahogany could be seen. Certainly, Kent was discouraged from exploiting the veneer which had its own quieter virtues, although he did somehow achieve the distinction of being the first English architect to consider furniture as interior decoration.

If Kent had one patron of long standing, Chippendale had many of them who were gathered together by his publishing activities which provided literally hundreds of craftsmen with the opportunity to copy his style. Thomas Chippendale (1718–1779) promoted designs which at that time appeared idiosyncratic but nevertheless fashionable, but they undoubtedly contributed greatly to surface finishing, notably by a much more restrained use of gilt and colouring than Kent ever managed. It may well be that he actually reversed many of the heavy-handed trends set by Kent. Chippendale's *Gentleman and Cabinet-Maker's Directory* first appeared in 1754 and then again in 1755, and it was revised and enlarged in 1762, and while it was not wholly and entirely the work of Chippendale himself, it nevertheless set the 'Chippendale' style and quickly became an almost universal source of inspiration. Towards the end of the period of rococo in the 1750s John Linnell (1737–1796) appeared. A cabinet-maker, carver and designer, he may well have extended the life of rococo with his bold and vigorous ideas, many of which are available for inspection at the Victoria and Albert Museum, London. It was due to Chippendale's influence that he created the Chinese Bedroom at Badminton.

William Vile (d.1767) was another London master who played a role in the short period of rococo, using gilt and heavy carving to a point of visual oppression. Yet later on in his career Vile became restrained to the point of being non-committal. He used mahogany in such a way that reliance was placed upon polished surfaces rather than on the types of decoration which had in previous years created so much distraction.

Under the sustained impact of several different phases of development and the whims of fashion, furniture began to fall into a state of gracelessness, and it seemed that the patrons of the craftsmen never seriously considered the question of its utility. They required something to look at rather than use, something to boast about. It was some years before the wood was permitted to speak for itself. Even so, the material did have its own champions, including George Smith who in 1808 published *A Collection of Designs for Household Furniture*. In his preface he stated: 'I have great pleasure in declaring, that very extensive and liberal encouragement has of late been given by our Nobility and Gentry to various artists in manufacturing cabinet-work, the good effects of which will, I doubt not, soon be felt in bringing forward a supply of able workmen, and in promoting an increase of skill and taste in their several departments: for as the beauty of the Antique consists in the purity of design, and what was pleasing centuries ago continues to be equally so now; so I do not despair of seeing a style of Furniture produced in this country, which shall be equally agreeable centuries hence.

'The following practical observations on the various woods employed in cabinet-work may be useful. Mahogany, when used in houses of consequence, should be confined to the Parlor and Bedchamber Floors; in furniture for these apartments the less inlay of other woods; the more chaste will be the style of work; if the wood be of a fine, compact, and bright quality, the ornaments may be carved clean in the mahogany; where it may be requisite to make out pannelling by an inlay of lines, let those lines be of brass or ebony. In Drawing Rooms, Boudoirs, Anti Rooms, or other dressed apartments, East and West India satinwoods, rose-wood, tulip-wood, and other varieties of woods brought from the East, may be used; with satin and light-coloured woods the decorations may be of ebony or rose-wood; with rose-wood let the decorations be *ormolu* and the inlay of brass; bronzed metal, though sometimes used with satin-wood has a cold and poor effect; it suits better on gilt wood and will answer well enough on mahogany.'

Smith was so specific that he must have been inspired by somebody or something, and it could have been Robert Adam (1728–1792). The architect and furniture designer, who returned from Italy in 1758, set up an architectural practice in London with his three brothers to introduce a neo-classical style of decoration based on what had been seen in Italy. It was followed in 1772 by designs for a range of Etruscan furniture, again inspired by the Italian tour and using colours derived from Greek vases. Adam shunned any hint of heaviness to achieve a harmony between gilded and painted decoration of both room interiors and the furniture itself. He relied principally on the lighter-coloured woods mentioned by Smith and now and then the contrast provided by ormolu on a plain mahogany background.

Thomas Sheraton (1751–1806) finally managed to extinguish what has been called the 'stiff artificiality' of Adam, although he did pursue similar ideas in the London workshops which he set up in 1790 after his earlier years at Stockton-on-Tees. He achieved the distinction of giving a new complexion to the natural tones of mahogany and satinwood, his surface finishes on furniture produced between 1790 and 1805 being restrained and not as flamboyant as that of his contemporaries. It was Sheraton who disclosed further trade secrets with particular attention to surface finishing in his 1803 *The Cabinet Dictionary, containing an explanation of all the terms used in the Cabinet, Chair and Upholstery branches, with directions for varnishing, polishing and gilding.* With its 88 engravings and a detailed text, the publication put into the hands of the reader not only design and construction modes but also many surface finishing techniques hitherto unknown to those outside the trade. If he was not entirely original in his designs for Directoire furniture, culled from the French transitional style between Louis XVI neo-classicism and Empire, the 1793–1804 period, his notes on surface finishing were, and still are, invaluable.

The business of publishing designs and revealing methods of ornamentation and surface finishing did not start with Sheraton or Chippendale. George Heppelwhite (d.1786) came from Lancaster to London, where he founded his own firm in 1760. It was his widow, Alice, who brought out the handsome folio, *The Cabinet-maker and Upholsterer's Guide* in 1788, consisting of 123 engravings showing 260 types of furniture. A second edition appeared in 1789 and a third in 1794. While impressive in its scope, the Guide did not exactly innovate design, but it can be said that it did much to enhance and bring to the attention of craftsmen the possibilities of restraint in wood surface decoration. By sheer coincidence Lancaster, birthplace of Heppelwhite, can claim another distinction, for it was the site of the Gillow factory which in the early part of this century specialised in fine quality reproduction furniture, from a stool to an Elizabethan-style hall. Detractors of Gillows pointed out that the same firm also made mangles.

Certain woods have enjoyed a vogue at certain times, governed as a rule by their fortuitous availability. The Regency (1811–1820), for instance, had an ample supply of the close-grained rosewood with its fine texture and good working qualities. But other exotic woods were now common, including the light brown amboyna from the East Indies, dark brown zebra wood from South America, striped and mottled calamander from the East Indies and many of the sixty varieties of mahogany, decorated with metal inlays in the Egyptian and Greek styles. In many ways the Regency was a precursor of Early Victorian with such items as grand pianos inlaid with brass, and parlour furniture decorated with brass beading, scrolling and floral motifs. There was overall a growing clumsiness which may have been coincidental with the use of oak, which was highly stained and polished. Where tropical woods had previously been favoured as veneers, the demand was now for home-grown wood, fashioned in many instances by ornamental turning and wax polishing. Despite this, the Regent himself was influenced by George Smith's designs, mentioned earlier, and after the Bourbon restoration he inspired what amounted to a sweeping revival of Louis XIV and Louis XV furniture, all heavily gilded and full of sinuous forms with stump legs and a thickset appearance. It was a regressive step which did not last very long.

The urge to over-decorate furniture created by what amounted to industrial processes as distinct from hand craftsmanship coincided with the Great Exhibition of 1851, and a new commercial initiative, which sprang from a growing demand for cheapness and availability. These were the factors which contributed in no small way to a decline in design and appearance. Victorian showiness and the tendency of designers to gather together examples from all periods in order to impress was responsible for all that was fundamentally bad about the period. When Franz Sales Meyer's *Handbook of Ornament*, known as the 'Victorian Bible of Design', was first published in English in 1894 it contained more than 3,000 illustrations in 300 plates, and it provided manufacturers with virtually ready-made ideas. In his Foreword to a 1974 reprint Tony Birt commented: 'Undoubtedly Morris would have disapproved of Meyer, not for his well-intentioned labours to present systematically and elegantly the elements of decoration, but because he made it easy for designers mindlessly to apply and misapply the ornament of the past instead of seeking new principles as guidelines, and at a time when confusion in design both architectural and domestic was as its height.'

Confusion there certainly was, but it should be said that a few people were attempting to purify Victorian Gothic, and among them was A. W. Pugin (1812–1852), who tried to revert to the medieval as exemplified in the interior of the Houses of Parliament and in the Medieval Court which he designed for the Great Exhibition.

The desire to create what commentators insisted on calling an 'age of purity' was strong. It was an idealistic William Morris (1834–1896) who wrote: 'Everything which was made by man's hand (in the Middle Ages) was more or less beautiful . . . almost all wares that are made by civilised man are shabbily and pretentiously ugly.' Founder, with others, of the Arts and Crafts Movement, Morris was the universal man with influence in many spheres. Between them, Morris' co-workers produced a large range of furniture, most of it Gothic in concept and all of it relying upon the indivisible partnership of line and decoration, and best demonstrated in the 1860s and 1870s by the work of Bruce James Talbert (1838–1881), William Burges (1827–1881) and Charles Locke Eastlake (1836–1906), using medieval and Jacobean motifs. The move in this period was towards furniture in which the wood was totally obscured by painted decoration. In pale imitation of the Morris industry, the Omega workshop was set up in 1913 by Roger Fry (1866–1934) with the object of producing painted furniture and other articles. Certain members of the Bloomsbury Group were closely associated with it, but in 1919 it closed down due to lack of enthusiasm amongst its craftsmen. Omega products were not especially noteworthy.

The 1882 establishment of the Arts and Crafts Movement had the irony of isolating the craftsman so that he personally made very little commercial progress because he was held in check by either Morris himself or by the Morris legend. Individual craftsmen resented Morris to some degree because he was dominating the market and, some said, thrusting his designs down the throats of the public. This was in some contrast to the vociferous group founded by Morris which was in a strong position to promote itself and prosper.

Elsewhere, the Century Guild, established by Mackmurdo (1851–1942), a Scottish architect and designer who was much influenced by Morris, made furniture based on the designs of the eighteenth century. There was also cottage furniture marketed under the label of the Cotswold School. Surface finishing was remarkably restrained to such an extent that some of it actually looked unfinished.

Celtic imagery also contributed to furniture design and surface decoration. 'The Four', Charles Rennie Mackintosh (1868–1928), Herbert MacNair (1868–1955) and the sisters, Margaret Macdonald (1865–1933) and Frances Macdonald (1874–1921) shared talents in architecture, metalwork, jewellery and embroidery. Mackintosh and MacNair designed furniture at the Glasgow School of Art and the Macdonald sisters provided the surface decoration in leaded glass, embroideries, painted gesso panels and repoussé metal panels. The style of decoration and, indeed, the design of the furniture itself, is frequently termed Art Nouveau, but this is incorrect, for surface decoration is minimal yet still has an undeniable attractiveness. If London failed to acknowledge The Four, their influence was considerable on the Continent, notably in Vienna.

Art Nouveau itself first appeared in 1890, and it destroyed any idea that wood was finally to be given a chance of showing its inherent beauty. The movement was a conscious attempt to create new style as a reply to mid-nineteenth historically-based tradition. Based on natural styles drawn from the flora and fauna of Britain and the decorative Japanese genre, it attempted to cover and dominate the entire surface. Some counteraction was provided by C. F. A. Voysey (1857–1941), the architect and furniture designer, who became Master of the Art Workers' Guild in 1924. His philosophy, akin to that of Morris, stressed the importance of simplicity, and there is little doubt that Ernest Gimson (1864–1931), architect and worker in metal, plaster and embroidery, reinforced the contentions of both. Gimson joined W. R. Lethaby (1857–1931) to set up a workshop in the Cotswolds with Sidney Barnsley (1865–1926) and Ernest Barnsley (1863–1926). The firm was called Kenton and Company, and from it came Windsor chairs and other furniture, all of it notable not only for its rural simplicity but also a natural finish achieved by the action of oil, wax and friction.

Gimson, Lethaby and the Barnsleys were not alone in producing plain and attractive furniture. In London Sir Ambrose Heal (1872–1959) pursued the trail of the Arts and Crafts Movement and in 1898 influenced public taste with his Plain Oak Furniture catalogue. His surface finishes were wax rather than oil. Unlike many of his contemporaries, he chose not to shun the machine but preferred to go into partnership with it while still retaining all the elements of good design.

In France the Art Nouveau philosophy was modified. The ideal of 'truth to materials' was thwarted by furniture designers who treated ideas as though they were intended as sculpture, even going to the length of making clay maquettes, or models, and then employing carvers to create the final version. The result was some furniture with incredibly sinuous forms which were, in turn, implanted upon other forms. The workshops at Nancy used marquetry, adorning surfaces with representations of the cow parsley and thistles of the region. Emile Gallé (1846–1904), who led Art Nouveau in France and was a founder of the Nancy School, went to the lengths of designing a complete bedroom inlaid with cow parsley themes and a series of fretwork sprays. Once more the French tradition of earlier years was asserting itself, for very few flat surfaces were left uninterrupted by marquetry. But this sort of thing was not practised by all the followers of Art Nouveau in France. The cabinet-maker, Louis Marjorelle (1858–1926), revolted against surface decoration and contested the trends which stemmed from Gallé. He wrote: 'The first need of a piece of furniture is to seek a healthy structure capable of inspiring a sense of harmony and such that the essential lines should have an architectural sense of elegant proportion. Whatever the function of a piece of furniture, the craftsman must ensure that the lines can exist without decoration. The richness of a piece of furniture should owe nothing to a surfeit of decoration – elegant lines and handsome proportions should suffice.' Loud though it was, Marjorelle's voice was not strong enough, and by 1906 he had lost his position as an arbiter of taste. This may have been due to the oppressive activities of Samuel Bing, an impresario of sorts who provided patronage for large numbers of craftsmen and designers, pratically all of whom favoured a full surface decoration. They included the cabinet-maker, George de Feure, who specialised in what can only be described as 'feminine' finishes, best exemplified in the giltwood screen with panels painted in pastels, showing graceful women walking with greyhounds.

England's lead in Art Nouveau in the 1890s and even earlier was soon relinquished. Belgium was able to produce a number of designers and craftsmen, including Gustave Serrurier-Bovy (1858–1910), Henry van de Velde (1863–1947) and Victor Horta (1861–1947), practically all of whom employed the fine-grained woods from the Congo. They included new types of mahogany and citrus used in conjunction with beech and oak, and with a sparing use of decoration, though Henry van de Velde, self-taught and occasionally wildly idiosyncratic, did produce white lacquered furniture while working in Germany.

Early furniture design and surface finishing in America were more or less in parallel with those which prevailed in England and the Continent. A suitable starting point for present purposes is the seventeenth century, during which period the furniture was commonly based on the box-shape. It was cumbersome and lacking even a rude peasant style, although turned sections did provide some visual alleviation, being confined to legs, backposts, stretchers and rungs, much of it lightly carved but with little attention paid to surface finish. Even so, there was still a large amount of furniture which had its roots in the possessions of the first English settlers, who arrived between 1586 and 1603 and in the cargoes of the *Mayflower* and *Speedwell* in 1620. The carved oak furniture of the period was utilitarian rather than decorative, and between 1675 and 1740 there was a demand for chests, known to us as 'Hadley' chests and named after the area in which they were made. The emphasis from 1650 was more upon carved furniture than upon decorative finish. This continued until the eighteenth century, when the merchant firms of the east coast imported furniture from Spain, Holland, Italy and China, much of it for the moneyed classes. By this time the native American craftsmen were able to exercise their émigré tastes, and they produced fine examples of cabinet-making, using walnut with veneers of cherry, apple and a great number of other fruitwoods. Elegance bloomed during the William and Mary and the Queen Anne periods, when the close-grained walnut was used to innovate design, probably best typified in the 'highboy', which consisted of a chest of drawers on a stand.

The American influence demonstrated itself in many ways, including the surface decoration of the Windsor chair, brought originally from England in 1700 to reach a major place by 1736 as an item of furnishing, when it was often ebonised or simply painted black or apple green, with a series of multicoloured lines to delineate its graceful profile.

But it was the Revolution of 1775–1783 that created another upheaval, throwing up many entirely English styles executed in American woods. This actually happened between 1790 and 1825, and the driving forces were the design books of Heppelwhite and Sheraton, whose ideas were often modified by such designer cabinet-makers as Samuel McIntyre (1757–1811), who was largely responsible for bringing Adam's neo-classical designs to America. He is nowadays better known for developing the Federal style of architecture in New England, and it was from this that the inlaid and carved satinwood and mahogany cabinet and writing tables, secretaires and commodes developed. Here and there the Heppelwhite styles were made, but without any surface decoration and entirely exploiting the mahogany. McIntyre had many accomplished contemporaries, but it was the American trade practice to operate through a series of agents, who located craftsmen such as John Seymour, with workshops in Boston from 1794. His form of surface decoration included the painting of compartment interiors and a widespread marquetry which used a vast number of woods to form a half-ring inlay pattern on top edges. It was this wide choice of woods which enabled the American craftsmen to enhance the traditions of Chippendale and Heppelwhite. Cuban mahogany, for instance, provided a unique surface finish, flecked as it was with white marks, like chalk particles embedded in the pores. Some phases and fashions lasted for only a very brief time. A fickle public did not much care for cherrywood which, together with Virginian walnut, dominated the market for many years. When wood was displayed, it had to be perfect and without any imperfections.

By the second half of the eighteenth century a great deal of furniture making was mechanised, but if the products were depressingly plain, the very plainness encouraged decoration. Lambert Hitchcock (1795–1852), of English descent, started a factory at Barkhamsted in western Connecticut in 1818, adding to it in 1826, but by 1829 he was bankrupt and practically forced to go into partnership with his former employee, Alba Alford, until 1843. He then started his own furniture factory at Unionville. His chairs were birch or maple, and his early products were painted to look like rosewood or ebony. To disguise their kitchen-plainness, he also painted them yellow and added stencilled patterns of fruit and flowers. Other models had inlaid brass as a reminder of the Regency and Federal styles. He employed women and children to apply the background colour, and trained older children to pick out patterns and the ring turning on the legs with gilt. If credit is to be given to any single entrepreneur for bringing decorated furniture to the masses in America, then it must go to Lambert Hitchcock and his $1.50 chairs.

Certain schools of furniture led to the making of individual reputations almost despite themselves, and nowhere was this more strong than in the luxurious furniture produced by the Quaker concerns of the Goddards and Townsends in Newport, Rhode Island, and Savery in Philadelphia in the eighteenth and nineteenth centuries. Intermarried, their work continued through twenty members from three generations, providing not only designers and cabinet-makers but also innovators of the surface finish, using all manner of fine oils and varnishes to achieve results.

There is some irony in the fact that of all American furniture the products of the Shakers remain predominant, although they banned beadings, mouldings and cornices. The Shakers were founded as a religious sect by Mother Ann Lee, who left England for the Colonies in 1774. By 1860 the sect had fifteen settlements with 6,000 members in

New England, New York, Ohio and Kentucky. Mother Ann instructed: 'Do all your work as though you had a thousand years to live, and as you would know you must die tomorrow.' It was this kind of philosophy of excellence which undoubtedly influenced Shaker furniture making at a time when there was pride in honourable work. Old pine, maple, cherry, pear, apple and walnut were used for chairs, beds, presses, washstands and much more besides. The craftsmen believed that the designs were conceived in heaven and transmitted by angels. Looking at them today, one might well agree for they have the three qualities of regularity, harmony and order. Because the Shakers were permitted no excesses of any kind, the surface finish was simply oiled, waxed or faintly coloured or tinted, while the beauty of the wood was unconcealed. At the height of their commercial operations, the Shakers sold rocking chairs in 1828 for $2.50, while straight chairs sold for 75 cents in 1807. Nowadays the virile Shaker tradition of furniture making and finishing still maintains a predominant position, although the sect itself has been reduced to only four members, all women, in Maine. (For the brief technical note on Shaker finishes see Chapter 34).

Thirty years into the nineteenth century the Roman, Greek and Eygptian decoration of the Empire style began to supersede other styles. Heavily gilded columns and caryatids in marble and brass provided additional decoration. Duncan Phyfe (1768–1854) had been the leading late eighteenth century figure in furniture design and manufacture. Of Scottish descent, he went into partnership with the French immigrant cabinet-maker, Charles-Honoré Lannuier (1779–1819). Their New York workshop produced some of the most handsome pieces in the Directoire and Empire styles, based for the most part on the design books of Sheraton and using the metal mounts brought to America from France and using all the traditional forms of marquetry and surface polishing. There was still a certain amount of scope for more alien forms. For instance, this advertisement appeared on 8 November 1805, in the *Federal Gazette and Commercial Daily Advertiser:* 'Elegant, fancy Japanned Furniture . . . all colours, gilt ornamented and varnished in a style only equalled on the continent . . . with real views, Fancy landscapes, Flowers, Trophies of Music, War, Husbandry, Love, etc.' Painted furniture of all kinds flooded the market until 1820 and then it died.

The Victorian period in America was heavily marked by a series of infusions of ideas from the major exhibitions which were held with some frequency in London, Paris, Vienna and Philadelphia, and yet no truly native style emerged from the wooden torrent. The most noticeable development was the number of novelty finishes which were demanded by the store owners, whose stock was factory made and then conveyed to be surface finished in workshops run by the store. The leader in the trade was John Belter (1804–1863), a German-born and trained cabinet-maker who settled in New York and became successful from 1844 to 1863, building much of his gigantic fortune on polished rosewood and a form of furniture construction based on the lamination of layers of wood which gave strength and decorative effect at one and the same time. His early output was, however, in the traditional rococo style with Continental carving and gilded surfaces. It fell to an Englishman to unwittingly react against it. Charles Locke Eastlake (1836–1906) published his *Hints on Household Furniture, Upholstery and Other Details*, which led to the production of furniture in what came to be called 'Eastlake Style', based on medieval and Jacobean designs. But the new simplicity failed to hold its ground. Millionaire buyers exerted both their will and their chequebooks to such an extent that by the 1890s the scene was once again reversed. The mansions of the very wealthy closely resembled Versailles with acres of carved and gilded wood in a spirited attempt to cling to what were considered to be the old and trusted values in a period which commentators have since stigmatised as 'stagnant traditionalism'. It continued throughout the Twenties and into the Thirties with only brief revivals of interest in other modes of design, most of it sheer faddist.

In the period up to World War Two it was in Europe where the majority of experiments were conducted, marked most prominently by Scandinavia's work with plywood, a material which demanded new forms of finish, such as lacquer. Curvilinear furniture made from single pieces became possible, while such woods as alder, birch, ash, oak, redwood, Douglas fir, gum, maple and others presented the surface finisher with all kinds of possibilities.

In reality, however, lamination was not really a modern invention. It had a very long history, stretching back to the time when it was used for bedstead headpieces in Ancient Egypt, examples of which were discovered in the tombs of the Pharaohs by archaeologists.

Since the end of World War Two the furniture manufactures have used a host of non-wooden materials, including steel, leather and plastics, but several attempts have been made to re-explore traditional materials, including the wooden chairs of the Finnish designer, Alvar Aalto (b.1898) which were first exhibited in London as early as 1931. In his later years Aalto demonstrated the possibilities of laminated wooden strips as part of the design, using the lighter coloured woods with contrasting finishes.

Hand-crafted furniture in which the surface finish plays as important a part as the design itself has gained some ground since the end of World War Two. If there is any criticism of this it is that the products are expensive and invariably far beyond the means of the ordinary person. On the other hand, there has been a refreshing move towards design refinement and sheer craftsmanship, shown in the work of Finn Juhl,

Hans Wegner, Peder Oos in Denmark, Adolf Loos in Vienna, Gerrit Rietveld in Holland, Eero Saarinen and Charles Eames in America, and, more recently, in Britain by John Makepeace, whose Dorset workshops provide a sound and solid apprenticeship in which the pupil has the opportunity not only of studying design and manufacture but also marketing and general commercial practice.

When the plan and the purpose of this book were first discussed with the publisher, it was felt that the finished work should provide a bench manual for both the amateur and the professional. It was agreed that when any historical background was found to be necessary in order to explain the nature of a particular wood finishing process, then it should be included. But when the entire field of wood finishing and furniture is examined in close detail, a kind of continuity is apparent. That explains why this introductory chapter is an extension of the original idea and an exploration of the twin roots of design and surface embellishment.

For the rest, this is a practical book.

*   *   *

In the beginning there was simple polishing . . .

Beeswax and common turpentine were mixed together and used as a polish up to the beginning of the seventeenth century, to be followed by spirit varnish, which imparted a hard finish capable of hard wear and providing a glossy polish.

The appearance of English furniture was described by François de la Rochefoucauld in his *Mélanges sur l'Angleterre* of 1748: 'The chairs and tables are also made of mahogany of fine quality and have a brilliant quality like that of finely tempered steel.'

In the workshops many of the trade secrets about surface finishing were closely guarded, but in his *Cabinet Dictionary* of 1803 Sheraton did describe some of the processes; and he made no bones about the fact that in the case of inferior furniture only the front was polished, leaving the back in a very rough condition. Beeswax, one of the main agents, was applied with cork pads, using finely sieved brickdust. The finishing itself was done with a soft wax mixed with red oil to heighten the natural colour of the mahogany. In the general run, however, linseed oil and brick dust was applied. Sheraton stressed the necessity for allowing the oil time to permeate . . . 'if the wood be hard, the oil should be left standing upon it for a week; but if soft it may be polished in two days. The brick-dust and oil should then be rubbed together, which in a little time will become a putty under the rubbing cloth, in which state it should be kept under the cloth as much as possible; for this kind of putty will infallibly secure a fine polish by continued rubbing; and the polisher should by all means avoid the application of fresh brick-dust, by which the unskilful hand will frequently ruin his work instead of improving it; and to prevent the necessity of supplying himself with fresh brick-dust he ought to pay on a great quantity at first, carefully sifted through a gauze stocking; and he should notice if the oil be too dry on the surface of the work before he begin, for in this case it should be re-oiled, that it may compose a sufficient quantity of the polishing substances, which should never be altered after the polishing is commenced, and which ought to continue till the wood by repeated friction become warm, at which time it will finish in a bright polish, and is finally to be cleared off with the bran of wheaten flour.

'Chairs are generally polished with a hardish compostion of wax rubbed upon a polishing brush, with which the grain of the wood is impregnated with the composition, and afterwards rubbed off without any dust or bran. The composition I recommend is as follows: take bees wax and a small quantity of turpentine in a clean earthware pan, and set it over a fire till the wax unites with the turpentine, which it will do by constant stirring about; add to this a little red leaf finely ground upon a stone, together with a small portion of fine Oxford ochre, to bring the whole to the colour of brisk mahogany. Lastly, when you take it off the fire, add a little copal varnish to it, and mix it well together, then turn the whole into a bason of water, and while it is yet warm, work it into a ball with which the brush is to be rubbed as before observed. And observe, with a ball of wax and brush kept for this purpose entirely, furniture in general may be kept in good order.'

2

Wood Structure & Characteristics

Species; Drying; Defects

PAINT can be applied to practically anything, but a good wood finish must take into account the nature and the sensitivity of the material itself in its many varieties. It would be ignorant and short sighted to suggest that practically any wood finish can be applied to any wood with startling success. At the same time, there remains a vast area for experiment providing the craftsman knows something about the nature of wood, its growth, its seasoning and its various ills. This chapter deals with such matters.

Experimental surface finishing is not something which is usually indulged in by professional wood finishers. They have to create finishes according to the dictates of tradition. Thus, oak is finished in a particular way, and mahogany is finished in another. Craftsmen who follow this trade are hampered by trade practices, as a consequence of which there is a lack of innovation. The customer expects the modern surface finish to mirror tradition. If any note of criticism is to be injected into the argument then it must be that craftsmen seldom if ever attempt to introduce customers to alternative possibilities. It is in direct contrast to, say, the French craftsmen of the eighteenth century who successfully interested the patrons of their day in the idea of painted wood. As it happened, this was a move which brought about a wave of true artistry, for it was the painter who became instrumental in creating some of the finest harpsichord cases and the decoration of other musical instruments, exemplified in the japanned case and chinoiseries on the Pascal Taskin harpsichord, made in Paris in 1786 and now in the Victoria and Albert Museum, London.

Although the present chapter is concerned with the physical structure and ailments of timber, it is not intended to be anything like a heavy-handed yardstick to which the reader must adhere with grimness and determination in relation to what he should or should not do. A surface finish can have its own perfection independently of the wood to which it is applied. If there is any inference to be drawn, then it is that a particular surface finish must have its own quite unique perfection, achieved by adapting a series of techniques, some of which will have their own tradition with roots in the established practices of workshops long gone, or else they will be modifications of the old methods. As we have already inferred, the choice of surface finish is generally dictated by the customer if the craftsman is working on a commercial basis. If he is working for himself, then it is quite another story, because he is at liberty to do as he wishes. It is quite obviously a personal choice. Too much is said about aesthetics and the rightness and wrongness, and yet a blue stained piano decorated with yellow roses in gesso may well look extremely attractive in a certain environment. On the other hand, it will probably look that much better if it is finished in such a way as to exploit the fine wood which forms the case of the instrument. Choice may be governed more by the nature of the wood itself rather than personal taste and inclination.

There are in the timber trade two types of wood, hard and soft. These are simply trade and technical terms. Their use does not necessarily imply that a wood is soft because it can be scratched with the fingernail or a screwdriver. In fact, certain softwoods are a great deal harder than hardwoods. This is a bewildering business for the amateur, and it is something which has grown with all the developments in wood technology. Before man began to understand wood, it was the craftsman's habit to use practically any wood which came to hand for certain jobs, and in any case he seldom had much choice. In particular, the medieval carpenters and joiners worked principally in oak, and they knew very little about its properties. They took it in a virtually 'wet' and unseasoned condition, and incorporated it into buildings which were often put up in a hurry, without any knowledge of foundations and stress and strain. Such a combination made the wood develop serious shakes, or cracks, in a matter of years. It must, however, be admitted that many of these medieval timbers managed to endure for centuries and to such an extent that the faults eventually became part and parcel of the building. In our own time many of these little disasters are becoming more evident, and the faults, combined with attack by parasites, have required their replacement. In the process of making them good, we have learned something about early cabinet making, building methods and the ways of our tradesmen forebears.

The choice nowadays of wood and the purpose to which it can be put must dictate the consideration of how it will eventually be surface finished. As part of his basic equipment, the wood finisher must have a working knowledge of the structure of the material with which he works. Wood is not metal. It is not inert. It once had life and even in its converted form it still has life. Wood is, above all, individualistic and even personable.

Texture and figuring are probably the predominant characteristics of all surface finished wood. They are the two elements which make certain woods instantly recognisable and identifiable, especially in the case of such standard materials as maple, oak, mahogany and others which have for the last two hundred years represented the mainstay of cabinet-making in Britain, the Continent and the United States of America. What makes these particular woods stand out is that the visual characteristics frequently obscure the fact that every single piece of wood has its own unique qualities.

Trees are, in fact, much more primitive than the herbs, which pass prolifically through the cycle of the seasons, producing their seeds and propagating their own kind. A tree cannot live on such a basis. There is all the difference between the flea and the elephant. Trees are with us for a very long time in comparison with other forms of life, and during their growth they have to be fiercely competitive in the need for light and air and even for the soil itself. A natural forest is a battleground, packed in tropical climes with the twisted and turned trunks, and yet, despite the struggle for survival, it has been found that such forests still produce timber which is superior to wood which is grown under carefully cultivated conditions, where man's well-meaning interference and tampering is constant. The eye of the experienced craftsman should be able to detect the differences between forest grown timber and cultivated wood, and it will soon become evident that the more interesting material has always been drawn from the natural forests of the world. Unfortunately, it is now a decreasing asset. This may help to explain why the furniture of some antiquity is interesting for the wood finisher because all of it was made from the natural wood brought from the areas which have now been thinned out by man's incursions or even wiped out totally and completely. Most definitely, there is a world of difference between eighteenth century mahogany and the thirty or so different kinds of mahogany which can be bought today, just as there are differences between the standards of craftsmanship of the two periods.

A brief reference was previously made to the curious anomaly that some softwoods are harder than hardwoods. It is most important that the wood finisher should know exactly what he is talking about in this respect, particularly if he has to work with the better class of antique restorer who is in possession of a wide and extensive knowledge of his many materials. In this respect it should be borne in mind that 'softwood' and 'hardwood' are simply commercial terms, used by timber dealers rather than those engaged in the restoration of antiques. In dealing with fellow craftsmen it is wise to adopt the commercial jargon. Here are the broad definitions: *Softwoods* are produced by gymnosperms and are represented by the conifer with needle-shaped leaves and naked seeds. *Hardwoods* are produced by dicotyledons, which means that the trees are broad-leaved with seeds in seed-cases.

There has in the past been a certain amount of confusion about the naming of timbers, due to the botanists who used one system, the timber trades merchants who used several more, and the rest of the fraternity sticking doggedly to its own terms. To these were added the vernacular names current in the area in which the trees grow, thereby adding to the international confusion. Some years ago the British Standards Institution cleansed the Augean stables by producing BS881 and BS589, consisting of the standard names for timbers as they were known in the United Kingdom. Although the two Standards did help to some extent, much work still remains to be done in this area if only because they apply solely to the United Kingdom. It is obviously desirable that an international standard should be produced to which all countries could subscribe. As in politics, it is irritatingly difficult, and probably quite impossible, to get entire nations to agree on this relatively simple subject, although the respective blocs appear to be in wondrous accord when it comes to the less important matter of armaments and the defence of territories.

Wood is produced by a simple process. It may be helpful to regard the tree as part laboratory and part factory consisting of four main parts, the roots, the stems, the leaves and that great conduit, the trunk. Roots nurture the structure on water which is drawn from the earth, and in the water are mineral salts which are present in the soil. The liquid and mineral solutions pass upwards to the leaves, whose function is to store the nutrition and at the same time absorb atmospheric gases and energy from the sun. The trunk is covered with bark, which is a protective covering to prevent the enclosed wood from high and low temperatures and to provide protection against injury. Apart from its role as a protector, the bark contains dyes and tannin, which are useful by-products. Between the wood and the bark there is the cambium, a tissue which covers both trunk and branches. Cambium is responsible for creating bark and it governs the trunk girth. In function it is not unlike one of the main glandular governors of the human body because it looks after the growth of the wood itself. Growth occurs according to the nature of the tree and its environment. In spring there is great activity in the tree in the temperate regions, but this slackens off in winter with a period of virtual non-growth during the most extreme part of the year.

Although they are not visible to the naked eye, a multitude of minute cells compose the materal which we now call wood. They are variously shaped and can be likened to tubes or bricks with pointed or blunt ends.

Some are empty, others are used as repositories for certain essential materials. In size they are from 0.025 to 0.5mm.

One of the remarkable facts about the tree is that it continues to increase in girth for a period, after which it reaches its optimum height. How that height is determined and governed is still something of a mystery. Growth means that the cells continue being added to. In theory there is no reason why growth should cease at all.

Softwoods have a strongly resinous odour, caused by the resin in the ducts. A softwood which lacks this odour can still be a member of the same family, and this is illustrated by such timbers as yew, sequoia and the true firs, all of which lack ducts and thus have no distinctive odour.

Hardwoods, on the other hand, have an entirely different microscopic structure, and this in turn presents a surface appearance which differs drastically from that of the softwoods with their pronounced pores. Oak and chestnut are two prime examples. The hardwoods have very narrow cells and in character are fibrous.

The craftsman has to consider all aspects of the woods with which he works. The surface finisher is concerned primarily with colour and hue. Antique wood has already attained its colour and become stabilised, but in the reproduction furniture trade the toning of new wood is a major consideration. The skilled and practised finisher knows how to disguise appearance, and he can make one wood look exactly like another. Although it is probably stretching the truth to suggest that pine can be made to resemble mahogany, just as one mahogany may be disguised to look like another mahogany, it remains true to say that certain woods will with some attention resemble what they are not and never could be. The line is a thin one and we may pass into the sphere of outright fakery. Regardless of the tricks of the trade, nothing can be better than the enhanced colour of a fine timber. Once the wood has been through the seasoning process it will already have changed colour not once but perhaps several times. It is a transitional process. In its rough sawn state mahogany does not at all resemble the usual conception of a wood which enjoyed its heyday in Chippendale's era. When left to season in the strong sunlight, it fades and can look somewhat bleached, yet when it is stored in sheds with the benefit of only a minimum amount of daylight, it soon begins to darken until it takes on the characteristic colour. Other timbers pass through a colour spectrum. Sycamore, for instance, will turn green if it is left in normal daylight. Today, with the universal use of artificially controlled kilns, the commercial timbers undergo colour changes by the use of moisture and temperature modification. In some forms of timber processing hydrogen peroxide is used to lighten woods and make them more marketable than they would otherwise be. The wide range of oak, much of it imported from the Orient, means that it must be controlled within a series of colour ranges which are acceptable to Western buyers. This is done by fuming, a process involving the exposure of the wood to varying intensities of ammoniacal gas during drying. If this appears to be disguising the wood and making it look what it is not, then it should be remembered that buyers are as selective and discriminating when ordering shipments for the mass production of furniture as are women when choosing fashionable hats. Mass production implies uniformity, and it is understandable that the buyer who orders a consignment of timber only to find that it differs radically between batches can be in a difficult position because the manufacture of long runs will then be quite impossible. The recourse to the surface finisher is frequent at a time when timber quality unavoidably varies.

Here are a few of the commonly used timbers which have played an important part in the trade since the eighteenth century. They are, so to speak, the 'standards' and should be known to all surface finishers.

AFRORMOSIA (also known as kokrodua)
A substitute for teak, but with its own 'trademark' of ripple markings. It does not bleach very well when used in furniture manufacture, but is considered to be one of the most reliable substitutes. Accepts a fine quality surface finish and is yellow-brown with streaks.

AFZELIA (also known as aligna, apa, ariyan, uvala, chanfuta, mbem-
  bakofi)
A wood which darkens during exposure to air, starting from a light straw colour deepening to honey.

IROKO (also known as kambala, moreira, mbule, odum, tule)
Generally used for construction work, but also in furniture when a tough and resilient material is required. Light brown with a hint of green when in the early sawn state, but darkens to a distinctive teak-like colour and finally becomes a deep rich brown.

MUNINGA (also known as bloodwood, mninga, ambila, mlombwa,
  mukwa)
A red-brown wood with red streaks or brown with black streaks. Widely used in the modern furniture trade at one time, its use is now much reduced due to a reduction of exports from Africa.

BURMA TEAK
The well-known very stable timber with innumerable substitutes. In its natural state it is yellow-brown when first sawn, gradually turning dark brown and with the colour of ancient leather.

ABURA
Used in the past for carved ornamentation on high quality furniture, yet not always a very reliable wood because it tends to display patches of

dark or even dense black colour. In its usual state it is light brown with a subtle hint of pinkness.

AFRICAN WALNUT (also known as bibola, dibetou, noyer d'Afrique, alona, lovea)
One of the major cabinet making woods with all the appearance of European walnut, and widely used as a substitute.

AGBA (also known as Nigerian cedar, moboro, ntolas, tola, branca, white tola)
A softwood substitute for mahogany, though more subject to parasitic invasion. Pale yellow-brown with some pinkness which is persistent even after lengthy exposure to the atmosphere and it must therefore be stained if it is to resemble mahogany.

AMERICAN MAHOGANY
Used extensively in cabinet-making, regardless of its highly variable colour qualities and possibly difficult hardness. Light red-brown when cut, it quickly darkens, but has a tendency to fade when exposed to direct daylight. This can be prevented by surface finishing.

GUAREA (also known as scented guarea, obobonufa, bosse, Nigerian cedar, Nigerian pearwood, cedar, mahogany)
In the thirties this wood was widely used as a substitute for mahogany. It was all the more attractive for its wavy or curly figuring, which has all the appearance of fine watered silk. It yields an excellent surface finish which enjoys a long life.

MAKORÉ
Has a mottled appearance which is not immediately apparent when first sawn, but shows itself when the pink and brown colour darkens to a uniformly deep red. It was widely used for veneer, and still features in cabinet-making.

SAPELE (also known as aboudikro, cedar, sapele mahogany, scented mahogany)
One of the most common of all mahogany types with a typical rich brown colour after sawing. Used extensively for the production of veneers, but also as a face timber in cabinet-making.

UTILE (also known as assié, acajou, assié, sipo, acajou sipe)
One of the mahogany family with an almost identical finished appearance with sapele, though it does not have the same striking figuring.

KERUING (also known as apitong)
A substitute for the traditional oak, though without the typical dark colour. When cut it is dark brown to red-brown. Occasionally used in

large pieces of furniture for the sake of its qualities as a material for reproduction work.

OBECHE (also know as wawa, ayous, samba)
When cut it has a rich cream-white colour which will accept many different kinds of surface finish. Sometimes regarded as a utilitarian wood for carcase and internal wood, but it has possibilities as a material for decorative finishes.

RAMIN (also known as ramin telur, melawis)
Exhibits a straw colour when cut but there is a darkening in older growth. Subject in its original environment to attack by parasites. Sound wood is used for furniture, and it provides a highly polished appearance.

LIGHT RED MERANTI
One of the major woods used for veneers with a light pink to reddish colour when cut. A very stable wood used for furniture and other applications where surface appearance is all-important.

DARK RED MERANTI
With the foregoing, a wood for veneer production. It has a hint of purple when cut and becomes dark red-brown, resembling mahogany.

EUROPEAN BEECH (also known as beech with a prefix to denote the country of origin e.g. Slavonic, French, English)
White or brown when cut, and remaining pale after seasoning. Used nowadays on a small scale for selective cabinet-work.

EUROPEAN BIRCH (when originated in various countries, the name of the country is used as a prefix e.g. Swedish birch, Finnish birch)
White to yellow-brown in colour, and used extensively for the production of veneers. The more exotic figurings are found in Karelian and masur birch, while flame and ice birch provide the more exotic figurings. In some wood finishing techniques which involve the application of fluids, there is a tendency to shrink.

ENGLISH ELM
Red brown and dull, sometimes with a touch of purple. It is used traditionally for small woodenware, coffins and other items. It takes all kinds of surface finishes. Likely to become somewhat rare in Britain due to the incidence of Dutch elm disease.

SWEET CHESTNUT (also known as Spanish chestnut, European chestnut, American chestnut)
It has the appearance of English oak but lacks the figuring. Cream to light yellow-brown in colour. Used up to recently for furniture, but not so much nowadays. Takes all surface treatments very satisfactorily.

EUROPEAN OAK (prefixed by the name of the country to indicate origin:
  e.g. English oak, French oak, American red oak, American white oak,
  Japanese oak)
A favourite target for the death watch beetle. True oak is generally
red-brown in colour, and is traditionally enhanced by a waxed finish. A
great deal of inferior oak is generally on offer in the trade.

A great many wood finishers do not quite understand the seasoning
process, although it can have a considerable effect on the finished effect
in new furniture. This does not apply to furniture which is over one
hundred years old and can therefore be regarded as antique, although it
should not be forgotten that even ancient wood has a habit of reacting to
the environment in which it rests. This has often been illustrated with
the installation of central heating in panelled premises, resulting in the
panels buckling, bowing and eventually splitting. Wood is not an inert
material, like metal or glass. Even though it may have been 'dead' for a
century or more, it still consists of a series of cells and retains a cellular
structure.

Fluid substances are applied to the wood during finishing. This can
create changes, either immediately or some time in the near future. A lot
depends on the nature of the fluid and the quantity which is applied, but
even a small amount can cause changes in delicate surfaces, particularly
those which are veneered with the paper-thin slices of wood. Some
veneers will curl and crackle when affected by spirit or water based
solutions. Even when the wood has been well and truly seasoned, it can
develop bad habits.

The process of seasoning has purposes other than imparting a certain
appearance. It also creates a degree of stability and acts as a
preventative against the growth of sap-stain fungi. Faults such as these
can develop only when the moisture content of the timber is more than
twenty per cent. But if the wood should happen to develop a moisture
content above twenty per cent after it has been seasoned and made into
furniture or other objects, such as sections of panelling or sculpture, then
a number of conditions can develop quite rapidly, and they include
buckling, warping and pest invasion.

The tradesman who makes a living from surface finishing antiques
will encounter all manner of wood and his discrimination should reflect
his experience. It is an error to believe that all ancient wooden furniture
is 'fine', and it should be appreciated that furniture aged up to two
hundred years has passed through many extremes of temperature during
its lifetime. The odds are that it will have developed some noticeable
flaws and faults. Swollen doors will have been planed down or, worse,
modified with a saw. Flat surfaces may have developed bumps and
lumps, and they, too, will have been flattened, often by crude means,

using blunt planes and leaving an unsightly scarring. The furniture has probably shrunk during dry periods and then taken on moisture during the moist and humid months. With age the majority of woods become slower to react to environmental changes, but the first fifty years or so of life will represent a series of internal changes. In the ensuing hundred years these changes will become more sluggish until the wood finally settles down and becomes stable to all intents and purposes. The initial seasoning prior to manufacture was not always as carefully controlled or even known about, as it is in our own times.

There are two methods of seasoning, by air or in a kiln. Air seasoning is more traditional, involving as it does the stacking of the timber in seasoning sheds, which look like Dutch barns, sometimes with slatted walls or adjustable louvres to regulate the flow of air. Practically all the exotic tropical hardwoods are air seasoned because kilning is too abrupt and apt to create faults in what is, after all, a very valuable material.

FIGURE 1. A timber stack in process of being air dried with the interleaving sticks ensuring an even flow of air throughout. The temporary roof protects the timber from rain, although any dampness is rapidly dispelled by the circulating air. Craftsmen who tend towards the traditional attitude favour this form of seasoning, which is slow and gradual.

Any material capable of holding moisture is shunned in the construction of drying sheds and the floor is made of concrete. Air circulation is encouraged by stacking the timber in layers, each layer being separated by 'stickers' of varying width to stimulate the air flow. These stickers, which are nothing more than lengths of wood, are selected with great care when they are used to separate the length of timber, and they are made from a wood which is not itself harder than the wood to be seasoned, otherwise indentations will occur, creating faults which can be cured only by machining the wood. This can represent a considerable financial loss to the timber merchant if a large quantity of timber has to be rectified.

In contrast to air seasoning, kiln drying is automatic, creating as it does a wholly artificial and instant environment of air circulation, temperature and humidity. It may be argued that kiln seasoning can be accomplished with greater precision and sureness of purpose than air seasoning. There is some truth in this, because the moisture content of the timber can be made uniform. This creates a standardisation of the quality of the material.

The kiln consists of brick with wood or metal doors and the heat supply is from steam-heated coils across which the air passes before circulating in the stacked timber. Water vapour can be admitted to the drying chamber as and when needed, and the sprays can inject steam into the internal atmosphere. The measurement of humidity is done precisely by hygrometers located at various points within the kiln and visible from outside to enable readings to be taken.

Air and kiln seasoning of timber are in general use in the industry, but chemical seasoning presents an alternative but lesser used system, and it achieves much the same objective. It is used mainly in countries where timber is prepared for shipment on sites adjacent to forestry areas, and it works on the principle that some chemicals in aqueous solution have much lower vapour pressures than ordinary water. When wood is coated with a solution the vapour pressure of the internal moisture of the timber will be much reduced. The most common chemical employed for this purpose is urea. When wood is coated with it there is deep penetration, leading eventually to a stabilisation of the internal structure.

Wood is just as prone to ills and ailments as are human beings. The faults, flaws and idiosyncrasies of the various types of wood can present individual difficulties for the wood finisher, and he should have a comprehensive knowledge of the causes. Certain defects which occur during growth are, in fact, quite beautiful and may even form a feature of a particular piece of furniture, the best known being the burr, causing a gnarled mass which interweaves and twists in upon itself. Knots, for instance, form patterns and, when polished, can enhance the appearance of furniture. Mineral streaks, too, have a singular beauty, often looking

FIGURE 2. Timber entering kiln at the Timber Research and Development Association.

gemlike under the polish and patina. Knots may be of almost any size, determined by the growth of the tree. They are the result of branches which are embedded in the trunk during growth. It requires only a small section of branch to create a knot, and in some trees, notably pine, they appear in remarkable profusion. In others, such as lime, they are rare. Knots may be round or spiked, and the term refers to the location rather than the size and shape. When they occur on the edge of a sawn piece of timber they are known as arris knots. Round knots are those found in a flat surface. The physical effect of a knot is that it weakens the section of wood. This is an important consideration when it comes to patching in of new sections to replace weakened parts of furniture.

Pith flecks are caused by the invasion of insects during tree growth. The visual appearance is that of a tunnel, cut longitudinally. The flecks are commonly found in maple, sycamore, alder and birch. When a timber is so affected, it is unlikely to be used for quality furniture.

Pitch seams or streaks are caused in softwood by the deposit of resin in 'tubes'. When cut, a tacky half hole is left. They generally follow the outline of the growth rings.

FIGURE 3. Numerous pin-like holes in chair legs or small piles of 'sawdust' under the dining table are often the first clues householders have that woodworm are attacking their furniture. Here a table has been severely attacked by wood boring beetles which have reduced the inside of the wood to a mass of sawdust.

Gum veins sometimes resemble varicose veins in human beings, and they appear between the growth rings. As with some other defects, the veins can look attractive in such cabinet woods as African walnut.

Mineral streaks are caused by canals cut lengthwise and it is generally assumed that they are caused by the taking up of trace elements from the soil.

The most common defects have now been described in broad outline. In past years any timber with such flaws was generally discarded. Apart from the growth faults there are others which are caused by the behaviour of timber under certain conditions. Some of them commence during faulty seasoning, but they can also develop in elderly pieces of furniture. Bowing, for instance, is a kind of sagging between the ends of a piece of timber so that the centre is lower than the ends. It can be caused by an incorrect spacing of the stickers during seasoning. Another fault, known as checks or shakes, happens when the grain separates, and it can sometimes be cured by the application of damp cloths to both affected and surrounding surfaces to stabilise the wood. Something should be said about timber worms, which the surface finisher in the restoration trade will often come across. While he is not a pest consultant, he should nevertheless know how to deal with them. It is not simply a matter of injecting a patent preparation. These invaders often have complicated life cycles and need to be understood. In the antique furniture trade it is not uncommon to come across very fine pieces which are so worm ridden that they are nothing more than shells, likely to fall to pieces under the weight of a few knocks. The probability of the worm being one type or another is narrowed down when it is appreciated that some insects will favour only certain types of wood, or wood which happens to be in a certain condition. The furniture beetle and the notorious death watch beetle are members of the *Anobidae* family. Furniture beetles belong to more than one genus, the most common one being *Anobium punctatum*. The death watch beetle is *Xestobium rufovillosum*.

The common furniture beetle does not necessarily start its life inside the house, but may be found in rotting trees. It divides its attention between decaying wood and other targets, including well seasoned wood in furniture. Larvae hatch from eggs which are tucked away in small cracks and joints. After the eggs hatch the holes become elongated not in any particular pattern but in a maze of holes and tunnels, which become filled with a substance like fine sawdust and is known as 'frass'. Ordinary sawdust is fairly coarse, but frass is more granular. In May, June, July and August the adult beetles appear and start mating, and once more the eggs are secreted in suitable crevices. As soon as they hatch, the tunnelling starts again, and so the cycle continues. The life cycle of the beetle is three years. Once the beetle is established, it is tenacious and hardy, but it cannot withstand the patent preparations

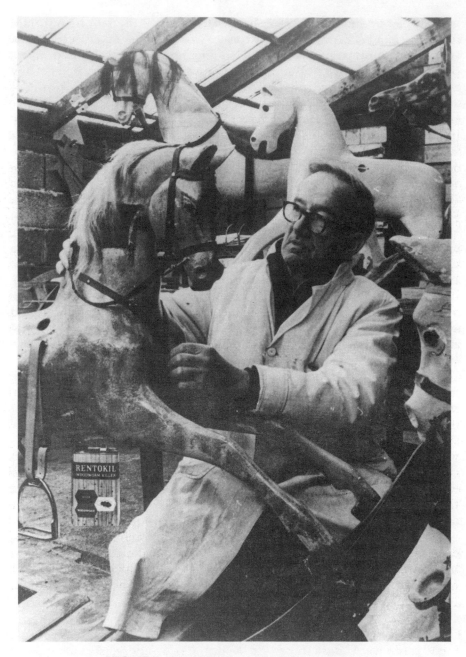

FIGURE 4. 'Galloping Woodworm'!
Treatment of rocking horses for woodworm.

now on the market, and it can be destroyed by fumigation. After the furniture has been treated, all the holes are sealed with wax. From the surface finishing point of view, the holes can be disguised with stain and polish. It is not advisable to use plastic wood for this purpose because a good colour match is difficult to achieve, and the result can look speckled. It is not, of course, advisable to allow infested furniture to stand close to sound pieces, because this will lead to a more widespread infestation not only in furniture but also floorboards and structural timbers.

The death watch beetle feeds on wood and is capable of creating widespread destruction at a very rapid rate, tunnelling deeply and through the wood. Although it seems to prefer ancient wood, it has also been known to attack softwood. The conditions in which the beetle is spurred to attack will probably be damp and there may also be a certain amount of existing decay, hence the presence of this pest in church timbers, generally in the neglected roof beams. One of the marked features of the tunnelling is the wide aperture, which can be up to ⅛th inch diameter. Although the life cycle of the death watch beetle is but one year, it can in that time still cause a tremendous amount of damage, including the weakening of the joints of heavy furniture. The best treatment for death watch beetle infestation is to call in a specialist. It is most certainly not a job for the surface finisher.

Many owners of fine furniture become alarmed if they discover as much as a single needle-like hole in one of their prized possessions, but some of them panic unduly. The presence of such miniscule evidence does not necessarily mean that the entire piece is radically infested. In such cases the unwelcome visitor is likely to be one of two types of boring weevil, either *ernobius mollis* or *Pentarthrum huttoni*. Their trademark consists of fine sawdust, or frass, and they are generally very easy to deal with by the application of patent preparations. It has to be admitted that the most sure and effective antidote to infestation has not yet been devised, although success can be achieved by brushing the affected wood with one or other of the home-made preparations, including paraffin and even creosote. Obviously, a lot must depend on the value of the piece being treated, and one should not give valuable furniture too much rough and ready treatment. In a word, it is a case of horses for courses.

3

Traditional Preparation Methods

using Bleach, Fillers, Abrasives, Shellac and Varnish Application

IN the medieval period, when England's supply of wood was taken from the forests which covered large tracts of the country, furniture was sturdy, perhaps even clumsy to our eyes, and it was designed, if it was designed at all, in a strictly utilitarian fashion. Very little rounded section was used, and the legs and the supports were cut on the square, using the adze, plane and chisel, and the various pieces were either dowelled or pegged together. Quite a lot of this early furniture from the thirteenth, fourteenth and fifteenth centuries has survived, perhaps due to its sheer bulk, and it is significant that while it was not elaborately surface finished, it has nevertheless managed to last for five hundred years or so without losing any of its formidable charm.

Any surface decoration consisted of carving. In the later period turning, moulding, inlay in the form of parquetry or marquetry, paints and stains, gilding and silver leaf and, finally, the surface finish proper arrived. With it came craftsmen from other countries, sometimes as immigrant refugees and sometimes as service contract workers to the Crown. Painted or stained furniture held its popularity in England, and there are museum examples dated pre-1550, some of it betraying traces of gesso, which was used not only as a base for the paint but also as a grain filler or sealer. By the second half of the sixteenth century the amount of painted furniture tended to decrease, although large quantities were still being commissioned by the aristocracy. The most common colours of the day included red, blue, yellow, black and white, using egg white, glue size and gum with water or oil as a mixing agent.

After the decline in the popularity of painted furniture it was soon discovered that the surface of the wood itself was capable of providing a beauty of its own. Prior to 1660 the finish was very rough, created as it was with wax or oil. The lack of technical information relating to this early period is probably due to the fact that much of the work was carried out by workshops manned almost entirely by apprentices. Because of the jealous position of the trade guilds it was not a good idea to share trade secrets and therefore livelihood with others by describing processes and techniques in anything other than word of mouth surrounded by the secrecy of the guild. But it is certain that these same workshops made extensive use of varnishes manufactured from linseed oil or spirits of wine and copal glue, the recipes for which were to eventually appear in books written by John Evelyn and John Stalker. Evelyn wrote about 'Joyners Vernish' and 'Japan and China vernishes, which infinitely excels linseed oyl'. They may well have been made from wine and gum lac brought from the Orient.

Precisely why varnishing was adopted and used so extensively in the finishing trade in the first place is still not exactly plain, but there is a strong possibility that furniture makers first found it in the shipyards, where it was used as a preservative not only for the exposed timbers of the vessel itself but also the fittings and general furniture of the ship.

Before varnish was used it is certain that beeswax, which continues to form the basis of some high quality finishes, was in use from a very early date, but another finishing agent was oil, the use of which would account for the typically dark and even black appearance of much early oak furniture. The chemical action of the oil, which we know as oxidation, may account for it, whereas wax will not darken oak to any appreciable extent. Some schools of thought believe that all traces of original polish must surely have vanished years ago, and ancient furniture could not have been darkened by any of the oil available at that time. Modern experiments have shown that if oil is used to stain a wood like oak, then the typical darkening will develop. However, there is, on the other hand, yet another theory which states that a great deal of traditional English oak furniture was either heavily or lightly painted black and later oiled. The idea would not seem to hold more than a spoonful of water, because there is seldom any evidence in the shape of flakes of paint or, indeed, any trace of paint which has worked its way into the grain. It is preferable to believe that oil was used with beeswax being introduced at a later date. Finally, varnish gained a hold and held it.

The history of furniture is a history of one wood following another due as a rule to the development of trade routes. Surface finishes have kept pace. Walnut furniture, for instance, was made between 1660 and 1700, and it was enhanced with a finish of a clear oil varnish. In this period the finishes had to be compatible with the intricate and colourful veneers which became the fashion. The oil varnish was mild and would to our eyes be very 'thin', probably brushed on very lightly and allowed to dry simply as a means of protecting the decorated wood and at the same time looking attractive to the eye. This was in some contrast to the practices followed by the Chippendale workshops in about 1770, when mahogany replaced veneer. The veneer of the time gave the client a wide choice of figuring, which included what the Chippendale tradesmen referred to as 'plum pudding,' 'fiddleback', 'ocean figure' and others equally picturesque. Exactly how it was discovered that the pink-yellow and brown mahogany could be brushed with a solution of bichromate of potash to create the typical rich red of mahogany is not clear. Quite possibly it was the result of a workshop accident, but it was not long before the majority of Chippendale designs were realised in this way, the surface finish of the wood consisting of linseed oil which was brushed on and allowed to soak into the grain, then later rubbed down with a cork pad and powdered brickdust. There were, of course, alternative finishes, but by 1803 Sheraton in his *Cabinet Dictionary* was advocating the Chippendale method at a time when other workshops still favoured the use of copal varnish. It is still possible to emulate the Chippendale method, and while the results may not always be up to par as far as brilliance and sheen are concerned, this may well be the fault of the quality of modern oil and wood rather than of the method itself.

Before any surface can be properly finished, it must be prepared in a rather traditional way around which there are no short cuts worth considering. A lot of amateur finishing fails because insufficient attention is paid to preparation. This consists not only of sanding the wood and ensuring that it is free of all foreign particles but also the removal of film-like residues. If the wood is simply washed down with caustic, or lye as it is sometimes called, it is quite possible that the characteristic soapiness will sink into the fibres of the wood and remain there, unnoticed, until the actual finishing process is carried out. More often than not, this will result in the development of mysterious milky patches or blemishes, caused by the finishing solutions, and the stains will resist any uniformity with the rest of the area. Some of the cheaper Thirties furniture was blemished in this way. Until the craftsman became more fully recognised in recent years, it was the understandable habit of the ill-paid jobbing finisher to rapidly clean down the surface, apply the surface finish and then get away as quickly as possible. Today, when the proper rate for the job is paid to the craftsman who really knows his job, things are different, and most customers will recognise the worth of the investment. Even in a world of instant this and instant that, it is acknowledged that the properly crafted finish will take time which must be paid for. A good surface finish is not achieved in minutes, perhaps not even in hours.

First of all, we should consider new wood, the sort of material used for making furniture of all kinds, from the kitchen to the lounge, bedroom and leisure areas. Even when wood looks bare and brand new, and is fresh from the cabinet-maker, there will usually be a large amount of dust and wood particles adhering to the surface. If it is going to be given a surface finish, it must be dusted down, taking care to remove any specks of paint or plaster, as happens in newly built houses. All the spots and marks should be wiped off with petrol or spirit, using just enough to lightly moisten the surface. Woods such as oak, walnut and the other open-grained species are likely to harbour grease, and if it is not entirely cleaned at this stage the result will probably be an irregular speckling. These suggestions apply to a wood which is going to be enhanced in such a way as to exploit the grain by the application of a stain and polish. If it is to be painted, then any little stains or blemishes need not be attended to in the same way because the paint will obviously cover them, though care should still be taken to remove any wood dust before the painting is done. Some new wood bears red or brown rust marks, the result of contact with wet metal. Even though the wood is going to be stained and polished, the marks will probably show through and flaw the final appearance. Such stains should be bleached out. Detailed instructions for bleaching are given later on in this chapter. The technique has many uses. Woods like maple and birch can be greatly enhanced by bleaching before surface finishing, for this is a process which lightens the wood while leaving the figuring, or grain, alone. Exactly what to bleach is a matter of choice. It is, for instance, a good idea to bleach panels in order to make them stand out from their surroundings and create contrast. When a section has been bleached and dried out, it must be sandpapered, because this is a process which raises the grain and causes furriness, like small hairs over the surface. This preparatory work occupies time, and the temptation to rush on should be resisted. While working on a section there may be one or two small dents caused by hammers and screwdrivers. Accidents happen in the best of workshops, and such faults can be tackled not by using fillers or plastic wood but by placing a thick wet cloth over the area and then laying an ordinary hot domestic iron on top. Even very severe dents can be treated in this way with some success. What happens is that the damp heat relaxes the impacted wood fibres in the dent, and they will then raise themselves to form a flat surface. But it must be said that this does not always work the first time, and several applications may be needed. Once the surface has been restored and flattened, the wood can be sanded smooth. Another common fault, particularly in cheap kitchen furniture, is the nail or screwhead which has been driven into the surface and left. They are quite easily dealt with. Nails can be driven further in, using a nail set, while screws should be removed and then countersunk. The hole can be filled with beaumontage or some other filler. Beaumontage is a very useful substance because it can be used to fill all kinds of holes. It is made by taking equal quantities of beeswax and resin and dissolving them together in a double boiler. It should be stored in an airtight tin. When used to fill holes it should be mixed with pigment or stain to match the surrounding surface.

Sanding is one of the most important stages in surface finishing, and a knowledge of the various abrasives is invaluable. The craftsman does not use any old piece of sandpaper, for this is a material which comes in a series of different grades, each of which has its particular use. Here is a comparison table of the various papers:

Glasspaper	Garnet	Aluminium Oxide	Flint Paper	Emery Cloth
–	10/0	10/0	10/0	–
–	9/0	9/0	9/0	–
–	8/0	8/0	8/0	–
–	7/0	7/0	7/0	–
00	6/0	6/0	6/0	–
0	4/0	4/0	4/0	FF
1	3/0	3/0	3/0	F
1½	2/0	2/0	2/0	1
F2	0	0	0	1½
M2	½	½	½	2
–	–	–	–	2½
S2	1	1	1	3
2½	1½	1½	1½	4
3	2	2	2	–
–	2½	2½	2½	–
–	3	3	3	–
–	3½	3½	3½	–

The following notes on abrasives will be of use:

General sanding is done with grade 1 or M2. In use, it is important that it follows the grain, because if it is worked across the grain it will cause a series of scratches which may be difficult to remove. Because certain woods have their own delicacy and call for special attention, grade 1½ should be used.

Certain woods are tough and resilient, and so they have to be smoothed with garnet paper, which is made by powdering the stone and then bonding it to a backing material. While it is very effective on most hardwoods, it works with much less efficiency on soft woods.

Most abrasives are available on either paper or cloth backings. There is a considerable price difference, the most expensive being aluminium oxide, which has a long life and gives a sustained performance.

There is an alternative to hand sanding, and this is to use the powered disc sander. However, this is not to be recommended for very delicate work, because it is in the habit of biting deeply and often unexpectedly, and resulting in a surface composed of a series of ups and downs which will show up when the final surface finish is applied. Such faults are

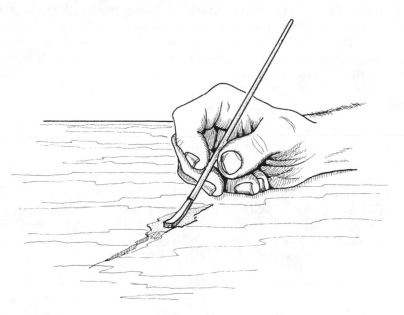

FIGURE 5. Filling an imperfection with beaumontage ensures a perfectly smooth continuation of the surface, and the beaumontage itself will accept practically all forms of finish.

obvious in reflected light. If a powered sander is to be used at all, there is always the gentler orbital sander, followed by hand sanding, using a cork or wood block to hold the sheet of abrasive and ensure an even pressure.

Sanding should be carried out in three phases, commencing with the coarse grade and moving along, or with, the grain. Depending on the amount of pressure which is applied, the coarser scratches will be an immediate eyesore. But they can be ignored at this stage. They are simply part of the process of creating a new surface which will form the base for the final finish. The next stage is to use a medium grade of sandpaper and spend somewhat longer to create a feeling of smoothness. It is useful to constantly dust the surface during sanding, because this enables the craftsman to note any changes in the nature of the grain. Indeed, this is the best way of actually creating distinctive grain patterns which will look attractive after the surface finish has been applied. In the final stages of sanding only the finest grade of paper is used, and the surface should be inspected by viewing it in an oblique light. The beginner will probably find a number of flaws, including all the bumps and scratches which should by rights have disappeared during sanding. It is also useful to wipe the surface with a cloth damped with turpentine before the final sanding. The dampness will show up any bumps or marks which should be removed. If there is any trick of the trade to hand sanding, then it is that the pressure must always be constant, and the strokes must always overlap to avoid creating small islands or areas untouched by the treatment.

Obviously, not all surfaces to be sanded are as conveniently flat as a tabletop. Edges, for instance, should be smoothed with a medium sandpaper, never a coarse one which will effectively chamfer away the edges and probably create a wavy effect. When sanding curved surfaces, use a very light touch and wrap the sandpaper round a piece of wood cut to pencil proportions to follow the shape of the curve. When used in this way some new sandpaper has a tendency to crack, but it can easily be made flexible by running it over the edge of the bench in an up and down motion.

One other matter should be mentioned in connection with sanding. It concerns the wide and versatile range of waterproof fine-grade garnet and aluminium oxide papers, which are best used wet to enhance their cutting qualities. They are used by the surface finisher between the coats of shellac or varnish to give tooth, or grip to the successive coats and this also acts as a bond of one coat to another. Water is used to dampen these papers. Up to now the discussion has concerned the sanding of solid wood, but the sanding of the fragile veneer calls for a much more delicate touch. In some older work they are as thin as the sensibilities of beautiful women, and in treating them it is necessary to cajole them with the finest garnet paper, exerting only a negligible pressure and always using a cork or felt sanding block. Because each individual piece of veneer has its own grain which may run in a contrariwise direction, it is no longer possible to follow the earlier suggestion that sanding should always be done in the direction of the grain when pieces are placed for decorative effect. The garnet paper is so fine that it is unlikely to scratch the surface. The secret should be obvious, use only the finest grade and practically no pressure. If the veneer is very deeply scratched, there may be no other alternative but to replace the afflicted section, and this will be a job for a craftsman experienced in the art of veneer patching.

One of the most valuable tools is steel wool. It can be obtained in the following grades:

No 3   Very coarse and of little use for present purposes.
No 2   Coarse but useful for smoothing down exceptionally rough surfaces.
No 1   A general utility wool to be used sparingly.

No 0   Somewhat finer and useful for all grades of smoothing.
No 00   Useful for the smoothing of fairly fine surfaces.
No 000 Superfine wool, almost equivalent to F2 glasspaper.

Steel wool should be handled as one would handle a tough, wiry little wrestler. It is most certainly not an alternative to abrasive paper, but it is best used for preliminary smoothing. Even grade No. 000 has a much keener cutting quality than any sandpaper, and it perhaps has the disadvantage that it leaves microscopic fragments of metal on the surface of the wood. It may also discolour some woods. But despite these drawbacks, it will still do a very good and worthwhile job if wetted with methylated spirit. Generally speaking, it is used in the following manner. A handful is taken and rolled into a ball. It can be used dry or dipped in methylated spirit. In use, it is gently moved backwards and forwards with the grain. The cutting action will be very noticeable if it is tightly wadded under the fingers. The ball should be turned over and inside out at frequent intervals to maintain new cutting surfaces. The sign that it has done its job is a sheen combined with a remarkably smooth feel to the surface of the wood. Note: steel wool has a habit of cutting into your fingers as well as the wood itself, and it is advisable to wear thick leather gloves to prevent injury.

A brief mention was made of bleaching earlier on in this chapter. It is used in various sectors of the antiques restoration trade when it is desirable to make areas lighter and then re-stain and polish them to give a more authentic appearance. The edges of chests, drawers and the front sections of chairs are similarly treated to suggest worn areas and in general mock the inexperienced buyer with the 'antique look'. It is certainly more subtle than simply rubbing files and rasps along edges to create the appearance of wear and tear, not to mention the chains and hammers which are used to batter otherwise harmless furniture into submission so that unscrupulous dealers can add a few years and make a little more profit.

Some woods bleach better than others. Here is an outline guide:

Good for Bleaching:
Ash, beech, elm, avodire (the latter is an African wood which resembles sycamore).

Difficult to Bleach:
Cherry, rosewood, padouk, iroko, ebony, satinwood.

There are several different varieties of bleach and various ways of using them. Bleach, including the domestic variety, can be bought ready made, although it is, in fact, much more economical to make your own and carry out a series of experiments. While ready-made bleach is extremely efficient, it has the drawback of being a standard mass-produced product, which makes it unsuitable for some jobs, taking into account the qualities of different woods.

Here is a formulary and technique guide for various bleaches, but first a cautionary note: WARNING always wear rubber gloves when mixing and applying these solutions, and ensure that any splashes on the bare skin are immediately washed off with clean water.

Two-stage Bleach

No. 1 solution. Take 4 parts of .880 ammonia, one part of water and mix.
No. 2 solution. Take one part of hydrogen peroxide (100 vol) and mix with 4 parts of water.

The No. 1 solution is alkaline and it will momentarily darken the wood as soon as it sinks into the fibres. When the No. 2 solution is put on the wood, there will be a chemical reaction and the bleaching will start.

It will be helpful to consider the process as a series of steps.

Step 1: Apply No. 1 solution plentifully and allow between five and ten minutes to penetrate the fibres.

Step 2: Apply No. 2 solution, using a broad, soft brush along the grain of the wood.

Step 3: Observe the action as the bleach dries. An appreciable lightening of the wood should now occur.

Step 4: As soon as the required degree of bleaching is reached, wipe the surface with a cloth soaked in methylated spirit.

Step 5: A white chemical residue will probably materialise on the wood when it is completely dry. If it cannot be wiped off with methylated spirit, use a fine sandpaper to clear the area.

If the initial bleaching fails to come up to expectation, go through the entire process once more. Unless something happens to be seriously wrong, such as an incompatibility between the wood and the bleaching solutions, the results should prove satisfactory.

The bleached wood should be allowed to stand in a well ventilated place for two or three days until it completely dries. The surface finish should be applied as soon as possible, otherwise the wood will begin to darken again.

Oxalic acid bleach is an alternative solution. 16 ounces of oxalic crystals are purchased from a chemist, and dissolved in one gallon of hot water. It is essential that the solution is applied as hot as possible to the surface of the wood, using a broad soft brush for the purpose. The proportions suggested above should be quite suitable for general bleaching, but an appreciably stronger solution will be needed to remove all the stains and black sap and mineral streaks. A very strong solution can be made by dissolving 12 ounces of oxalic crystals in ½ gallon of water. When the dark marks caused by mineral and sap streaks feel waxy or greasy to the fingertip it is a good idea to thoroughly wipe them with methylated spirit before applying the bleach, otherwise the film will form a barrier which prevents the bleach from doing its job. Neutralise with clean cold water.

Here is a third and even stronger bleach, consisting of chlorinated soda. It has to be made up in three stages.

Solution 1

Dissolve 10½ ounces sal soda in ¾ gallon of water.

Solution 2

Take 5 ounces of domestic chloride of lime and dissolve in ½ gallon of water. Stir constantly and allow it to settle. Decant the clear liquid into another bottle and add ½ gallon of water to it. Stir well. Now add a small quantity of water to the sediment, agitate and then strain it through a filter paper into the solution.

Solution 3

Now mix the two solutions together. It should turn green and smell strongly of chlorine.

The method of application is precisely the same as with other bleaches, including the final washdown, and while it works hot or cold, the hot solution is the most effective.

There are other bleaches, including peroxide of hydrogen, which is used by antique restorers, who apply it on small areas of furniture. It is brushed on and then permitted to dry, after which the area must be thoroughly washed. Peroxide of hydrogen works rapidly and its action should be carefully inspected, otherwise the result is a series of unsightly white patches.

Some professional finishers use a solution of 10 fluid ounces of hydro-sulphite in 90 ounces of water. This is applied in a series of coats, the stages of bleaching occurring as each coat dries. The amount of bleaching can be judged to a nicety between coats, and when the required degree is reached, the wood is washed with clean water.

Permanganate of potash can also be used for bleaching. It is dissolved in water and then brushed over the surface, causing a purple colour, which is dispelled by a saturated solution of hypo-sulphite, causing a bleached area to appear. An alternative to the hypo-sulphite is oxalic acid in water to a five per cent solution.

The effect of bleach can be mimicked if the wood to be treated is already light coloured. This is done by taking a 50/50 mixture of ordinary matt white paint and white spirit, and applying it with a coarse brush. A pad soaked in spirit is then wiped over the surface, using enough pressure to ensure that the grain or figuring shows through the thin layer of paint. When dry, it can be finished with an ordinary wax polish. This method is used extensively in stage set decoration and for exhibition stands. It is both cheap and quick, and it can look effective on pine.

Some General Notes about Bleaching.

1. It is debateable whether bleaches are universally successful in the treatment of old wood which has previously been varnished or stained. It is advisable to strip off the old material before attempting to bleach. But see below.

2. Bleach stored in plastic bottles will expand and may burst the bottles if they are left in a heated workshop. It is advisable to loosen the bottle caps if bleaches have to be stored.

3. Do not mix different blends of bleach and attempt to use them. It seldom works. To be effective, bleaches have to be made up in balanced quantities.

4. Do not store bleach in metal containers which can rust and contaminate it.

With reference to 1, above, old wood can be stripped and cleaned by first soaking it with a water-based solution of tri-basic phosphate consisting of 1 lb to one gallon of the chemical. This will remove much of the old staining and general surface debris, leaving a clean neutral field for bleaching purposes.

WARNING: wear rubber gloves and instantly wash skin splashes with clean water.

The preparation of the wood for surface finishing must include the use of fillers and sealers to provide a good sound base. Filler is used mainly by french polishers to secure the polish in a film and prevent it from sinking into the grain. What it accomplishes, in effect, is an equalisation of the surface by providing it with a tough skin, and reducing the risk of an uneven finish. Open grained woods are porous and they need a filler, whereas most hardwoods do not. Woods which most benefit from a filler include ash, oak, mahogany and walnut. Ash and oak are known as 'hungry' woods by professional surface finishers, because they are coarse, and unless they have fillers they will continue to swallow up finishing fluids for a long time and refuse to give the desired finish.

Before the filler is applied, the surface must be thoroughly dusted and cleaned. This happens to be a crucial stage in the finishing process, and any dust, however microscopic, which remains will probably cause trouble later on. In its most basic form the filler will consist of glue or size mixed with an appropriate colour, and its purpose is to fill the wood pores. Thus, if a piece of mahogany is to be finished, the colour will be Venetian red. Walnut requires brown umber, pine will call for yellow ochre. The glue or size is applied very hot with a broad brush and rubbed well into the grain with a cloth, wiping it firmly along the direction of the grain.

There are more traditional methods of filling the wood. Superfine plaster is a most efficient filler. On the assumption that the wood has already been stained to the required colour, two coats of thinned shellac are applied and given ample time to dry. It is absolutely vital that the shellac is completely dry and hard before the filler is applied. The next stage is the application of the superfine dental plaster, and it is carried out in the following manner. The dry plaster is placed in a tray next to the surface to be treated, and with it is a bowl of water. A clean cotton rag is damped in the water, then dipped in the plaster. It is then rubbed vigorously into the surface of the wood. The plaster will now begin to form a thickish paste on the wood. When the point is reached before the plaster begins to get lumpy and granular, use a piece of clean coarse sacking to wipe it off. The surface will now look white and streaky. This can be removed by wiping it off with a cloth pad soaked in raw, not boiled, linseed oil. This is known as 'killing' the plaster. Ideally, the oil should mix with the plaster and prevent it from setting any further.

When a colour is required to reinforce the stain, powdered pigment can be added to the plaster, but it should not be overdone.

A note here about other oils which may be used. While raw linseed oil is quite suitable for the darker tones, it is probably better to employ a thin, clear mineral oil for the lighter hues because the heavier oils will as a rule stain the wood.

As usual, oak, the grandfather of woods, demands a separate consideration due in this case to its wide pores. It can be left in its natural state, or it can be waxed, or it can be finished in a variety of other ways. When it is desired to fill the pores, the material to use is french chalk, a handful of which is mixed with the chosen liquid surface finish to give it some body. Mixing with shellac or varnish can be a strenuous and sweaty business, but once it begins to mingle with the liquid, it should not be too difficult. The mixture is then brushed on to the oak. It takes an hour or two to dry and harden, after which it can be rubbed down with a medium grade paper. The result should be a very

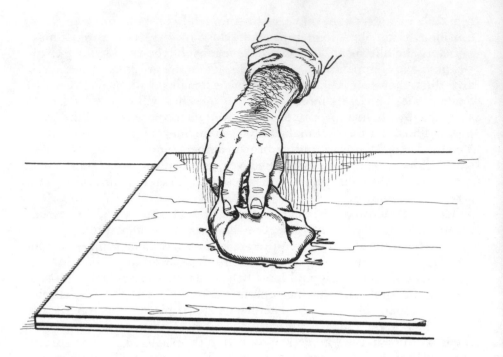

FIGURE 6.   Before using a wad of rag to apply a superfine plaster filler to the surface, make sure that the rag is thoroughly soaked, but not dripping with water, to make it pick up the powdered plaster, then rub with a firm downward pressure to force the plaster into the grain, or pores, of the wood. The plaster will form into a thick cream as the work progresses and make penetration easy.

smooth and attractive surface which will endure many years of hard wear.

Another traditional filler for oak and ash consists of water, methylated spirit and plaster of paris. The plaster is sieved and put in a tray. Into another vessel is poured methylated spirit and water in a 50/50 solution. Soak a clean cotton rag in the spirit and then dip in the dry plaster, then rub into the oak until it absorbs the plaster. Two or three coats should be sufficient. The methylated spirit will evaporate with the friction set up by the rubbing, the water will soften the plaster as it fills the large pores, and the finishing can be done with a wax polish a few days later, when all the dampness has disappeared. One of the secrets of this particular method is not to over-saturate the wood, otherwise the grain will be raised and it will prove difficult to sandpaper perfectly smooth without interfering with the action of the filler.

When using paste fillers on softwoods it is necessary to take into account the structure of the wood itself. The filler should always be thinned down until it feels slippery rather than resistant to the touch. The purpose is to create a substance of sufficient thinness as to be capable of being forced into the pores of the wood with a stiff brush.

There is another method of treating softwood, and while it is perhaps more elaborate it is still very efficient. The paste filler is first thinned down to the consistency of thin treacle, using the following formula: 1 gallon of varnish; 1 quart of turpentine; 1 pint of japan drier; 2½ lbs of silex. The silex is mixed with some of the varnish, after which the other liquids are added and stirred to a smooth consistency. It should then stand for five days, after which it is strained through muslin to get rid of any lumps or stringiness. The rest of the varnish should also be strained and stirred in. The silex is then folded in. When in use, the mixture should be constantly stirred to ensure that the silex is evenly distributed. Being heavy, it will sink to the bottom of the pot. When first applied, it will have a remarkably high sheen, but it will become dull as it dries. As a filler, it is practically unbeatable.

The surface finisher craftsman should know the best sealer to use for a surface which has a varnish or a lacquer base. It happens that this one

FIGURE 7. Forcing filler into softwood requires the use of a stiff and well worn brush which is used only for this particular job. The action should be downwards so that the bristles carry the paste or liquid filler straight into the pores.

can also be used for painted surfaces. The sealer is shellac, which is applied in a 2 lb cut (see below). It is sanded when dry between coats. In the case of sealing lacquer, three coats of thinned shellac are used with a thorough sanding between each coat.

The uses of shellac in french polishing will be dealt with at length in a later chapter of this book, but its other applications should be considered, firstly as a sealer. In this respect it is hard to surpass when used in a 2½ lb cut. It can also be used as a top coat, applying up to six coats which, when hard, can be polished with steel wool. Another use of shellac is for a coloured surface finish. Certain dyes are soluble in shellac, and it is possible to patch-in worn areas with some precision. Again, a 2½ lb cut is recommended.

Shellac is not simply slapped on like paint. It has to be applied with a wide double chisel fitch brush, using an even and well considered stroke, moving to and fro until the loaded brush is exhausted. When it has been recharged, the next area is covered evenly with a thin film. Because shellac in a 2½ lb cut dries fairly swiftly, the coats have to be put on with a sure touch. It can take up to a couple of hours for the coat to dry, and each one should be rubbed down very thoroughly with a fine garnet paper, softened in water to a point where it is flexible. Rubbing should be light, not forced, otherwise the garnet will cut through the layers. If it is properly and evenly rubbed, the result should be the typical satin-gloss. This can also be achieved with a very fine steel wool or a mixture of powdered pumice and oil. The grade of pumice to use is FF, a quantity of which is placed dry in a tray. The medium for rubbing is felt, perhaps a piece cut from an old hat. This is soaked in machine oil and pumice is coated on it. Then it is placed on the surface and the rubbing is done with a medium pressure, continuing until the friction and touch make it evident that renewal is required. It is a good idea to use two or three pads in rotation. Each pad will end up coated with grime, and this is the signal for a new one to be pressed into service. The accumulated grime should be completely removed before being re-coated.

Shellac has a long history, and it has been a favourite finishing material for centuries, probably because it endures and has its own mellow beauty. Yet it is not entirely waterproof and will be unsuitable for external use where dampness penetrates to cause milkiness and eventual flaking. It is made from the residue exuded by the lac bug *(Laccifer Lacca)* in Sri Lanka and India. Ironically, the exuded material eventually encloses the bug and kills it, after which it is gathered in large quantities. Then it is warmed in bags over fires and melted down, refined and flattened into thin sheets, cooled and hardened, and then crushed into small flakes which are dissolved in denatured alcohol. The usual proportion is the 5 lb cut, which means that 5 lbs of shellac have been dissolved in one gallon of alcohol. There are, of course, price considerations, and a heavily loaded shellac will naturally cost somewhat more than the 2 lb cut. It should be mentioned in passing that some inferior shellac is very thin and of no value. If it is intended to use a large quantity of shellac, then it is advisable to buy the 5 lb cut and then reduce it according to requirements, as below:

(To convert shellac use methylated spirit)

5 lb cut to 3 lb cut	⅞ pt to 1 qt shellac
5 lb cut to 2 lb cut	1 qt to 1 qt shellac
5 lb cut to 1 lb cut	⅔ gal to 1 qt shellac
4 lb cut to 3 lb cut	½ pt to 1 qt shellac
4 lb cut to 2 lb cut	¾ qt to 1 qt shellac
4 lb cut to 1 lb cut	2 qt to 1 qt shellac

Orange shellac is used on the darker woods, such as oak, mahogany and walnut, but it is unsuitable for lighter woods and bleached surfaces in which it is necessary to retain the lightness. For this purpose a white shellac is suggested, and when applied it will resemble a clear varnish, though there is a disadvantage in that it quickly reacts to any traces of dampness by developing milky streaks. A further disadvantage is that it does not store well even under ideal conditions and more often than not it goes off in a matter of weeks.

Shellac is occasionally eccentric as far as the drying time is concerned, but it can be retarded by adding a few drops of almond oil.

In the family of finishing materials, varnish is second cousin to shellac. The best quality varnish will last for years if it is looked after, and if it is to be successful it has to be treated carefully like a baby right from the start. There used to be an expression in the old-fashioned finishing workshops about varnish. If it was to perform well, it had to be 'tender and soft'. This meant that it must give to the movements of the wood and be capable of expanding and contracting, yet still continue to enclose the wood and hold out against heat, cold and moisture. Where a spirit varnish will harden to a glass-like finish, the oil varnish is preferable because it has an elasticity due to the addition of gums which mix but do not cause a firm setting when the varnish dries on the surface. Old varnishes had the addition of such exotic substances as oils of lavender, spike, rosemary and turpentine combined with linseed oil.

Up to the beginning of this century spirit varnishes were used very widely for many things, from furniture finishing to painting the exterior woodwork of houses and industrial premises. They fell into certain groups, such as alcohol and mastic, alcohol and copal, alcohol and mixed resins. Modern pre-mixed varnish is standardised and generally very reliable indeed, and the art of using it consists largely of knowing which method to use. But whatever the vitues of modern formulae, there are some old workshop recipes which tantalisingly suggest that it may be interesting to experiment with methods capable of providing something more than what can be a visually boring surface finish.

1. Brown spirit varnish
Take 2 lbs of shellac; ½ lb gum sandarach; 1 gallon methylated spirit. Shake until the gum is dissolved, then add two pints turpentine. Strain and store in a closed bottle for four weeks before using.

2. Spirit varnish
Take 4 ounces shellac; 2 ounces resin; ½ ounce gum benzoin; ½ ounce gum; 1 pint methylated spirit. Granulate the gum and resin and then mix them with the methylated spirit. Shake and store in a warm place and strain before using.

3. White varnish
Take 2 ounces of bleached powdered shellac; 1 pint of denatured alcohol. The shellac is dissolved in two-thirds of the alcohol, filter and add the remaining spirit and then dilute. Orange shellac can be used if a red varnish is required.

4. Dark varnish
Take 3 ounces of orange shellac; ½ ounce of turpentine; 1 pint of denatured alcohol. The shellac is dissolved in the alcohol and turpentine, using a hot water bath, not over a naked flame.

The recommendations for using these varnishes are much the same as the branded product, but personally prepared varnishes may call for slightly variable handling. A slow-drying varnish takes about twenty-four hours to dry under normal conditions, and the work must be done in a temperature which is stable and lacking humidity. A fast drying varnish takes up to five hours to dry, and is used as a rule for exterior woodwork. One of the fast-drying varieties is known as cabinet varnish, and it can be polished to a mirror-like gloss if rubbed with pumice. Another variety is called rubbing varnish, and when buffed with oil and pumice it will yield a high polish. In fact, there is little to choose between cabinet and rubbing varnish apart from personal preference, but if anything the cabinet varnish will give a much harder and more shiny final finish, and it will probably last a great deal longer.

Flat varnish, as its name implies, dries to a non-shiny finish, and it can be put on over a gloss to create a kind of dull glow providing it is applied to a suitable wood. Walnut is one of the best. Flat varnish requires no rubbing.

It is not generally appreciated by amateurs that the application of varnish calls for conditions as close to the ideal as possible. The biggest enemy is dust. Dust is everywhere, in the air, on the floor, and it appears like some form of evil magic as soon as the varnish is applied to the wood. For several hours after application the wet or drying varnish is a very efficient dust trap. If there is a single particle of dust in the air of the room where varnishing is done, it will beyond all doubt end up on the varnish. Doors and windows must be shut tight when varnishing although some ventilation is necessary, and it is always a good idea to put a prominent do-not-enter notice on the door to thwart callers and idlers who have nothing better to do than drop in for a chat. If the floor of the workshop is wood, brush it down with oil to keep the dust down. Cover it with sheets to make doubly sure. The other point to watch out for is room temperature, because varnish is so temperamental that it will not work in temperatures under about 65 degrees Fahrenheit. If it is more than 85 degrees Fahrenheit, the varnish will run like water. Thus, temperature should be maintained at a constant level between 70 and 80 degrees Fahrenheit, not only during application but throughout the drying time.

But if a variable temperature can cause problems, the condition of the wood itself may well be the worst miscreant. There is a more dominant need for surface cleanliness in varnishing than in any other form of finishing. If the wood has already been sanded, then all traces must be removed, using a well washed cotton cloth damped with a very small quantity of varnish. It is made into a pad and rubbed across the wood until it becomes tacky and lifts any debris and dirt. The tack rag, as it is called, is the varnisher's secret weapon, and it should be kept stored in an airtight jar. The second secret weapon is the varnish brush itself. Any old brush which has already been used for a hundred other painting jobs is no good at all. No matter how clean it looks, it will probably contain traces of past work in the shape of dust and paint particles. New brushes are to be preferred, but they must first be well soaked in the varnish and then worked out on a clean wooden surface, not the surface which is going to be varnished. Alternatively, a new brush can be well washed in turpentine and the bristles well frisked between the fingers. It is amazing how many loose bristles will fall out, saving a few irritations later on. Likewise, when the varnishing is finished, it is essential to preserve the cleanliness of the brush. This is done by preparing enough 'brush keeper' varnish to completely cover the bristles and keep them supple. Brush keeper is a mixture of two-thirds turpentine and one-third varnish, and the brush is simply suspended in it by hanging it from a wire crossbar across the top of the container. It is useful to cover the container by putting a piece of polythene over it to prevent dust entering.

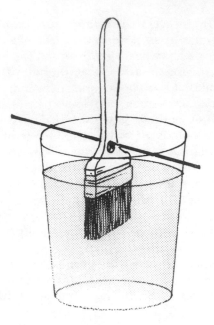

FIGURE 8. Suspending the brush in keeper varnish is a method of ensuring that the bristles will retain their straightness and at the same time remain supple for future work. The crossbar need not be elaborate, merely a length of thick wire placed across the mouth of the vessel. As an added precaution a polythene bag can be placed over the vessel to prevent dust particles from settling on the surface of the keeper varnish and transferring to the brush when it is removed.

The process of varnishing may seem pretty simple when seen from afar, but it is something which calls for a distinct technique, and it can be considered in some detail. The best brushes are a fitch or a double-chisel camel-hair, the width being three inches for general furniture finishing. The workpiece should be set in a good strong light, preferably daylight, because surface examination has to be frequent. When the brush is loaded, or charged, it should be moved with the grain in very even strokes, without faltering. The method of covering the surface should be systematic, not erratic, and there should be a generous overlap of each section. The first covering can be put on with some energy. While it is still wet, the second varnishing can be started at the initial point, this time holding the brush vertically so that the bristles delicately pass over the surface. This is done in order to smooth out the varnish, and so it is unnecessary to load the brush as generously as in the first coat. One of the initial faults of the beginner is that an excess of varnish will gather in corners and crevices. Blobs, sags and runs show that too much varnish has been used. They can be smoothed out with a deft and dry brush, often by simply flicking them with the bristle-tip.

It will probably take between six and eight hours for the first coat to set and harden if the room is at the right temperature and a good quality varnish has been used. But there are variables in every job, and so the time may be longer or shorter. The varnish has to be tested to find out whether it has set or not. All that is necessary is to push the finger-nail down. If it makes a dent, then the varnish is obviously still soft. But if it does not make a dent, the second coat can be applied.

The new coat is not slapped on like paint, because this will cause peeling and blistering within a short time. Such a failure is caused by not giving the second coat a good ground, or base, to which it can adhere. The first coat must be thoroughly rubbed down, using a wet/dry medium garnet paper. Petrol is a good lubricant, and the rubbing action

FIGURE 9. Varnishing should be done against natural light with each stroke slightly overlapping to ensure an even coverage of the wood. If the craftsman stands in such a position as to be able to see the light as it reflects on the wet surface, the completed job should be devoid of any areas starved of varnish.

should follow the grain. After the surface has been wiped clean, use the tack rag to pick up any remaining particles.

The second coat of varnish is applied in the same way as the first, and it may dry more rapidly. If it shows a certain number of imperfections, generally in the shape of small bumps and rises and falls, these can be rubbed away with garnet paper.

After a third coat the dry hard varnish is polished. This is done with a felt pad and a quantity of fine pumice powder, using mineral oil. The pad is soaked in oil and then coated with pumice, and it is then placed on the surface and rubbed with what can only be described as a medium pressure in long even strokes rather than a circular motion. The varnish should begin to polish almost at once. This action will also flatten out any uneven areas. When the polished area is complete, it should be wiped with a clean cotton cloth.

Despite the vast number of polyurethane and instant finishes which can be brushed or sprayed on, and the claims made for them by the manufacturers, there is still an enormous amount to be said for varnish. But it does call for an almost fastidious approach to the job, and this may well go against it as far as some of the more profit-minded craftsmen are concerned.

4

French Polishing

IT would be quite pointless to pretend that french polishing can be done by anybody who is blessed with only a slight knowledge of the materials and the process itself. If it is to look right and if it is to wear well for many years, then french polishing must be done in an expert fashion, employing methods which are among the oldest in the wood finishing trade.

Throughout this chapter, and indeed, elsewhere in the book, the word 'French' will be expressed as 'french' in accordance with modern practice. Although this particular treatment of the wood surface is said to have its origins in France in the seventeenth and eighteenth centuries, it has since Georgian times become international and is in use wherever fine furniture is made and antique pieces are restored. At one time not only furniture was so treated but also internal casements, doors and architraves, especially when mahogany was used. In its heyday french polishing was not, however, applied only to mahogany. When the method was first introduced an enormous number of woods were so treated, sometimes with success, often with failure.

The modern wood finisher uses it with some discretion. For example, it would not usually be used on oak which, by and large, is improved with a wax finish, but it is essential to underline the fact that of all woods it enhances mahogany best of all. It can be applied with success to other woods. For instance, it can give spectacular results to walnut and to the lighter woods, such as pine, when there is a good stained surface.

The preliminaries are similar to those required for shellac or varnish. The surface of the wood is smoothed and then, if necessary, stopped to fill the pores of open-grained wood. The purpose is to achieve a very smooth surface and prevent absorption by liquid polishes. Obviously, a lot depends on the wood to be polished. The light coloured soft woods can be stained if required, then filled, using the methods described elsewhere and wiped over with a liberal coating of linseed oil. Boiled linseed oil will enhance the eventual tone of the majority of lighter woods, but it is not always a good idea to apply it to the darker ones, which will become even darker and obscure any distinctive figuring. But these are preliminary considerations and they will, of course, vary from one job to another, as, for example, walnut, which is a darker wood and is oiled to bring out the figure.

As in the application of varnish, the place in which the french polishing is done should be kept at a temperature of about 70 degrees Farenheit. If the air is humid the polish will work badly and this will result in a cloudy and opaque finish due to moisture in the air. The french polisher often finds himself working in some strange locations, and it is not always reasonable to expect to have a perfectly even temperature when working on say, a grand piano in a church, or a mahogany commode in the hallway of a stately home. So sensitive is the process that it is possible to bring a source of warmth to the surface of the workpiece and still get reasonable results. Even a low voltage electric fire suspended over the surface will prove effective. It has even been known for the resourceful craftsman to lay a piece of brown paper or a blanket on the wood and then iron it until the wood fibres are warmed, then work quite successfully on the surface. Wood will hold heat for a considerable time. It will also absorb dampness, and this happens to represent one of the major nuisances of french polishing. A damp patch in the wood fibre will show up during polishing, but if it is found early enough it can be dispelled, using several layers of brown paper and a smoothing iron. Occasionally, there are dangers in doing this, in particular, for example, when french polishing stained work. The water-based dyes and stains will react, showing up as dull patches which cannot be removed. If one persisted and went ahead with polishing the result may be so bad as to call for complete stripping of the job and a fresh start. The moral may well be to use spirit stains whenever possible, although this is not always the best treatment for a particular piece of furniture.

The french polisher works with comparatively few materials, but one thing he will need is a plentiful supply of wadding or lint-free cotton wool, flannel and cotton sheet and linen.

The proverbial well-washed bedsheet is ideal, provided it is not at the point of falling to pieces with all the traces of starch removed. Mixtures of man-made fibres and cottons are no good at all because they are only partly absorbent. Cotton sheeting is used to make the rubbers which perform a very important function. The rest of the french polishing materials reside in a selection of bottles and will be considered later on.

What we are looking at are the tools for the job.

There is, quite rightly, something of a fetish about the rubber. Almost as old as wood finishing itself, this pad is fashioned from wool or flannel and rags in a size which is dictated by the job in hand, and all are home made to the same pattern. This is a prime tool of the trade. If it is properly made and correctly charged, it will help perform miracles.

To Make the Rubber

Make the inner wadding pad from, say, a 9 inch square folded in half lengthwise and then into three to make a $4\frac{1}{2}'' \times 3''$ rectangle. Fold the top right and left-hand corners to the base which will leave a triangle and from this fold the base-points towards the centre, leaving about a $1\frac{1}{2}''$ base to form the heel of the final wedge. Before you are ready to start polishing, the wadding should first be thoroughly dampened with polish to maintain its form while folding as above; if you wish to practise folding, simply dampen with water or use a 9 inch square of paper. The square size may be reduced or enlarged according to requirements.

Cover the pad with a similar size square of linen or cotton and hold them together at the heel end with the folds of the linen hanging down. With the other hand make the linen taut at the pointed end and fold the surplus drape at the point into two or three long narrow triangles, each folding over the other to meet the face edge of the rubber. Make sure that the point is maintained. Now turn the rubber face down, having the heel end resting between the thumb and index finger. Any loose linen at the heel end can be gathered together with the folded material from the point and 'screwed' together at the rear top edge. This top 'knot' will sit comfortably towards the palm of the hand while the fingers at the pointed end and the thumb against the side of the heel propel the rubber when in use. The objective when covering the pad is to ensure a tight overall wrap, ensuring that the flat wedge-shape is maintained; also it should have an easy access to the wadding, through the 'screw-top', to enable simple recharging with polish.

The secret of the success of the rubber is the internal wadding because it is absorbent and should be completely dry. Many a job has been ruined by an inexperienced polisher using any old material for the pad and not noticing that it happens to be slightly damp. Some brands of wadding have a 'skin' on one or both sides, and this should be stripped off before use, leaving some pure soft material.

There is no greater enemy than dirt in french polishing. Even a few wandering specks may ruin what is otherwise a fine piece of work. The expert polisher knows almost by instinct when the rubber has picked up some grains of dirt, even when the rubber is almost black with use.

Rubbers can be stored in airtight tins and kept supple with a few drops of methylated spirit or alcohol every now and then. When the outer cover eventually wears out it can simply be replaced.

FIGURE 10. How the inner wadding is folded for the rubber.

Use a 9″ square of wadding, and fold ,in half, then into thirds. Now fold the other two sides underneath, centre right, finally forming the material into a wedge or tear shape, (bottom). If properly made, the wadding should form itself into a convenient shape with some material on top for easy handling. It is advisable to soak the material in polish, let it dry, then soak with spirit for ease of manipulation.

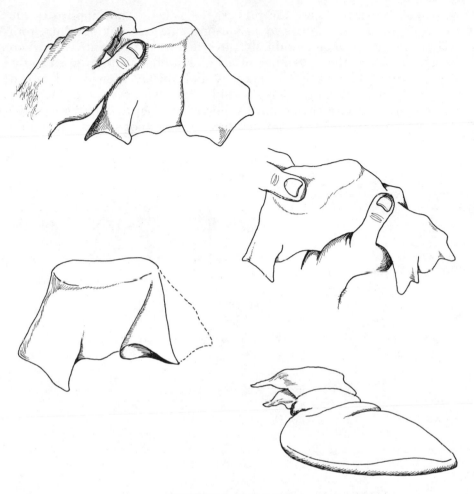

FIGURE 11. Making the rubber.

A piece of well washed cotton rag or linen is placed over the folded inner wadding, keeping the heel two inches from the rear edge (top). Now hold the other hand underneath with the fingers firmly against the point of the wadding, pulling the rag tight. Place the left hand to hold the rubber at the point. If the wadding is well soaked in spirit, the wadding and the cotton rag should stick together. Now make two or three folds as shown and then turn the rubber over in the left hand and gather together the surplus cotton rag and turn it round and round to form a 'screw' top and to exert a uniform pressure on the rubber which would cause the polish to be exuded when charged.

When preparing to use the rubber, the polish is not applied to the external surface, it is dripped inside onto the covered wadding from whence it soaks through gradually, governed by the pressure exerted on it. This is where the advantage of using a rubber with an open top is demonstrated, because it can be easily and quickly opened and spread out, ready for recharging. This should be done with care, and the bottle containing the polish should have a pierced stopper to help regulate the flow just enough to simply moisten the wadding, not saturate it so that

FIGURE 12.   Using the rubber by pressing the flat surface down on the wood while the forefinger provides the necessary pressure, which can be modified as the build-up of sheen is created:

the entire rubber is dripping wet with polish and virtually unmanageable. No advantage whatever is gained by using a rubber which throws drops of polish in all directions. When the wadding is damp, the sides of the covering cloth are gathered together and tightened, and the rubbing surface is pushed against the palm of the other hand, creating an even flow of polish through the linen before it comes into contact with the surface which is about to be polished. At this initial stage the objective is to spread an even film of polish on the wood, working in long, even and firm strokes, first across the grain and then with it. As soon as the rubber feels dry it should be removed from the wood, opened and replenished with a few more drops of polish. The rubber is again applied to the surface, making sure that the entire area is thoroughly covered. An erratic scrubbing action should be avoided, for all it will do is scuff the surface and probably spoil it. There must be constant motion, and the rubber must always be kept on the move. This is particularly so when it makes initial contact with the surface and when it leaves it; in such cases remember to commence and finish the contact each time with a sweeping motion, rather than simply placing the rubber down or lifting off the work. If there is any pause or hesitation or an action in an uncertain and jabbing way, it will result in a series of ridges.

This first initial film is followed by a second application, known as 'bodying-in', and is applied in much the same way as previously described. The workpiece should then be allowed to stand overnight in a well balanced temperature to give the polish time to harden in a sound and firm skin, which is the foundation for the subsequent applications known as 'bodying-up'. Regardless of how much bodying up is done, the surface of the wood will not be affected. The initial film will have taken hold and the further applications will not penetrate the wood. What does occur, in fact, is a gradual growth of the sheen which is the hallmark of the technique.

The correct procedure is the one which is used by craftsmen who polish the cases of grand pianos and it is from them that we can take a lead. Each 'coat' on a traditional grand piano is thoroughly smoothed and examined before the next coat is put on. The smoothing tool is home-made, consisting of what is known as a pounce-bag, and it is no more than a square of soft cotton sheet into which one ounce of very fine pumice powder is placed. The edges are lifted up and tied, some looseness being left for the pumice to move about inside. The pounce-bag, slightly damped with denatured alcohol, is rubbed over the surface of the hardened polish, occasionally being tapped to release a little pumice powder which grinds flat any irregularities.

There is always room for some adjustment of a coat of french polish, and if a particularly fine sheen is needed, then steel wool should be used as an abrasive, taking care to use the tack rag to remove any loose particles. Use of fine steel wool will ensure a deep sheen and it is, if anything, superior to the pounce-bag technique of surface grinding.

When bodying-up it will be found that somewhat less polish will be needed and the glossy surface will start to appear very quickly as each coat dries. During this stage the polish will dry more rapidly and because of this the rubber should be provided with boiled linseed oil as a lubricant. Use only a few drops at a time, simply enough to help the rubber to glide over the polish. During the application of the polish the

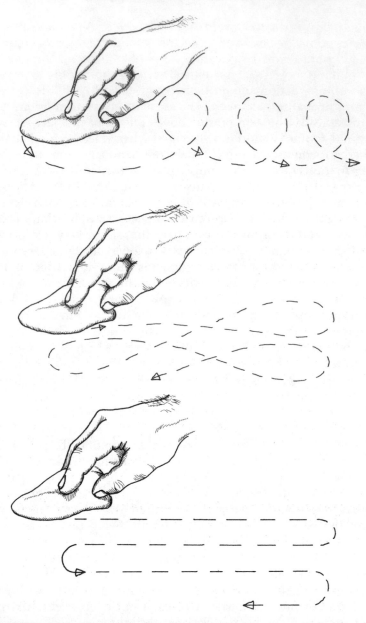

FIGURE 13. The sequence of movements when using the rubber, starting, at the top, with a generous circular movement, ensuring that a scaled down movement is used to cover the edges, followed by the elongated figure-of-eight, at which stage it is likely that more oil will be needed to aid lubrication, completing with long and straight movements, (bottom). By following this sequence it is possible to create an even covering and a sound foundation for subsequent polishing.

surface will look quite dull at the start but the sheen should appear after only a little light rubbing. The oil itself is not a contributory factor to the success at this stage. All that it does is keep the rubber on the move. Some craftsmen simply smear it on the areas in need rather than applying it to the rubber. This method may have an advantage, because the quantity required can be judged more finely if it is put on the rubber. If oil is on the surface in too lavish a quantity, it will 'sweat' between coats and appear as globules. It should be wiped off with a clean cloth. The results will look encouraging. The movement of the rubber should

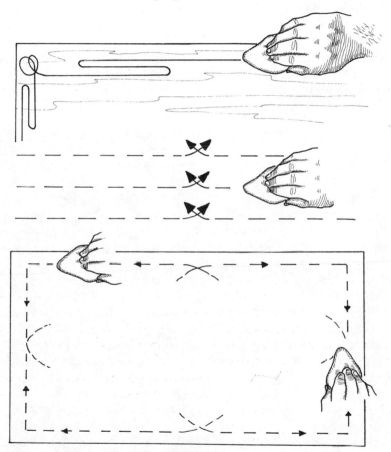

FIGURE 14.   Awkward corners and contours are tackled by following a definite sequence of movements. The top movement is designed to ensure a good covering of right-angled corners, using a rubber with a finely formed point. In the centre is the movement known as 'stiffing', when the rubber is glided off the surface where it is unable to finish at either edge due to mouldings or other obstructions. At bottom is a method of tackling edges and corners: rubber is glided off in the centre of each side.

by now be in a figure-of-eight, along the grain, and the pressure need only be slight to get results. Each application should begin at the edge and move inwards towards the centre so that the figures-of-eight overlap. Too much pressure at this point can cause streaking, due to the softening of the under-surface of the polish which has not completely set. Streaking and smearing can be avoided to a great extent if the later coats of polish are much thinner in consistency than the initial ones. To achieve this the polish should be thinned down with either denatured alcohol or methylated spirits in a 50/50 proportion. The thinner the polish, the quicker it will dry and harden. But it should not be thinned down too much, because a surfeit of methylated spirit will also act as a solvent and soften whole areas of the coating.

If smearing continues, the workpiece should be left to dry and harden. This will not necessarily cause the smears to disappear, but the resting time will at least stabilise them, ready for spiriting out. To do this a

FIGURE 15.   Applying a rubber of french polish and creating one of several coats to build up to a fine deep finish.
(Photo by courtesy of Arthur Brett and Sons Ltd, Norwich)

special rubber is needed with a two-layer cotton outer cover. Methylated spirit is dropped into the felt or cotton-wool core and allowed to thoroughly permeate. The rubber should feel no more than slightly damp, and the spirit should not run straight through it. The entire area of the smeared wood is rubbed over very lightly, followed immediately by rubbing along the grain with a clean cotton cloth. If the smearing is quite pronounced, then strong circular strokes can be used, finishing with lighter ones along the figuring. And that is just about all there is to it. Spiriting out needs to be done with judgement and discretion. If it is badly handled, it can result in a wholesale disturbance of the surface.

If french polishing has any drawbacks, then the main one must be that it achieves a mirror surface which is not always demanded, especially when refinishing antique furniture. During the Thirties there was a vogue for highly polished furniture of all kinds. Some of the pieces executed in so-called bird's eye maple looked as though they were surfaced with glass. Times change, perhaps thankfully, and people now seem to prefer a soft satin sheen type of finish, which can be developed from conventional french polish. It can be done very simply by placing a quantity of pumice powder in a tray, making a cotton pad and soaking it in linseed oil, picking up a quantity of dry pumice and then rubbing it along the grain of the wood. This should instantly dull the surface. It takes only a short time to get rid of the gloss and the oil and pumice will not inflict smears. The only danger is of cutting through one or more coats of polish, but if a fairly delicate pressure is used, the dulling should become quickly apparent and present the required appearance.

While there is little to be said against the french polish which can be bought readymade, it is still an advantage to make it up personally, especially in the small business where it is necessary to provide a wide range of finishes to meet the needs of each client. Using a standard readymade polish can lead to a mass-produced appearance in everything handled. In an age which is once again beginning to patronise the solitary craftsman, it is an obvious advantage to revive old methods rather than operate what may well amount to a mini-factory.

Two polishes are used, and they are both based on shellac. The first is made by dissolving six ounces of shellac in a pint of methylated spirit. This is a standard mix and it can be reduced or increased according to need. As a general rule, however, the standard mixture will be suitable for the first four to six applications of polish, after which the proportions can be modified to thin it down. If a great deal of french polishing is to be done, it is advisable to make up sets of polish in separately labelled bottles, marked either '1' and '2' or 'A' and 'B'. The second mixture will be made out of the first one, diluted either 50/50 or one to two-thirds. It is rather like cutting shellac. When mixing the basic polish it is not strictly necessary to weigh out the shellac. All that is necessary is to crush the flakes to a coarse dust and then half-fill the bottle, regardless of the quantity which is being made up and then fill it with methylated spirit. Ample time should be allowed for it to dissolve, and it should be well shaken daily while being stored in a cool, dark place.

The second preparation is known as white polish because it is made with white shellac. It is a good idea to keep in stock a selection of both standard brown and white polishes ready-made if any commercial work is to be undertaken. White polish will not colour the wood, and so it is suitable for ash, sycamore and similar woods. The standard mix is used for darker woods.

The differences between ready-made and home-made liquid polish can be very marked, and while some manufacturers may claim to include certain resins and gums in their preparations, it is noticeable that quality varies as much as price. One somehow never achieves exactly the same degree of perfection which becomes possible with home-made polish. Certainly, there can be no special or magic ingredient in the readymade polish which will lead to immediate success.

A variation of french polishing is known as glazing, and it is applied to carved wood or, indeed, any intricate surfaces. It cannot be considered as a substitute for french polishing, because all it consists of is a coat of spirit varnish. One frequent criticism of glazing is that it lacks the durability of french polishing, although it can look pretty much the same. On the other hand, it can look superior when applied by a skilled craftsman, many of whom use it as a final finish. The basic difference is that a true finish is made by friction whereas glazing is simply painted on. If it has anything to commend it, then it should be its use on pieces which cannot be treated with ordinary french polish. A carved area is the best example. Other awkward or difficult areas may be the rails of chairs and the edges of some tables, and inlaid work, including marquetry and parquetry in which the individual pieces may be disturbed by vigorous rubbing. Pierced wood is practically difficult to polish, and so here again a glaze is the answer.

Glaze is made by mixing gum benzoin, also used as an incense, with methylated spirit. As with shellac and methylated spirit, a 50/50 mix is effective. Before mixing, the gum benzoin should be broken down to a coarse powder and sieved to remove any thick particles and foreign matter. After it has been mixed, it should be strained and then stored for up to a month or two at house temperature and shaken frequently.

Glaze can be applied with a rubber, a brush or sponge. The method does not much matter as long as an even coating is achieved. It has to be applied to a surface which already has a sealing coat of shellac polish. If it is applied to naked wood, absolutely nothing will happen because it will simply sink into the fibres and vanish. Glaze should be applied very lightly, not forced into the wood. If a sponge is used to apply it, then a dabbing action should be adopted and the work should be done very quickly. If it is painted on, the brush should be well loaded and rapidly passed over the surface in an up-and-down motion.

Although it has been said that glaze is best used for difficult areas, it can also be applied to large flat surfaces, using a rubber. Several coats may be necessary. Using a second rubber kept for the purpose, apply a minute quantity of oil and methylated spirit to achieve a final effect.

Glaze can also be used to revive old french polish, and it has advantages over other methods, such as waxing, which simply provides a protective coating to the old finish. Glaze will revive old french polish without the trouble of completely refinishing the entire surface.

It is possible to expand the limitations of french polishing by the use of colour for spotting-in as and when it is needed. A fine piece of wood may be enhanced simply by the use of a process which heightens its natural hue, whereas a piece which suffers from colouring faults can certainly be improved. Colour application has many advantages when french polishing has lost its charm through misuse and fading. Although the entire question of wood staining is dealt with in the next chapter, it may now be useful to consider it in relation to french polishing.

The materials used for colouring are simple enough and while they need not represent a significant outlay, it is nevertheless a good idea to lay in as wide a selection as possible to meet all colour requirements. Certain colours are available in powder form, including bismarck red and gas black. The spirit-based colours include yellow, green, mauve, and brown. A suitable brush is a No. 7 camel hair mop.

The principal use of colour is for spotting-in and retouching areas where furniture has had the full blast of sunlight and partially faded. Victorian furniture does not as a rule suffer from such blemishes, but earlier furniture does exhibit the fault. The Victorians were in the habit of closing the curtains in rooms not in use to protect the furniture from direct sunlight.

The purpose of spotting-in polished areas with colour is to apply the tint over the film of polish. This means that the colour will ultimately be sandwiched between layers of polish.

As with fine art retouching, the first move is to mix the colour to achieve an exact match with the surrounding areas of the wood to be treated. Both colour and polish are mixed together, but first a mixture of 50/50 methylated spirit and standard polish is made up. In the case of darker woods, such as mahogany, it is necessary to create this 'body' which will act as a carrier for the colour itself, and this is done by putting a few drops of gas black into the polish, followed by a very small amount of bismarck red, which should give a particular shade of brown. The precise colour will probably be slightly off at the first attempt, but an adjustment of colour can be made by the addition of more colour. It is better to start by using very small quantities and adding to them than trying to make the required colour in a single bold attempt. When the colour is judged to be right after testing by dabbing on a piece of scrap wood or paper, take a folded cloth and lift the paint on to it, using the brush. Do not over charge the cloth, otherwise the result will look like a stuck-on patch which will be difficult to remove. The cloth is now dabbed down on the faded spot. It should not be held down, but repeatedly dabbed. When it shows signs of taking, the rubber is lightly run along the direction of the grain so that the colour is evenly distributed. The cloth should be used in the style of a brush, flicking to ensure that the area is equally covered. If it is not possible to use a cloth in this way, then a brush should be charged with colour and squeezed to a point, removing most of the surplus colour. The point of the brush is then delicately used to apply the colour to the area. One of the common faults is that the beginner will work too close to the surface and in so doing lose sight of the area which is being treated, ending up with patchiness. It is advisable to work like an artist, standing back from the easel, so to speak, and getting an overall view. It seems scarcely necessary to stress that all this takes time, especially in the final stages, when further retouching becomes necessary.

The coloured area should be polished very gently, using a rubber made for the purpose, but it will not be necessary to apply the same amount of pressure which is used for conventional french polishing. The colour may well move if too much vigour is used, and this will ruin the job. Once the familiar lustre appears, stop.

The use of colour is admittedly a very tricky business, and most craftsmen encounter difficulties when trying to get a perfect match. It will pay the craftsman to experiment with the colour range, especially those which are spirit based. Spirit colours can supplement the basic method of fixing certain colours. Yellow can be added to red to tone it down, while green will convert red into brown. But spirit colours should be used with great discretion, and it will be found that the smallest quantity will be sufficient to achieve an effect.

5

Stains and Staining

Materials and Methods

EVEN the most experienced craftsman may occasionally find that he has a less than perfect knowledge of the range of stains. It is noticeable that there is an innate kind of conservatism when it comes to experimenting with colours and hues which are outside the conventional. This is a pity. In the last few years many entirely new stains have appeared, including a number with a polyurethane or varnish-like base which enables even the most inexperienced amateur to achieve results previously unattainable. They have brought a range, albeit a somewhat narrow one, of wood finishing techniques and possibilities within the reach of people who would never attempt the skill, though it is debatable whether any true skill is needed to obtain satisfactory results. It would be pointless to scorn these instant finishes. At least they introduce the beginner to some of the possibilities and may even lead to craft-finishing, using the more traditional methods and materials.

The three reasons why stains are used are:

(1) to make inferior woods resemble better woods;
(2) to match some woods with others;
(3) to serve a function in decorative work and antique refinishing.

Thus, in (1), a common pine can be made to look like walnut, rosewood or even oak. In (2), oak and other woods can be enhanced to look like more elite brothers. In (3), unobtainable woods can be imitated in marquetry and other specialised techniques, and touched up to resemble ancient furniture.

There is one school of thought which objects to any staining of wood on the grounds that it constitutes fakery, and yet in the craft of marquetry certain woods have been dyed and disguised ever since the craft began for the simple reason that it is not always possible to obtain sufficient matching exotic wood to complete a particular job. On the other hand, it should be appreciated that the common woods in ample supply can be used for interior furnishings, and stained and polished in such a way as to resemble something rather better than they basically are without detracting from their functional rôle.

Regardless of the many arguments in favour of disguising wood, there remains the overwhelming fact that staining happens to be one of the aspects of the finishing trade which can offer a wide spectrum of possibilities at the lowest cost. The materials are cheap. No elaborate equipment is needed. All that is required is an understanding of the properties of the colours and the fluids in which they are suspended.

The purpose of wood stain is to colour the surface. It is as easy as that. Some schools of thought stress the importance of deep-staining the wood, but depth is actually irrelevant because it does not necessarily achieve any particular or remarkable strength of colour or even affect the polish when the piece is finally finished.

Wood can be stained with practically any form of water soluble dye, including the cold water variety used for clothes. Patent aniline dyes are freely available in chemist shops in two varieties, one being soluble in water and the other in spirit. While anilines are quick to react to the wood, they will not necessarily endure for a very long period, although, if they are mixed with a spirit base and quickly varnished, this should prolong their life. Water-based dyes will have a longer life if they are strengthened by the addition of a small amount of vinegar. If it is required to add spirit stains to varnish and apply direct to the wood, it may take some time to achieve exactly the right colour, because the varnish will mask the colour, and it will be found that colour diminishes in proportion to the thickness of the varnish. Thus, it is better when working with colour to use thinner varnishes.

Apart from stains already mentioned, it is also possible to colour wood by using natural substances. Beetroot, for instance, will give a typical red-purple tone, and blueberries boiled with alum and a solution of copperas will give a blue colour. Privet leaves can be boiled in a salt solution to yield a yellow-green. A delicate yellow can be made from apple tree bark if it is boiled in a solution of alum.

The choice of material to use as a wood stain is governed by the inclination of the craftsman who may want to develop colours which are unobtainable in the commercial range. However, the commercial range is now wide enough to meet practically all needs, and there is also the advantage of standardisation of colour. It is one thing to distil yellow from a quantity of privet leaves only to discover that the supply runs out at exactly the moment when more is needed, but it is a more comforting thing to know that further supplies are available from the nearest chemist or hardware store. While the manufacturers supply shade cards and examples to show the stains on pieces of wood, it is still unlikely that exact and precise matches will be achieved. They are no more than a broad guide. Some idea of stains now available can be gained from the following examination of the range:

OIL STAINS

Fumed Oak	Weathered Oak	Cherry	Brown Flemish
Dark Oak	Early English	Rosewood	Walnut
Golden Oak	Brown Mahogany	Malachite	Jacobean
Mission Oak	Red Mahogany	Grey	Antique Mahogany

SPIRIT STAINS

Brown Oak	Light Mahogany	Flemish Oak
Bog Oak	Dark Mahogany	Moss Green

DRY ANILINE AND COAL TAR STAINS

Mahogany Fast Red, water soluble
Mahogany Fast Brown, water soluble
Walnut, water soluble
Walnut R, alcohol soluble
Golden Oak, alcohol soluble
Bismarck Brown, water or alcohol soluble
Black Nigrosine J, water soluble
Black Nigrosine WN, alcohol soluble
Yellow Acid H.M., water soluble
Orange Y, water soluble
Scarlet 2 RB, water soluble
Green M. X., water or alcohol soluble
Methylene Blue 2B, water and alcohol soluble
Fuchine Magenta RT, water and alcohol soluble
Violet 3 BPN, water and alcohol soluble

PERIOD STAIN FINISHES *Acid (water) stain*

Brown Hepplewhite	Baronial Oak	Butler Oak	Fumed Oak
Chippendale	Cathedral Oak	Old English	Flemish Oak
Sheraton	Hungarian Oak	Kaiser Grey	Austrian Oak
Colonial Mahogany	Antique Mahogany	Adam Brown Mahogany	

PERIOD STAIN FINISHES   *Oil Stain*

Early English	Antwerp Oak	William and Mary
Weathered Oak	American Walnut	Louis XVI
Flanders Oak	Jacobean	Mission Stains
		Queen Anne

The choice of material to use as a wood stain is governed by the individual craftsman who may want to create colours which are outside the normal range.

Although water stains are said to have a shorter life than spirit stains, they remain the most widely used. A water stain means that the colour is dissolved in water. There are four different types: water soluble aniline and coal tar dyes; chemical acid and alkalines; colour pigments and, finally dyewood stains.

Aniline and coal tar dyes are the biggest group and they are used in the construction industry for the finish of some exteriors and interiors. Oil and spirit aniline and coal tar dyes are used for the rest of the work. Chemical acid and alkaline stains are used in parts of the furniture industry. Colour pigments are manufactured and blended for specific purposes by the craftsman, using dry powder colours. Colour pigment water stain has now passed out of use, but may still be available from isolated suppliers. Dyewood stains are no longer available.

Water stains are popular because they can be used to cover large areas of wood, such as cupboard doors and panelling. The most usual form for this type of staining are the aniline and coal tar dyes which can be bought in both dry and liquid form. If there is any disadvantage in using a water stain on large areas, it is that it will raise the grain and need to be sanded before it is finally finished. If that is a snag, then there are definite advantages. For instance, water stains do not obscure the grain, or figuring, of the wood, and they can actually enhance it. When used on good quality plywood a fine birch grain will be beautified by a suitable stain. If water stains are not permanent, a more lasting effect can be achieved by using the corresponding spirit or oil aniline stain.

The ease with which water stain can be applied is quite remarkable, and a job can certainly be done much more quickly with it than with spirit stain. This is due largely to the absorbent qualities of the wood. One of the tricks of the trade in water staining is to heat the stain to a temperature of about 90 degrees Fahrenheit, which makes it take far more quickly than if applied cold to the wood. Water stain can be used on wood surfaces which are subject to intense sunshine and weathering, such as shop fronts, and the external surfaces of window frames and sills. If they are treated with oil or spirit stains, they will fade in a year or two.

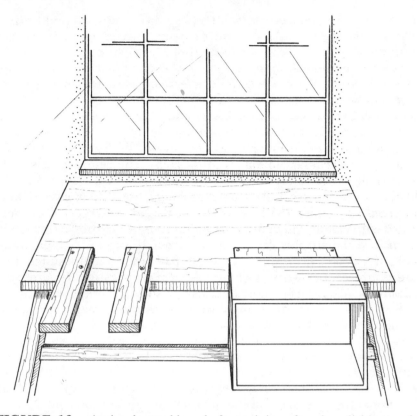

FIGURE 16. A simple workbench for staining, french polishing and other finishing techniques, consisting of sturdy battens fastened to the bench in such a way as to securely hold workpieces. The battens may be grooved or bored, to hold spindles, rails, dowels etc. The recommended bench height is three feet with as much natural light as possible.

Water stain, on the other hand, is equally effective for both light and dark colours, and can be executed in all shades of gray, the lighter shades of green, and Circassian and French walnut.

What the craftsman most needs to appreciate is the quality of water stains. While the effect produced is rapid and dramatic, this stain is more sensitive to aberrations in the surface of the wood, most notably to absorbency. When wood is machined, the grain is sometimes crushed, and this creates a less absorbent surface causing patchiness when the stain is applied, though this can be remedied by a generous application of clean water which should loosen and raise the fibres.

It is preferable to apply water stain in two coats, sanding after the first to smooth the surface. It should not be necessary to sand after the second coat has been applied.

Applying water stains does call for a modicum of skill, and beginners will find that laps and joins will demand heavier brushing to avoid creating dark marks. This cannot happen with spirit stain to which a very small amount of thinned shellac has been added. In water staining laps and joins can be avoided if the wood is first brushed over with clean water, followed by the stain itself, using a generously wide brush. The first reaction may be of a darker colour than is required, but if the surface is kept wet it can be sponged and lightened. The most common fault is to apply far too much stain, soaking the entire surface to such an extent that the colour runs in all directions. The rule is that sufficient stain to colour the surface is applied with just enough wetness to enable adjustment to be made. But adjustment of the colour should not be attempted on a piecemeal basis. Even though a large flat surface is flooded with colour which is too strong, it should carefully dabbed with a sponge and the surplus gradually removed. If an area is lightened too much, the final effect will be one of patchiness, more suited to the antique appearance when the highlights are emphasised. In antiquing it is desirable that darker colour should lodge in the corners and the crevices, but in the normal run of water staining all that is needed is an overall and well distributed colour.

A word of warning should be sounded about applying water stain to any veneered surfaces. The glued underside of veneer often dries out and granulates as time goes on, and this makes the individual pieces weak and unable to withstand dampness. If water is applied it will penetrate the edges of the pieces and seep into what remains of the glue, then soak the wood beneath. When the inevitable expansion occurs, the damp veneer will be forced upwards. That is why the faster acting spirit or oil stain should be used on veneered surfaces.

Water stain has its own idiosyncrasies, but it shares the same basic requirement as other staining techniques in that two thin coats are always preferable to one strong one. A thin and light coat is simpler to apply and it is much easier to avoid laps and streaking. The first coat must be thoroughly dry before the second one is put on and the effect observed. Colour may change as the wood dries, and this enables the craftsman to decide how much colouration is required for the second coat.

One gallon of water stain will treat up to 500 square feet of softwood and 700 square feet of hardwood.

Formulary of Water Stains

Weathered Oak water stain for use on chestnut or oak
Dissolve four ounces of walnut aniline crystals in one gallon of hot water. Apply generously to the wood and allow to dry, then sandpaper smooth and dust clean of particles.

Dissolve 6½ drams nigrosine, J, dry, water soluble and 1½ drams scarlet 2RL aniline, dry, water soluble, in one gallon of hot water. Apply to wood and dry. Used as a surface finish either an orange shellac and a wax or a flat varnish.

Golden Oak for use on oak and a wide variety of woods

Dissolve 3 ounces of loutre aniline, dry, water soluble, and one ounce of napthol yellow, aniline, dry, water soluble in about one gallon of hot water. Apply to the wood and allow to dry before thoroughly sanding. If oak is being stained, use a silica filler darkened with Vandyke brown in oil

The finish should be orange shellac and varnish.

Fumed Oak for use on oak

Dissolve ½ ounce bichromate of potash and ½ ounce carbonate of potash in one gallon of hot water. Brush on generously, allow to dry and then sandpaper smooth.

Take the following and mix together as dry powders:

> 2 drams acid brown aniline, dry, water soluble
> 2 ounces walnut aniline powder, dry, water soluble
> 1 ounce nigrosine black, dry, water soluble
> 1 dram napthol yellow aniline, dry, water soluble
> 1 ounce and 6 drams sulphur brown M, aniline, dry, water soluble

Take 3½ ounces of the mixed powders and stir into 1 gallon of hot water. This should be brushed on to the wood, allowed to dry and then sanded. The surface finish should be as follows: mix 2 ounces of boiled linseed oil, 1 ounce of japan drier and 5 ounces of benzine. This should be rubbed in and the surplus wiped off at once. A second coat is brushed on and allowed to soak in. When dry, apply a coat of thinned orange shellac, followed by a flat varnish.

English Oak for use on oak

Dissolve 10 ounces of walnut aniline, dry, water soluble, and ¼ ounce of caustic soda in one gallon of hot water. This is brushed on to the wood and allowed to dry before the surface is sanded.

The filler should be silex mixed with Vandyke brown for colour.

The final finish should be orange shellac, suitably thinned and applied in two or three coats. Alternatively, a varnish can be used if preferred.

Early English for use on oak

Take 2½ ounces mahogany brown aniline, dry, water soluble, 13 ounces nigrosine, black, dry, water soluble, ½ ounce picric acid and dissolve three ounces of the mix in one gallon of hot water.

If a filler is required, use silex mixed with Vandyke brown and a little black. The final finish can be a gloss varnish rubbed dull or, alternatively, orange shellac.

Antique Early English for use on oak

Take ¼ ounce walnut aniline, dry, water soluble; ½ ounce mahogany brown aniline, dry water soluble; 4 drams caustic soda, dry, and mix in 5 quarts of hot water.

Apply to the wood with a sponge, allow it to dry and then sandpaper smooth. A second coat will increase the darkness. Use silex as a filler and mix it with Vandyke brown, oil based.

A suitable finish is shellac in a mixture of ¼ orange and ¾ white. One coat should be sufficient, followed by waxing and then dulling down to a lustre.

Flemish for use on oak

Take two ounces bichromate of potash and 1 ounce of caustic soda and dissolve in one gallon of hot water. Apply generously to the wood, allow it to dry, and then sandpaper smooth.

Now apply the following: 2 ounces nigrosine black, dry, water soluble; 1 dram, sulphate of iron, dry; 2 ounces acid brown aniline, dry, water soluble. This should be brushed on and allowed to dry.

Apply the following to the wood: 2 ounces boiled linseed oil; 2 ounces japan drier; 4 ounces benzine. Several coats may be required before the wood begins to respond.

Tobacco Brown for use on oak, chestnut, pine

Mix 8 drams naphthol yellow, aniline, dry, water soluble and 1 dram bichromate of potash in one gallon of hot water. This should be brushed on in a generous quantity and the wood sanded.

The next part of the treatment consists of the application of the following: 28 drams walnut aniline crystals, dry, water soluble; 3½ drams mahogany brown aniline, dry, water soluble.

Mix in 2½ pints of hot water and then brush on to the wood and allow it to dry, after which it should be covered with a very thin coat of 50/50 orange and white shellac. The filler should be silex coloured with Vandyke brown, oil based.

The final finish is the shellac, as before, followed by a flat varnish, which is then waxed.

Malachite suitable for oak or chestnut

Mix the following in one gallon of hot water:

¼ ounce methylene blue 2B aniline, dry, water soluble

1 ounce green M. X. aniline, dry, water soluble

One coat is applied to the wood, which is sandpapered when dry, and a second coat is then applied. The filler is silex, darkened with 6 ounces of drop black, 1 ounce Vandyke brown and 1 ounce dark chrome green, oil based. The final finish should consist of two or three coats of thin white shellac, rubbed down to a dullness.

Sheraton Mahogany suitable for mahogany, birch and other woods

Mix the following in one gallon of hot water:

1¼ ounces bichromate of potash, dry

2 drams black P.B. aniline, dry, water soluble

1 dram mahogany red, aniline, dry, water soluble.

Brush on two coats and, when dry, sand smooth and then cover with a single coat of orange shellac.

Use silex as a filler mixed with 5 ounces of Vandyke brown, 4 ounces of burnt umber and 3 ounces of rose pink, oil based.

The final finish should be orange shellac, rubbed to a lustre.

Mahogany for various woods

First, dissolve 4 drams of caustic soda in one gallon of hot water and apply plentifully to the wood. Allow to dry, then sand smooth.

Dissolve 6 ounces mahogany red aniline, dry, water soluble, and 4 ounces mahogany brown aniline, dry, water soluble, in 5 quarts of hot water. Apply generously to the wood, allow to dry, and then flat varnish or put on one coat of orange shellac and rub dull.

Silver Oak for oak and various other woods

Dissolve 12 drams of bichromate of dry potash and 12 drams of caustic soda in one gallon of water. Brush on to the wood, allow to dry and then sand smooth.

Dissolve the following in one gallon of water: ½ ounce bichromate of potash; 2 ounces brown aniline, dry, water soluble; ½ ounce naphthol black aniline, dry, water soluble. Brush on and, when dry, sand smooth. The filler should consist of zinc oxide in oil and a small quantity of dry whiting, reduced to a paste with boiled linseed oil, 1 ounce of japan drier and 6 ounces of benzine. Some silex filler can be added but is not strictly necessary. The final finish should be paraffin wax thinned with turpentine and benzine.

Mention has already been made of aniline and coal tar dyes, which are the by-product of coal. Although the water stains are highly recommended, this does not mean that the anilines are in any way inferior to them. It is simply a matter of finding the best material for a particular job. Something like two thousand different aniline colours and their variations are available, and most of them can be bought in a powder form which is mixed with alcohol or spirit staining or oil for oil staining.

Coal tar stains can be used as acid spirit and direct colours. While they are not commonly used nowadays, the acid colours are mixed with acid and are water soluble, whereas the direct colours are mixed with acid colours. Spirit and oil colours do not mix, they are quite incompatible. Their colour range is strong rather than restrained and delicate. In one group the eosine red coal tar dyes have a distinctive appearance, as does mauve. Alizarine red, for instance, will last for years when applied to internal decor, but it will quickly fade if used on areas subjected to strong sunshine. The coal tar dyes suffer from lack of permanence, but they will endure once they are covered with varnish, shellac or a waxed finish.

One of the drawbacks to coal tar dyes is that they quickly reach their saturation point in spirit or alcohol. The working implications are obvious, because in the repetitious treatment of furniture quantities of stain must be made up in batches and stored for use in order to create colour standardisation. In use, such a stain can be temperamental and affected by extremes of temperature. Like water stain, is should be applied hot, the temperature being maintained by resting the container in a water bath. If it falls below the required temperature, the colour will descend to the bottom of the container and finally crystallise.

Coal tar dyes can be dissolved in water apart from spirit, and they have the distinction of being very strong, only one ounce being needed to colour a gallon of water. Because variations of colour are often called for, the craftsman should keep a variety of strong colours in stock to enable him to make the dilute mixes. The basic colours will yield practically every single variation, including:

In the black range: nigrosine, naphthalene.
In the brown range: Bismarck, loutre, seal.
In the brown mahogany range: orange, naphthalene black.
In the red range: scarlet, carmosine.
In the orange range: orange Y, orange G.
In the yellow range: naphthalene yellow, auramine yellow.

The stock solutions should be stored in dark glass bottles and well shaken prior to use.

Spirit stains naturally dry very quickly, aided by evaporation, but they do not remain permanent in strong light, and the colours are occasionally uncertain, though modern preparations which are bought ready mixed have shown some improvement in recent years. Once applied, a spirit stain should be covered as soon as it is dry, using varnish or shellac. Such stains do not penetrate very deeply because of their quick drying properties, and they should be put on very quickly, using a broad brush. There is always a chance of making laps or streaks, which cannot immediately be brushed out. The standard solution is to apply a second coat as soon as possible. Another way to avoid laps and streaks is to airbrush the stain, though this calls for a certain technique to ensure that the stain is applied equally and evenly.

When varnish or shellac is applied over the spirit stain, use a very thin solution which can be put on in sweeps. Any airbrushing will probably affect the spirit base of the stain and cause muddying or smearing.

One gallon of spirit stain will provide a coat up to 400 square feet of softwood, and up to 700 square feet of hardwood.

Formulary of Spirit Stains

The usual proportion for spirit stains in their dry form is between one and four ounces to one gallon of denatured alcohol, dissolved by using a water bath with one container in another and applying the heat indirectly by means of hot water.

The working range of spirit soluble aniline and coal tar stains is as follows: Walnut R. Golden Oak. Bismarck Brown – red. Black nigrosine W. N. Green M. X. Crystals. Methylene Blue 2B. Fuchine Magenta R. T. Violet R. B. P. N.

Mahogany

4 ounces Bismarck brown, dry, spirit soluble is dissolved in one gallon of denatured alcohol. It should be added very gradually, ensuring that the stain does not become cloudy.

English Oak

4 ounces nigrosine, spirit, soluble, dry; 8 drams auramine, spirit soluble, aniline, dry; 2 drams malachite green aniline, spirit soluble, dry. Dissolve in one gallon of denatured alcohol.

It is brushed on and, when dry, sanded smooth, followed, when clean, with a single coat of shellac. When the shellac is applied, it should be done quickly and with the shellac well cut to ensure flow.

If a filler is needed for certain open-pored woods, use silex mixed with Vandyke brown and black. Classically, the English oak effect should have no sheen and be rubbed dull.

Old Oak

4 ounces nigrosine black, dry, spirit soluble; 1 ounce scarlet aniline, dry, spirit soluble; 1 dram auramine, aniline, dry spirit soluble. Dissolve in one gallon of denatured alcohol.

The stain is brushed on and allowed to dry, followed by a single coat of orange shellac, applied rapidly and in such a way as not to disturb the stain. The final finish should be orange shellac followed by waxing.

After the water stains the oil stains are probably the most useful, and they have the advantage of offering slow drying times in which troublesome areas can be rebrushed and any alterations made as far as colour distribution is concerned. Oil stain does not, however, penetrate to any great extent, although this is not considered to be a very serious drawback. The most popular form is the aniline coal tar stain, which is available in several hundred colours and has a strong penetrating quality.

Formulary for Aniline Oil Stains

Golden Oak

8 ounces nigrosine black, oil soluble, dry; 4 ounces yellow, auramine, aniline, dry, oil soluble; 1 ounce walnut aniline, dry, oil soluble; 1 quart hot turpentine; one gallon black varnish.

The turpentine is heated in a double boiler of hot water away from direct heat, and the yellow, nigrosine and walnut are stirred into it. When it has cooled, the varnish can be added. It is then painted on the wood and rubbed in with a hessian pad. If a filler is needed, silex can be used. The final finish should be orange shellac, rubbed to a dullness.

Jacobean Oak

2 ounces walnut aniline, dry, oil soluble; 1 ounce orange Y; 1 ounce nigrosine black, dry, oil soluble; 8 ounces drop black; 1 pint hot turpentine; ½ pint boiled linseed oil; 2 quarts benzine. Naphtha as required to govern drying time.

Heat the turpentine in a double boiler and then add the walnut, orange and nigrosine, followed by the drop black. Stir in the oil and when cool add a quantity of naphtha gradually, stirring and ensuring that too much heaviness is not created. Apply generously to the wood but do not overload in nooks and crevices, otherwise a deep darkness will be caused which can be troublesome to lighten. The final finish should be orange shellac, rubbed to a dullness.

English Oak

1¼ lbs nigrosine black, dry, oil soluble; 2 ounces and 8 drams yellow, naphthalene, dry, oil soluble; 8 drams walnut brown, aniline, dry, oil soluble; 12 ounces boiled linseed oil; 1 quart turpentine; 1 gallon benzine.

The turpentine is heated in a double boiler and all the colours are stirred in until they dissolve. Remove from heat to cool, after which thin down with the benzine.

Use silex filler if required, and flat varnish as a finishing coat.

The even staining of any surface, whether it happens to be a floor or a piece of furniture, requires a definite working system, and the method of application must be worked out beforehand, governed by the type of stain to be used. Water stains permit a certain working time, as do oil stains, but others, which are spirit stains, demand quick action and a pretty decisive touch. These are the sort of things to take into account before starting the job. The actual working method is, of course, standard and varies little from one workshop to another. Regardless of the nature of the job, it is usual to start at one side and work towards the other. This rule applies equally to a ballroom floor, a piece of furniture or a small box. In the case of panel staining, the beginner will more often than not use a spirit stain around the side mouldings and then begin to work inwards towards the centre only to end up with a kind of darker tone on the edges. But if the job is worked from one side to the other, including the moulding, using broad and even strokes and a well loaded brush, the effect will be uniform. By using this system, there will be only one wet working edge at a time.

Some of the best effects are obtained by toning. This means that a second colour is mixed with the stain. The second colour should not be in violent contrast unless some kind of novelty effect is deliberately sought. The most obvious application is the lighter coloured woods in which the compatible tones are brown, red, orange, straw, grey and amber. The scope as far as the darker woods is concerned is strictly limited, though burnt umber can be applied with some success. The versatile burnt umber can also be used on lighter woods to create an aged effect. Cherry, on the other hand, will give a mahogany appearance by the application of burnt sienna, while a mixture of burnt sienna and yellow ochre can impart an orange appearance to pine, maple and teak.

The tools required for staining are few and they are simple, including a two-inch soft-bristled brush, a second brush with stiffer bristles to use when the stain has to be forced into the wood, a selection of artist's brushes to reach the more difficult areas, a quantity of cotton rags and some brush cleaner. The stock of stains is optional, depending on the type and the variety of work to be done, and there should also be a

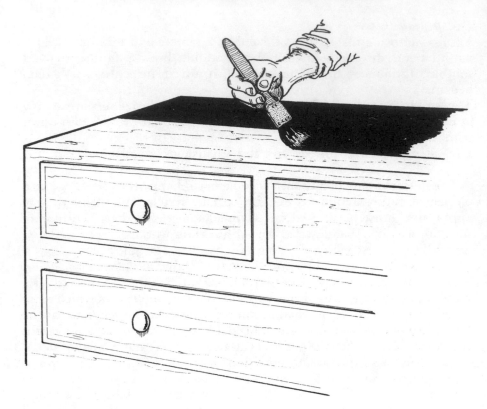

FIGURE 17.   The staining of large areas.

The brush should not be too large but manageable and flexible so that it can be easily drawn across in even swathes to form an even coat. It is advisable to apply one base coat without attempting any touching up of faint or fault areas. When a second coat is applied, this will generally correct itself. It is very important to keep the brush on the move and to use diluted stain rather than attempt to get the final colour in two coats.

selection of artist's oil colours for touching in faded areas, including the basic burnt umber, burnt sienna, yellow ochre, white, black, chrome yellow and orange. They are mixed with artist's oil as a medium when using with spirit stains. If water stains are used, the equivalent colours can be some tubes of water colour pigments. Apart from this basic equipment, various sodas are handy for the treatment of greasy and dirty surfaces before any staining is carried out. There will always be areas in a workpiece in which the stain does not seem to make any impression at all, including resinous knots and mineral streaks. Unless they are properly dealt with the result will be light areas or dark areas.

The treatment consists of brushing with a one per cent solution of water and potash and then washing clean. A single application may, or may not, remove the oiliness or resinous film on the wood. If it does not have any effect, then a generous coat of methyl alcohol can be used.

While attractive as panelling and in some types of furniture, pine also happens to be one of the most troublesome of all woods to stain satisfactorily due to the many knots. In such cases the entire area should first be washed with soda and water, using about four ounces of soda to one gallon of hot water. The surface should be thoroughly washed with clean water before any stain is applied.

Wood staining is not in any way a precise technique. It is often a matter of carrying out experiments before the required colour and appearance are achieved. Practically all the methods described in this chapter are traditional, and most of them can be modified by strengthening or diluting the colour.

The difficulties in achieving precisely the right stain and the right finish are nowhere more aptly demonstrated than in the art of marquetry, where it is customary to use commercial veneers which may at the start be lighter than the required colour, and then stain them darker, using coloured inks, vegetable dyes, wood stains and many other less conventional materials. Modern marquetry artists frequently run into trouble not so much with the tinting and general colouring, some of which is done in situ, but when they reach the point where the work is complete apart from an overall shield-like finish which is required as a protection against dust, dampness and general wear and tear. While some may want a matt or gloss film, others search for a finish which will mellow the marquetry panel. This is the point at which the difficulties start, for it has been found that the veneers, being drawn from a wide variety of woods, both soft and hard, relatively speaking, and many of them coloured with different types of stain, begin to react in disparate ways. Some may begin to curl, others will crack or split, in others the tints may lift and merge with the finishing substance, badly impairing the intended effect. Both varnish and the polyurethanes are known to affect marquetry in these and other ways.

Marquetry is possibly unique as far as wood finishing methods are concerned, because the mixture of woods used combined with a variety of stains and tints makes it practically impossible to generalise about the surface finish to be employed. The professional finisher knows what to do for the best when it comes to oak or mahogany, but faced with a mixture of ten, twenty or thirty different woods he is often at a loss. While there may not be a single surface finish available or capable of being formulated, it is nevertheless possible to achieve some sort of compatibility without any fear of interfering with the colour range or the nature of the veneers by applying a wax polish. Chapter eight discusses the properties of waxes. As far as marquetry is concerned, beeswax mixed with turpentine is one of the best mixtures in view of the fact that the polishing can be halted at any point, depending upon whether a dull glow or a high sheen is required. Carnauba wax is another possibility when it is blended with ceresine wax, but the quantity of turpentine should be reduced by about twenty-five per cent in order to avoid a sudden high and mirror-like gloss which can seriously detract from the effect of a pictorial subject.

FIGURE 18.   MARQUETRY: 'Standing on the corner'.

6

Lacquer

History, Technique, Practice

The mystery of lacquer remains unsolved after hundreds of years. Relatively few Europeans have ever seen lacquer applied in the traditional manner, and even fewer have visited the Oriental workshops in which the work is done. There is no completely satisfactory formulary to tell us about its composition, although we do know something about its properties. Practically all our knowledge is broad rather than specific. Lacquer has been imitated in France, Germany and Britain, and some of these imitations may still be taken for the real thing. Even so, there are marked differences when the genuine Oriental and the fake European imitations are closely compared. The European version may look superficially right, but it lacks the Orientality. From a very early date there was no lack of instructional material for those who wanted to get to grips with the process. Stalker and Parker in their 1688 manual, *A Treatise of Japanning and Varnishing* told the reader how to make and apply 'chestnut-colour Japan' and 'olive-colour'. In 1701 William Salmon in *Polygraphic or The Arts of Drawing, Engraving, Etching, Limning, Vernishing, Japanning, Guilding, &c* included a chapter on 'Japanning Wood With Colours' and described 'Black, White, Blew, Common Red, Deep or Dark Red, Pale Red, Olive Coloured, Chestnut Colour, Lapis Lazuli'. Other sections dealt with 'Marble Japan' and 'Tortoise Shell Japan'.

By 1730 the French were in direct competition with the Orient, and they were adapting the French and Chinese motifs, and developing markets not only in France itself but also Russia, Spain and Portugal.

Lacquer originated in China in the Chou dynasty (1027–221 BC) and it was taken up mainly in Holland in the latter part of the seventeenth century, when furniture carcases were sent to the Orient for lacquering.

Other countries practised lacquering, including Korea, Japan, Iran and areas of India, no doubt under the influence of the French and English trading companies when the mercantile routes were being developed.

In China the technique was to use the prepared sap of the lacquer tree (*Rhus vernicifera*) which hardened by natural drying. Other countries more or less followed suit but introduced a number of adulterants. The enigma of ancient lacquer is that it was applied in the high temperatures of China and it was done in the very areas where it should have been difficult to retard the drying time which is essential to a successful finish. Yet the craftsmen of that time and place did somehow accomplish it to such an extent that the oldest lacquer will successfully resist even the strongest modern solvent. It has been claimed that lacquered wood can be boiled for hours on end without detriment. Under such rigorous treatment it is the internal wood which suffers, not the lacquer itself.

The modern craftsman is unlikely to produce an answer to the Chinese riddle about the composition, application and finishing of true lacquer. It is equally unlikely that commercial clients will commission finishes which resemble old lacquer. It is perhaps for the solitary craftsman to create pieces which can be sold not so much as furniture as works of art. There are possibilities of using modern lacquer techniques for modern designs, of course, and utilising traditional flat, raised or cut lacquer, then applying decoration in polychrome and plain gold, or by the use of the established colours, which include green, blue, gold, buff, red, yellow and black. Still in the commercial field, there are opportunities for the finisher/restorer who is capable of repairing old lacquer for antique dealers. That there is a sorry lack of good craftsmen for lacquer work is self evident, and it may be due to the fact that the work is time consuming, relatively expensive and, above all, slow.

Quite obviously, there is a disadvantage in discussing traditional lacquer work if the trade secret is not known. In Europe the term 'lacquer work' has for many years referred to a form of varnishing with decorative inlays, and it must be said that it is no more than tenth cousin to Chinese lacquer work.

In the present chapter we will content ourselves with a discussion of what can only be called polite imitations of the real thing. There is, however, no reason why the polite imitation should not display some degree of superior craftsmanship. All should be well providing we do not delude ourselves into believing that we are about to rival real lacquer work.

It is interesting to recall that in the 1907 edition of *Henley's Formulas* the article on lacquering gives the following account:

'The art of lacquering includes various steps which are divulged as little as possible. Without them nothing but a varnish of good quality would be realised. . . .' Later on, part of the process is described: 'When the Annamites propose to lacquer an object, a box, for example, they first stop up the holes and crevices, covering all the imperfections with a coating of diluted lac, by means of a flat, close, short brush. Then they cover the whole with a thick coating of lac and white clay. This clay, oily to the touch, is found at the bottom of certain lakes in Tonkin; it is dried, pulverised, and sifted with a piece of fine silk before being embodied with the lac. The operation is designed to conceal the inequalities of the wood and produce a uniform surface which, when completely dry, is rendered smooth with pumice stone.

'If the object has portions cut or sunk the clayey mixture is not applied, for it would make the details clammy, but in its place a single, uniform layer of pure lac.

'In any case, the pumicing, a third coating, now pure lac, is passed over the piece, which at this time has a mouse-grey colour. This layer, known under the name of *sou lot*, colours the piece a brilliant black. As the lac possesses the remarkable property of not drying in dry air, the object is left in a damp place. When perfectly dried the piece is varnished, and the desired colour imparted by a single operation. If the metallic applications are excepted, the lac is coloured only black, brown or red.'

Henley disclosed certain formulae, and while they are summarised below, they are curiously incomplete and, moreover, they stipulate ingredients which are no longer available and have no modern equivalents.

Black, for instance, is described as being one part of turpentine warmed for twenty minutes beyond the fusing point; then poured into three parts of lac. *Pheu deu*, otherwise copperas, is added, and the mixture is stirred for at least one day. Obviously, a somewhat impractical proposition for the modern finisher.

The description of the famous red laquer is somewhat more intriguing, for here the lac, which has already been stirred for six hours, is mixed with hot oil of *trau* and then stirred for a further day, after which the vermilion is then added.

Henley continues: 'After the lacquer has been applied, certain parts of the design must be gilded. The sections are covered with a mixture of lac and oil of *trau*, and the metallic leaves are then applied and protected by lac and oil of *trau*. All these lac and oil of *trau* mixtures are carefully filtered, which the natives effect by pressing the liquid on a double filtering surface formed of wadding and of a tissue on which it rests. It can only be applied after several months when the metallic leaf is gold. In the case of silver or tin the protecting coat can be laid on in a few days. It favourably modifies the white tints of these two metals by communicating a golden colour. The hue, at first reddish, gradually improves and acquires its full brillancy in a few months.

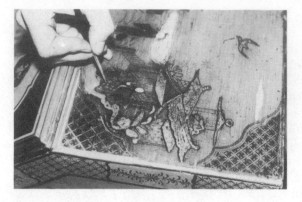

FIGURES 19 and 20.   Nicholas G. M. Atkins of Robertsbridge, East Sussex, is one of the leading exponents of traditional lacquerwork in Britain. He explains his method: 'The old gesso is chiselled and scraped away very carefully to achieve a clean, dry base, and the smooth surfaces are then coated with a suitable filler, such as gesso. The raised surfaces are applied later after the first layer of filler is dry. Gilding and colouring-in of treated parts may then be undertaken. Careful consideration must be given to the colours used because they may have to be toned down afterwards. The decoration of the gilded parts, known as "inking-in", is then applied, followed by a suitable varnish, the choice of which is decided by the base colour structure. After the varnishing and polishing the toning is done followed by another coat of polish, and then by a coat of wax. Between these processes the surface is rubbed down with fine wire wool or flour paper. One of the most important aspects of this work is that many pieces have individual chemical base colours, such as resin, lacquer or paint, and so considerable care must be taken to establish exactly what sort of structure you are working on before you actually make a start.'

'Little information is procurable concerning the process employed by the Chinese. The wood to be lacquered should be absolutely dry. It receives successive applications, of which the number is not less than thirty-three for perfect work. When the lac coating attains the thickness of ¼ inch, it is ready for the engravers. The Chinese, like the inhabitants of Tomkin, make use of oil of *trau* to mix with the lac, or oil of *aleurites*, and the greatest care is experienced in the drying of the different layers. The operation is conducted in dim-lighted rooms specially fitted up for the purpose; the moisture is maintained to a suitable extent by systematically watering the earth which covers the walls of this "cold stove".'

It would be a most exceptional modern craftsman who is able to spend time applying no less than thirty-three coats of anything whatever to a surface, meanwhile exercising patience to wait for each coat to dry before embarking on the decorative process. But it is quite easy to emulate the dense blackness of typical lacquer, using a very old formula which is as follows: take ⅓ ounce aniline hydrochloride, ⅓ ounce achohol; 1 part sulphate of copper; 100 parts of water. The aniline copper is dissolved in the alcohol and the copper sulphate in the water. The wood is first coated with the copper sulphate solution. After this coating has been given plenty of time to dry, the aniline salt tincture is applied. Shortly, the copper salt absorbed by the wood will react on the aniline hydrochloride, developing a deep, rich black which acids or alkalies are powerless to destroy. In its original form the recipe concludes: 'If coated with shellac and given a french polish, the ebony lustre will finish up to a unsurpassed lustre.'

If all that is required is a sound black finish without any ornamentation or decoration, then the following formula for gesso-lacquer can be applied to practically any wooden surface, which must first be throughly cleaned. An undercoating of flat white lead paint is prepared by mixing with turpentine and linseed oil in equal parts and it should be thinned down before application. Used as a primer, it will rapidly be absorbed by the wood. There will, of course, be a crosshatching of brush marks, but this does not matter because all traces will later vanish. Because this is simply an undercoat with a thin consistency, it should be possible to go on applying it until the wood is very well soaked. It may take ten hours or more to dry completely. An overnight stand in an even temperature should be long enough.

The materials required for the next stage are ordinary domestic powdered whiting, white polish, fine grade pumice powder, a two-inch camel hair mop and sheets of No 2 sandpaper. The whiting is broken down by crumbling into a basin and covered with cold water, then allowed to stand for several hours. The water is then strained off, and the mass of wet whiting is warmed on a low heat, stirring all the time and taking care not to let it dry out. The next stage is to warm a quantity of jelly size, obtainable from art restorers' suppliers or some decorators' shops. The quantity can be critical and should be just a little less than the whiting. Add three tablespoons of linseed oil. Avoid boiling the mixture, but stir or fold-in the whiting. If it is desired to make a mixture which will be extra hard when dried and set, then powdered resin can be added. A dessert spoon is quite sufficient. This gesso has to be applied hot and it cools rapidly.

The gesso is applied very quickly with a well charged brush. In appearance, it will resemble nothing more exciting than tacky flour and water, and the first coating will have a surface full of brushmarks, but they can be disregarded. The requirement at this early stage is to ensure that the first coat is ample without any air pockets trapped in it. It should be allowed to dry in a workshop or a room in which the windows are open to admit a strong passage of air. Gesso has a slight stink which tends to pervade a premises. The drying time is variable, but it will probably be from four to six hours, though it is wise to leave it as long as possible to make quite sure that the underlayer becomes hard.

The appearance of the hardened surface will be rough when dry, but it can be rubbed smooth with sandpaper, using a cork block to create a perfectly flat plane. Gesso is easy to make smooth and a silky touch will result. It is entirely a matter or taste whether only a single coat is necessary. If a second coat is applied, however, it will not be necessary to smooth the first. As many coats as seem necessary can be applied.

Gesso can be coloured without difficulty, using red, black or green. The colour must be applied in the form of a pigment in liquid suspension, and it should be placed in a double water boiler and mixed with equal parts of turpentine and gold size, and then applied with a soft brush. Because it dries almost as soon as it has been applied to the absorbent surface, several coats may be necessary. Indeed, the more the better in order to achieve a density of hue. It will take about an hour to dry and harden. If it is then rubbed with fine pumice, using water as a lubricant, the result should be something akin to a mirror finish.

What has been described can perhaps be described as the Western equivalent of Oriental lacquer. While it is suitable for an overall appearance, it also lends itself to the incision of patterns and figurative decoration. This is done by drawing or tracing a design in outline on the surface, and then cutting it out with a surgical scalpel. The dug-out area is then inlaid with soft metal or a contrasting colour gesso which, in turn, is polished in the usual way. A possible variation is the use of marquetry, for the gesso makes an excellent ground for exotic woods, which are held in the sunken areas with a suitable bonding agent. Granted, this is a precision job, but it does offer other possibilities. In the general run, however, the gesso-lacquer is intended to provide a covering which will wear for many years and withstand scratching and bruising.

The method of application of gesso must vary according to what is being treated. If it is on, say, a chest of drawers, then it will be advisable to remove the drawers and treat them separately, not in situ. The greatest advantage of gesso lacquer is that inferior furniture with dented and damaged surfaces can be smoothly coated and considerably enhanced. This may suggest possibilities for the small finishing workshop which happens to have access to quantities of secondhand furniture in need of refurbishing and profitable marketing.

Although it is possible to apply yet another surface finish to gesso

FIGURE 21. Restored early 19th century European lacquer work on a tabletop with engraved decoration against a grained background. The restoration was carried out by Alexandre Kidd of Ealing, London, whose workshop also deals with the repair of papier mâché, french polishing and a wide range of historical decorative techniques, including 22 carat gilding.

Photo: Andrew J. Gigg

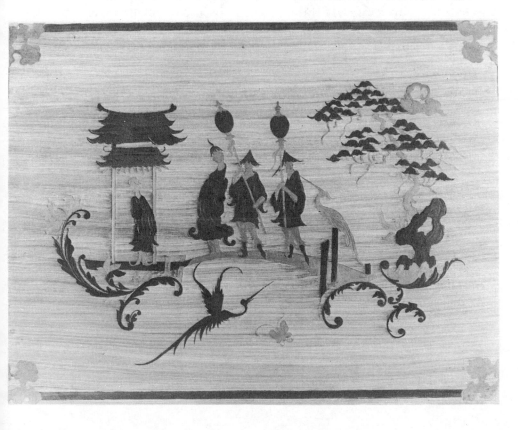

lacquer in the form of french polish, it is not strictly necessary. However, a plain surface of any size, such as a coffee table or a side table may look better if finished with a clear french polish, although it will not withstand high temperatures.

Today the word 'lacquer' has come to mean a synthetic preparation which can be brushed or sprayed on to the wood. It is made from nitrocellulose, resin gums, solvents, softeners and thinners. The solvents are made from ethyl and amyl acetates, acetone and methyl alcohol with the addition of softeners and plasticisers, and the thinner is manufactured from toluene, benzene and xylene.

Clear gloss lacquer can be sprayed and, if it is first thinned, it will dry within a couple of hours, after which it can be sanded to a high gloss. There are two varieties of clear gloss lacquer. They are gloss and flat, and there is also a lacquer enamel which is exactly the same material with the addition of pigment. For the craftsman who prefers to create his own colours, there are the so-called colours which are simply mixed with a clear lacquer. Not all lacquers are manufactured specifically for spraying. The slow drying variety is applied in the same way as paint, and it is available in many different colours. If a transparent finish is needed, then a water-white lacquer is used. Shading lacquer is transparent and it is used for highlighting areas when the workpiece has to be antiqued. It is also possible to obtain novelty lacquers to create crinkled and crackled finishes, which also have their uses in antiquing techniques.

Something should be said about lacquer thinners. They are categorised by a fast, medium or slow drying time. When the first experiments are carried out with lacquer there is generally a lot of haste to complete the job and see what it looks like. Even the modern form of lacquering must take time. When spraying in an environment which is too warm, the temperature can interfere with the finish because the lacquer will partly or wholly dry before it reaches the surface, resulting in powdering. A slow-drying lacquer, on the other hand, will start to run, causing 'tears' to form on the surface. Lumps and blobs created by this fault can be very difficult to remove. The other phenomenon common to spraying is the 'orange peel' finish in which the entire surface develops minute or coarse wrinkles, caused as a rule by too little solvent in the mix. A number of things can go badly wrong when spraying lacquer, which explains why so many experienced craftsmen prefer to follow the slower but much surer method of hand brushing. This makes it possible to correct any errors before it is too late.

Although there are many similarities to the technique of ordinary varnishing, it will do no harm to go over lacquering step by step, and it is proposed to break the process down into a series of basic stages:

FIGURE 22. Early 18th century European oak wall cupboard decorated with English lacquer in the Oriental style with raised figures. It was extensively restored by Alexandre Kidd of Ealing, London, who learned the art from Japanese masters.

Photo: Andrew J. Gigg

Stage 1

The workpiece is thoroughly cleaned by washing it down with water, followed by an application of animal glue. Two tablespoons to one pint of water will be suitable. It is then allowed to dry before being sanded down, using a fine grade sandpaper. All dust should be removed.

Stage 2

If desired, the wood can be stained at this stage, either by a surface stain application which should take on the glue size, or by the addition of stain to the wash-over coating of glue size, as in stage one. Make a mixture of one part lacquer sealer to 6 parts of lacquer thinner, or, alternatively, a mixture of one part of white shellac to seven parts of methylated spirit. Brush on and, when dry, paper to smoothness.

Stage 3

A filler is now applied, consisting of a branded preparation. It is essential that the filler contains no oil content. A heavy brand is used for open-pored wood and a thin or light brand for other woods. A coat of sanding sealer is applied, after which it is sanded when dry.

The lacquer is now brushed on with long even strokes and a fully charged brush. The first coat should dry within a couple of hours, and it can then be followed with a second coat. There is no need to sand between coats. Some craftsmen use a dull lacquer for all except the final coat and then apply a coat of gloss lacquer which will take well, but there does not seem to be any advantage in doing this, because the final result will look exactly the same.

Mention was previously made of staining. It may be useful to know that the method of applying the stain direct to the wood rather than mixing it with the transparent lacquer does offer certain advantages. It is much easier to pick out the characteristics of a well-figured grain by this method. The stain can consist of any wood staining agent, and it is advisable to use a spirit-based one which will dry quickly. While some craftsmen who are in a hurry will use a spray gun to apply stain, this is unnecessary. In fact, the concentrated rush of air will disturb particles of wood and dust and blow them into any nooks and crannies from which they will later emerge and get caught up in the film of lacquer.

A note should be appended about the fillers used for lacquering. An ordinary universal silex-based filler can be used for the job with a drying time of up to three or four hours. Prior to application it should be diluted with lighter fuel (benzine) rather than ordinary petrol, which has additives. One quart of benzine to every three pounds of filler plus a quart of lacquer thinner will provide a filler which can be brushed on. Alternatively, one part of finely ground silica, one part of cornflower mixed with thinner to a thin paste and a small amount of sealer will make a satisfactory filler.

Apply filler with a moderately stiff brush. After laying the coating to the surface of the wood, stab it down with the tip of the brush to force it into the pores of the wood. Follow this with another coat, this time working across the grain and then repeat the stabbing action. A coarse cloth should be padded and rubbed with and against the grain.

The secret of successful lacquer work is thoroughness at all stages. The basic sealing coats are just as important as the finishing coat. There are certain tricks of the trade, and in traditional lacquer establishments where furniture is surface-finished it is usual to put on a substantial shellac base after the filler. This can save at least one coat of lacquer, maybe more. There is a drawback to this, however, because if the shellac is not dry and hard, the finished lacquer will in the fullness of time begin to raise and blister.

Although application of lacquer by brushing has been advocated, there must still be a number of craftsmen who will prefer to use a spray gun for the simple reason that it is so much quicker and in their eyes, at least, just as effective. It is, after all, a matter of personal choice of the

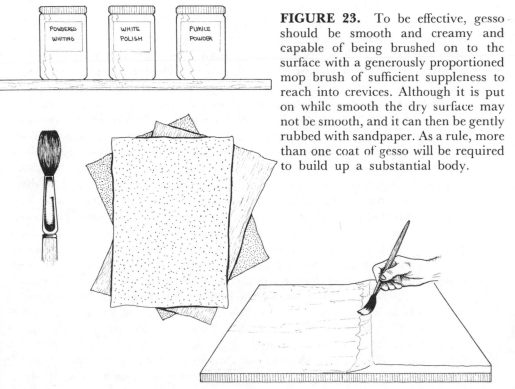

FIGURE 23. To be effective, gesso should be smooth and creamy and capable of being brushed on to the surface with a generously proportioned mop brush of sufficient suppleness to reach into crevices. Although it is put on while smooth the dry surface may not be smooth, and it can then be gently rubbed with sandpaper. As a rule, more than one coat of gesso will be required to build up a substantial body.

tools for the job. Spray guns operate either on suction feed or pressure feed. In the suction gun the pressure is at the nozzle and the liquid is emitted in a fan or fishtail pattern. The suction type spray gun is better for lacquer spraying because the fluid is first mixed and then poured into a glass container from which it is drawn upwards to be emitted through the atomiser. If it is to be at all effective for spraying purposes, the clear lacquers must be thinned by about twenty-five per cent, while heavily coloured lacquers must be thinned by as much as 150 per cent. This does not detract from the covering qualities of the lacquer, because it will, if correctly sprayed, dry almost at once and there will be much less risk of teardrops and other faults. In most types of spray lacquering the distance from the workpiece should be something like six inches and areas of about six inches at a time will be covered. The correct pressure should be about 40 lbs. When spraying small furniture it will make things easier if a simple turntable is used on which the workpiece can comfortably stand and be moved round while spraying is in progress. This will avoid the necessity of walking round the workpiece while spraying, trailing cables and leads and probably varying the spraying length. A sprayed workpiece should never be handled while it is still wet.

One distinct hazard is fire. Atomized lacquer and thinners are highly inflammable and if they come in contact with a naked flame the result can be a considerable explosion and a fire. The strict rule should be no smoking and no electric or gas fires during spraying.

When a lacquer mix has been made up and the spray gun loaded, it is advisable to carry out some tests on scrap wood to make sure that the nozzle is clear and the correct degree of spray is emitted. Never do this on the workpiece itself. There may be particles of material in the nozzle and they will be blown straight on to the workpiece. Correct spraying is a matter of practice, creating a central wet patch in the centre of a circular pattern, and tapering out to a perimeter of fine dots around the edges. If there is any coarseness and the spray pattern is uneven, this will cause sagging of the lacquer and probably the appearance of the orange peel surface which can be difficult to remove. Such a fault may be caused by the atomiser having too coarse a nozzle or else the lacquer is too thick and needs thinning.

Brushing lacquer is more in keeping with the traditions of this ancient craft. While there may be rather more points to watch out for than in spraying, there is much less risk of failure. The lacquer brush itself must have bristles set in rubber. Brushes with other kinds of bristle setting will be affected by lacquer solvent and quickly shed their bristles, which will get mixed up with the wet lacquer. In this event, the only remedy is to totally strip the surface and start again. The rubber-set brush will not shed its bristles. The general utility size is three-inch with one or two smaller ones for applying lacquer to edges and corners and crevices. As with any brush, it needs to be throughly cleaned before by washing in lacquer solvent and then allowed to stand in the lacquer itself so that the bristles become full charged. Unlike ordinary painting, the lacquer brush is not stroked free of surplus, although the tip should be lightened before moving it to the workpiece. Lacquer is put on in generous sweeps so that the liquid spreads evenly and smoothly. The habit of touching up any missed areas should be resisted. Trying to fill in this or that area will probably result in unsightly blobs appearing, and they will be difficult to smooth out. The term 'to flow lacquer' is often used in relation to brushing techniques. It is an apt description of how lacquer is put on to

FIGURE 24. When the gessoed panel is dry and hard, and has been sanded to a perfect smoothness, the pattern can be traced on to it and any sections for inlay can be carefully cut out with a surgical scalpel. The direction of the cut should be straight downwards, and if the composition of the gesso is correct, it will cut cleanly.

wood. If any streaking does occur, it can be removed by charging a separate brush with a small amount of lacquer thinner and deftly brushing until the streaks vanish.

As in varnishing, the atmosphere has a lot to do with the success of the work. In humid or damp weather there is generally moisture in the air, and it can cause opacity. It may not be immediately detected during spraying or brushing, but it will certainly show itself when the lacquer dries. Spray lacquering, in particular, will cause this fault, because the drops will pick up the dampness between the nozzle and the working surface. Brushing takes longer and it is more sure.

If popular taste has to be acknowledged at all, then the most favoured lacquered surface has a typical satin sheen. The Oriental mirror finish has an equal attraction for many craftsmen if only for the considerable challenge which it poses. The satin finish is not at all difficult to achieve, for it is done very simply by rubbing down with fine pumice. When lacquered furniture is produced commercially, the satin sheen can be imparted even more rapidly by applying a single finishing coat of flat lacquer, which requires no rubbing and dries very quickly. While it is not as a rule available ready-made, the satin sheen finish can be made in the workshop by taking a quantity of ordinary gloss lacquer and adding it to a small quantity of flattening pigment. Well stirred and kept in suspension during application, it will give the finish without any difficulty. Although drying time is rapid when it is sprayed, a brushed application will take three or four hours to dry. It is not possible to be dogmatic about the correct quantities of lacquer and flattener, and some experiment is recommended.

When it is necessary to rub down an intermediate or final coat of lacquer to create a high gloss, the preferred abrasive should consist of rottenstone and a fine pumice powder, well mixed and using either oil or water as a lubricant. As lacquer presents a much harder surface than other materials, it is advisable to rub the surface down with a very fine sandpaper. This should be applied in a circular motion, followed by rubbing along the grain. If the previously suggested finish for a satin sheen is used, the results will be better if it is rubbed down with a fine grade steel wool, using fluid wax as a medium. The residual wax can be removed by wiping with benzine.

A word can be said at this point about an unusual application of lacquer. It is now possible to create a suede-like or flocked finish, using a fibrous material which is available from suppliers. The method of operation is very simple, because the lacquer acts as an adhesive base which is sprayed, or brushed, on in the usual way. The fibres are simply scattered on in a layer while it is still tacky, completely covering the surface. Achieving an even layer which looks like suede is not quite as difficult as it may sound provided that no lumps or accumulations occur. When the lacquer is quite dry, the surplus fibres are brushed off. When this process was first developed there was a new passion for covering the entire external surfaces of pieces of furniture with suede or flocked finishes, but it did not, in fact, wear very well and is now very little done. But as a method of creating eccentric-looking furniture and even objets d'art of various kinds, it may have some attraction, and it can also be applied to wood sculpture and carved relief panels.

There have been recent technical developments in lacquer finishes for wood, and they include the catalyst lacquers, which have a polyester base capable of hardening when in contact with the catalyst. If there are any advantages, then they are that catalyst lacquers are heat resistant, they do not markedly age or chip or fracture, and they are, above all, very hard indeed. If there is a disadvantage then it is that many of them have a somewhat plasticised appearance. While they are surface finishes within the strict meaning of the term, they seem to lack the versatility which is associated with the more traditional finishes. What they do offer is a number of colour variations. They are made with resin in styrene, and they react to a catalyst, representing a very simple operation. The home surface finisher generally chooses the convenient cold-cure catalyst which contains a hardening agent. As soon as they are applied by the aerosol in which they are sold, they harden on exposure to the atmosphere. Relatively expensive in comparison to ordinary lacquer, they have the advantage in that they can be sprayed on in a thick layer without in any way affecting their hardening time, which is governed by internal chemical reaction. In one of the systems, a double aerosol can be used to enable the operator to spray equal quantities of the ingredients at the same time. In other systems the operator applies the hardening agent in a separate operation. But regardless of which system is used, the final effect is precisely the same.

Catalyst lacquers are widely used in commercial production, and they are now gaining ground amongst amateur craftsmen. In the last few years the manufacturers have introduced the same process for use without a powered spray or aerosol, the ingredients being supplied in separate containers. But before using them, it is necessary to appreciate their limitations. The material is applied as a film and put on in a single sweep, and the setting starts immediately and continues for eight to twelve hours. While brushing can present some difficulties due to the consistency of the material and the disconcerting knowledge that it is setting even while it is being applied, there is always the possibility of ridges appearing due to the brush action. It should be emphasised that there are safety hazards connected with the use of catalyst lacquers, and the manufacturer's instructions should be strictly adhered to.

The catalyst lacquer finish is permanent. Because it is unaffected by heat, solvents and other materials, it cannot be easily stripped off for refinishing. The most usual way is to remove it by gently scoring the surface with a scalpel and then lifting or chipping it off in small sheets or bits. It can also be abraded off, using a power tool. This rather dangerous operation calls for a delicate touch, otherwise the abrasive will cut straight through the lacquer and into the wood. The orbital sander, however, will be a better tool for the job, using a coarse sandpaper.

7

Gilding

THERE are some substitutes for gilding, including the use of a wax charged with metallic powder which is rubbed into the wood. Traditional gilding will be immediately obvious to the professional eye, and the various forms of gold paint and lacquer have a powdery look to them which quickly becomes shabby. The application of gold leaf, well laid down and expertly burnished, will always look superior and endure for a much longer time than any substitute.

Gilding has a longer history than any other form of surface finishing. The Pre-Colombian civilisations used it for the enrichment of jewellery, and in the Byzantine Empire it was used on the grand scale to embellish architecture. It was widely practised in the Twelfth Dynasty (2000–1788 BC) in Egypt, when the gold beaters reduced the metal to a flexible skin which was fitted to a wooden or other surface. Much the same art was followed in the Far East, Iran, India, Japan and China at a time when gold was regarded as a decorative material for robes, religious objects and sculptural enrichments. The *cassoni*, or clothes chest, of Italy in the Middle Ages and the Renaissance, said to be amongst the most beautiful furniture produced in this period, was often gilded, carved and finely decorated with marquetry. Between the late sixteenth and the eighteenth centuries gilding was part of the exuberance of design and decoration, but by the mid-eighteenth century it went into a decline and was only slightly revived in the latter part of the same century.

In his *Cabinet Dictionary* of 1803 Sheraton boldly defined gilding as 'The art of spreading or covering thin gold over any substance.' The earlier Vitruvius was fully aware of gilding as a technique in Ancient Greece and Rome, for in Book III of his treatise on architecture he stated that silver and brass could not be properly gilded without the application of quicksilver.

It is unfortunate that he does not describe the method of application, although it is unlikely that it would differ in anything other than detail, because gilding has been done in one way for thousands of years and it fortunately remains one of the crafts which has not suffered from innovation and sheer quickness for the sake of profit. Our modern practices have their roots in the late seventeenth century, prior to which the decorative artist was also a gilder. After the Middle Ages two methods were evolved, oil and water. Water gilding combined both matt and burnished surfaces, whereas oil gilding, which cannot be burnished, was used to cover wood or iron. Sheraton commented: 'As to lustre and effect, it has doubtless the advantage of oil gilding, but is attended by much more trouble and expence.' He was probably referring to the need to apply gilders' whiting or gesso and size in order to create a perfectly smooth surface before the gold leaf could be laid down and burnished.

By the eighteenth century gilding was extremely popular, and all kinds of furniture sported the distinctively opulent glimmer. As Sheraton remarked: 'Gilding in water is more operous and tedious, except on glass, which is more simple in itself than oil gilding, but as connected with the occasional ornaments attending it, it is sometimes more troublesome. Gilding upon glass is much wanted in the present mode of mounting prints and drawings.'

Gilding has always been an expensive process, which explains why various attempts have been made to make it more easily accessible to the client and his wallet by using adulterated and cheaper materials. In 1758 Robert Dossie said in his *The Handmaid to the Arts:* 'There is, besides the true leaf gold, another kind in use, called Dutch gold: which is copper gilt and beaten into leaves like the genuine. It is much cheaper . . . but, with any access of moisture, it loses its colour, and turns green in spots; and, indeed, in all cases, its beauty is soon impaired, unless well secured by lacquer or varnish. It is nevertheless serviceable for coarser gilding, where large masses are wanted; especially where it is to be seen by artificial light as in the case of theatres; and if well varnished will there in a great measure answer the end of the genuine kinds.' Despite Dossie's opinion about the use of varnish to seal it off from moisture, Dutch gold could not have lasted very long, and it obviously had a short life because it was unable to stand up to close scrutiny and wear.

Gold as a metal was not always used for gilding purposes. In the reign of Charles II there was a momentary interest in using silver leaf, and in the final thirty years of the reign it was applied to such items as cabinet stands, chimney glass frames and small tables. The methods used were not immensely successful, however, because when the metal was varnished or lacquered it immediately began to look tarnished and was occasionally mistaken for an inferior form of gilding. Nevertheless, John Stalker and George Parker included it in their *A Treatise of Japanning and Varnishing* in 1688, the process being detailed in a chapter entitled 'Wood with burnisht Gold and Silver.'

Gilding reached its greatest popularity in England due to the influence of the Adam style. It was Robert Adam, drawing on the Etruscan mode, who introduced furniture designed in the grand manner, made by William Linnell and the elder Chippendale, and creating a revolution in taste in which the furniture became the vehicle for decoration. Gilding had a large role to play. But the style was not without its critics, including Horace Walpole (1717–1797), who opined in a letter to Sir Horace Mann on 22 April 1775: 'Adam, our most admired, is all gingerbread, filigraine and fan-painting.' The disparaging reference to gingerbread concerned the cheap gingerbread sold at country fairs. We do not know what Mann, the American educationalist and statesman, made of it. Despite Walpole's views, the gilded furniture trade in London expanded rapidly, so that in the final ten years of the eighteenth century there were more than 150 master carvers and gilders, plus about 30 water gilders all making a good living out of it. So intense was the enthusiasm for the craft that many amateurs took it up, among them Lady Hartgood, who in 1741 wrote to the Countess of Pomfret: 'Within doors we amuse ourselves (at hours we are together) in gilding picture frames and other small things. This is so much in fashion with us at present that I believe if our patience and pockets would hold out, we should gild all the cornices, tables, chairs and stools about the house.'

Gilding technique has changed hardly at all, and it seems fitting that is should occupy its own place in the present book, because while it remains as costly and as time consuming as ever, it nevertheless remains a craft to jealously preserve and practise whenever the opportunity presents itself. The description which follows is based on historical technique.

What is known as the 'old world' style of gilding is used mainly for picture and mirror frames. While it takes less time than the gesso-ground system, it is simply a way of treating frames and is not necessarily the technique to use on large pieces of furniture.

The first requirement is the gold leaf itself, which is bought in the form of 'books', each containing 20 sheets about one ten-thousandth of an inch thick. It will probably be quite difficult to assess exactly how much gold leaf will be needed for any particular job, and so it is obviously a good idea to buy more rather than less. As a rule of thumb, a book will cover about 1½ square feet. Various thicknesses are available, including the double-weight, which is easier to handle and apply, and there are also variations of colour which are created by mixes with silver alloy. The grades are indicated by carat. The low carat gold will tarnish quickly. Thus, 18½ carat lemon gold, 16 carat pale gold and 12 carat white gold are among the most common, and supplied in squares of 3⅜ inches. A heavily carved frame will take more than a plain frame because the area to be covered will be substantially greater.

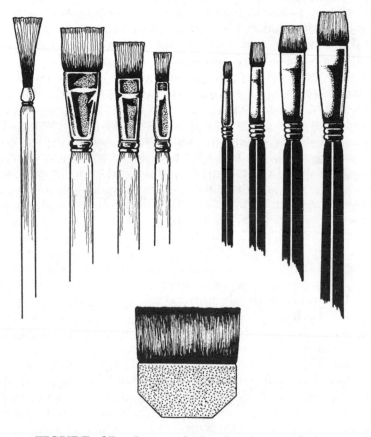

FIGURE 25. Some of the brushes used in gilding.

At the top from left to right: camel hair quill for adjusting the position of the leaf when it is first laid in place; three sizes of flat bristle for heavy flat surfaces; flat sable, available in four sizes; below, the gilder's tip used for lifting leaf into position.

As to the other requirements, they include a razor blade or a gilder's knife, a squirrel-hair brush or gilder's tip with two-inch bristles, which is used to lift the leaf on to the prepared surface. A small piece of pure silk will also be required.

The ground is japan size, which is quick drying and holds the leaf in place on the workpiece. A good gold size can be made by mixing one part of yellow ochre, 2 parts of copal varnish, 3 parts of boiled linseed oil, 4 parts of turpentine and 5 pints of boiled mineral oil. The ochre must be ground in oil to a paste before mixing with the fluids. This gives a thicker ground, almost a cushion, and is superior to japan size.

We will assume that the workpiece is perfectly clean and ready for gilding. Four coats of white shellac are applied to form a foundation, each coat being rubbed with fine sandpaper when it is dry. Then a coat of japan size or the preparation mentioned above is applied. If it stands up to about three hours it will become progressively more tacky, but it should not dry and harden.

The gold leaf is laid on a piece of chamois leather tacked tightly to a board about 4 inches wide and 8 inches long, known in the trade as a palette, and preferably fitted with a 3 inch high cardboard draught guard fastened round one end to prevent the leaf from lifting in the event of a sudden eddy of air. Gold leaf is a very fragile material and even a waft of air or a sudden puff of breath will disturb it, making it flutter away. For this reason it is advisable to lay out only a few sheets at a time. The razor blade or gilder's knife is used to cut the leaf into pieces to fit the various sections of the workpiece. The difficulty here for the beginner is that the areas cannot be measured by anything other than the eye, and the purpose throughout the initial stages is to cover as big an area as possible. Inevitably, when a complicated piece of carving is being gold leafed, there will be many areas in which only a small sliver is required, and the art is therefore to cut the leaf accordingly without wastage. Pieces are cut as required.

The brush is now stroked briskly on the silk to create a charge of static electricity, and when the tip approaches the gold leaf it will fly to it, making it possible to lift the leaf into position on the workpiece and the tacky gold size. It is gently laid down in position and manipulated accordingly. The same process is used to cover the adjacent area. And so on until the area is covered. Only small areas at a time are covered, and the leaf will probably look wrinkled and uneven, even when it is done by a professional gilder. The smaller areas are patched in with odd pieces of leaf.

When the area is fully sheathed in gold, a pad is made with a piece of silk using some cotton wool as a core, and this is used to flatten out the ripples and uneven areas, and it is then burnished with a piece of ivory or steel, made for the job, taking care not to penetrate the soft skin. If it is then left overnight the size will dry and harden. A final treatment consists of rubbing the entire suface over with bronze metallic powder to soften the somewhat hard appearance of the gold and give it a more mature look. An alternative is to wipe the gold leaf with turpentine. If the gilding is on furniture a single coat of thin orange shellac will protect it.

In furniture reproduction and faking the craftsman will often brush the gold over with Vandyke brown and umber mixed in turpentine,

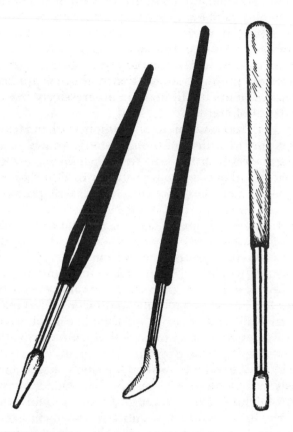

FIGURE 26. Agate burnishers.

Use only when the leaf has been laid down on a resilient clay size. There is no general utility burnisher, and the various configurations are intended to reach into all angles, utilising the broad, flat area of the agate tip rather than the point or end.

working the pigment into any cracks and fissures, and then burnishing the highlights with a silken pad or a wooden door knob. Another faking device is to apply the gold leaf over a red or blue ground. Fissures are made deliberately by cracking the leaf and then burnishing selectively to impart an impression of age with the pigment peeping through the lustre of the metal.

In the last half of the nineteenth century a somewhat questionable innovation occurred in the gilding trade when a varnish renowned for its lasting and resilient qualities came into common use. The ingredients consisted of 1½ ounces of gum sandarach, 1½ ounces of mastic, 1 ounce of elemi and 1 pint of spirit. The sandarach, mastic and elemi were placed in a double boiler with the spirit and raised close to boiling point for two hours, then put into a retort for distillation, resulting in about half a pint of fluid. One-third of this was placed in a still and boiled for a further two hours, followed by the remaining two-thirds. The varnish obtained by this method was excellent for use on gilded areas which were subjected to humid and wet atmospheres, and the preparation played a large part in many questionable trade practices where inferior gold or even a cheap substitute was used. There is no modern equivalent of the varnish, but the nearest is probably polyurethane, although its application should be resisted because it will in all probability react on the gold size and start to peel.

The more traditional and very ancient method of gilding requires the laying down of a bed of gesso prior to the application of the leaf. Gesso powder can be obtained ready made from any artist's supplier. It is mixed with water to a thin paste, left to dry and harden, and then rubbed down to as perfect a smoothness as can be obtained. It is then covered with glue size, and the leaf is applied while it is still tacky, then finished off with a silk duster and a burnisher, as in the previous method. Some gilders use bole as a preliminary to the glue size, although bole is itself a form of size, being made from clay, coloured variously from pink to near-purple. Bole can be bought as a paste, which is mixed to a light creamy consistency with some animal glue added until it looks like whipped cream. This is brushed on to the gesso to form a smooth even coat. When dry, it is smoothed by rubbing and shellac is painted on in one or two coats, followed by thin glue size and the application of the gold leaf.

Gilding is merely a matter of technique, depending for its success on the handling of the gold leaf, 280,000 leaves of which will just about make a one-inch thickness. The beginner will find that if it is too highly charged with static electricity, the corners will curl in on themselves and behave in a most stubborn fashion. Only practice will determine how much charge should be used, but if the leaf will not part company with the brush, then a smart tap on the wooden section of the brush will release it. And that is perhaps the only trick of the trade which is known to protect the beginner from a severe headache.

Quite a lot can be done to enhance the appearance of a gilded surface. In the Adam period it was usual to simply burnish the gilding and

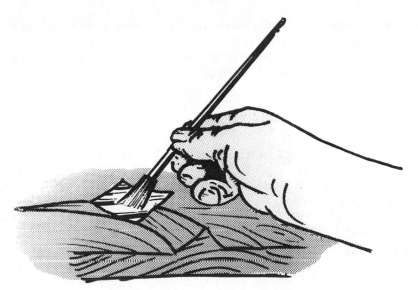

FIGURE 27. When properly charged with the right amount of static electricity, the gold leaf will adhere to the gilder's tip without curling in on itself so that it can be laid down on the sized surface without difficulty and then burnished. Here, the quill is adjusting the leaf into its required position after having been first laid in place.

simply leave it to gleam out its own opulence. Today, however, it is often felt that a shiny gold surface can look extremely garish and perhaps even cheap, and so it may be useful for the craftsman to have some knowledge of the finishes which are possible, the colour range of which is wide, from grey to yellow. It is also possible to deliberately tarnish the leaf to age it.

A standard antique appearance can be achieved by mixing burnt umber with shellac to a predetermined hue. This is soaked up on a pad of cotton cloth formed into a fad and then dabbed on to a surface which has been painted with a mixture of 60 per cent varnish and 40 per cent turpentine. By using the fad in a circular motion the tint will form an even coat which dries hard and slightly brown.

Another method of getting the antique effect is by spattering, using a mixture of japan colour, matt varnish and turpentine. The mixture should be as thin as water, though the colour must be fairly pronounced. It is then spattered on to the gold surface in such a quantity as to give greater density in some areas and less in others. When dry, it is lightly scrubbed with a very fine steel wool. A more restrained effect will result if the spatter is blotted here and there before it dries.

The question of when to stop burnishing gold leaf is better answered by practical demonstration than in the written word, but it may be useful to know that when the leaf is as smooth as stretched human skin, it is time to cease. Any joins in the leaf should be burnished with vigour until they are obscured, and any danger of the joins showing can be avoided by using generous overlaps.

FIGURE 28. Using the agate point to burnish the leaf.

The curved section of the burnisher is moved in a single direction, either left to right or vice versa, depending on the section being treated. Only a very light touch is needed, and no downward force should be exerted, otherwise the leaf may break up.

8

Waxed Finishes

Formulary and Application

THERE are many ready-made domestic wax polishes on the market, but what they do not provide is an actual waxed finish. Few of them can meet the quality which is possible by following the standard craft workshop formulary. Some modern furniture polishes contain silicones, which impart a high sheen almost at once, but this is self-defeating, because many pieces of fine furniture look tarted up if they shine like mirrors. Oak, for instance, is meant to glow, not emulate Eddystone lighthouse. What wax does is impart a dull sheen to bring out the beauty of the wood rather than obscure it with fairground dazzle.

A summary of the ingredients of different kinds of wax polishes will aid an understanding of application and effect. Probably the most important component is beeswax itself, and it can be either white or yellow, with a melting point of 152 degrees Farenheit. It is, of course, produced by honeybees. There is Brazilian, or carnauba, wax, a product of a certain type of palm tree, and it is brittle and pale yellow, melting at 185 degrees Farenheit. It is one of the principal ingredients of commercial furniture polish. Ceresine, another variety, is frequently mixed with carnauba to give it some bulk, and it has the same melting point. The cheapest of all is paraffin wax, which has a melting point of 131 degrees Farenheit, but it has only a limited use in the field of craft polishing.

The following formulae will be found in the recipe books of most workshops. All of them are very easily made and if there are any secrets to be revealed, then they are likely to be in the methods of application.

Antique wax is made by adding one ounce of rottenstone to one pint of liquid carnauba and a colouring of Vandyke brown. This is quite a good utility wax, useful for restoring oak or mahogany.

Beeswax polish also has a general application, and it is made by taking one lb of white or yellow beeswax and adding to it half a pint of turpentine, and dissolving the wax in a double boiler. *Note:* when using a double boiler attention should be paid to the risk of fire, which can be caused by the volatile fumes of turpentine. A low heat and ample ventilation is the answer to this.

White wax polish is made by shredding paraffin wax into a 50/50 mixture of turpentine and naphtha with a little colouring of zinc-white.

Carnauba polish can be used for all kinds of wax polishing. It is made by taking one lb of carnauba wax, one lb of ceresine wax and one pint of turpentine. The waxes are fine shredded and placed in a double boiler, the turpentine being added as soon as the waxes become liquid.

There are, of course, a great many coloured waxes which are used to enrich the tone of various woods. They are easily made by adding artist's oil colour mixed to a fluid consistency before being added to the wax while it is still molten. If a quantity of rottenstone is added to the wax, this can create an antique appearance. Coarse grained woods will often benefit from grey coloured wax, and a true effect can be achieved if it is scrubbed into the wood prior to applying a finishing coat of shellac, followed by a coat of soft paraffin wax on top of the dry shellac, then well rubbed with a piece of flannel or cotton cloth.

Putting wax on wood is not simply a matter of daubing it all over the surface and then rubbing hard until some sort of a sheen appears. Wax is a material which demands a firm base before it begins to work. While it may have some effect on a new surface which has been stained, a much more superior and satisfying effect will be gained if new wood is given two coats of thin shellac. When new wood has to be wax polished, then a paste wax with a soft cheese-like consistency should be used. The best way of applying it is by making a muslin pad about 6 inches wide, consisting of four or five layers with the wax amply placed between, like a multi-layer sandwich. This has the effect of forcefully feeding the wax through the muslin to the surface in gradual amounts and at the same time prevents any hard lumps of wax from finding their way to the wood. The first application of the polishing pad should be done in a circular motion, briskly rubbing to create a lot of friction which will soften the wax and make it flow freely. When the surface is completely coated with an even but thin film, it should stand for about fifteen minutes. A dry muslin cloth is formed into a pad and used in a circular motion. At this point the typical sheen should appear, and the strokes should move along the grain. If a considerable surface, such as a table, is being polished, a large pad should be wrapped around a wooden block to increase the downward force. The finished surface is tested by drawing the tip of the finger across the surface. If a smeared mark results, it means that too much wax is still present. A new clean cloth should be used to resume the rubbing until the surface will not show smear marks.

The craftsman finisher is sometimes called in by the customer who wants some valuable old furniture polishing. Most of the furniture in this category is actually very dirty due to wear and tear, the wandering hands of children and the application of many different kinds of polish. In the passage of time all of these will have deposited dirt and engrained it in successive layers of polish. For obvious reasons it is not a good idea to strip the surface and start all over again because this will probably mar the surface finish of what may well be very valuable furniture and create far more problems than it solves. The best treatment consists of wiping the surface over with a clean cloth wrung out in turpentine. This will shift a surprising amount of dirt within a few minutes, and the turpentine will at the same time also soften and lift at least some of the old wax polish.

White rings almost always mar old tables. They are caused by very hot plates and dishes. While marks like this can often be faded with methylated spirits, this will sometimes soften the french polish and create an even more unsightly mark. A better and safer treatment is to make a thin paste with wax and turpentine, and then gently attack the ring. Where methylated spirits can be savage and damaging in its action, turpentine is much more gentle and can be controlled. As soon as the white ring disappears, use either silk or flannel, and work it across the affected surface, finishing by rubbing with the grain.

One of the most arduous and protracted tasks, even for the experienced craftsman, is the refinishing of oak furniture. It is the kind of job which requires very careful planning if it is to be finished in a reasonable amount of time. We will take as an example a piece of oak furniture which has already been stripped, or is entirely new, and is therefore ready for surface polishing. First, it has to be stained, and any highlights should be sanded. The area should be sealed with a preliminary coat of thin shellac, rubbed down and then given a second coat of shellac, which is allowed to dry. Half a dozen coats of wax polish will finish the job. The secret of this lengthy but satisfying treatment is the amount of trouble taken with it. Regardless of the treatment, the nature of the wood must always be taken into account before starting the job. Walnut, for instance, requires a special preliminary treatment. It should be stained with a mixture of three parts of raw linseed oil and one part of turpentine. Boiled linseed oil contains driers and may unduly

FIGURE 29.   When treating bare wood, use a petroleum-based beeswax polish, which has a greater firmness than pure beeswax. It momentarily darkens the wood and can be hand-rubbed to a silky sheen or mechanically buffed to a near-mirror finish.   *Photo: Andrew J. Gigg*

hasten the process. The oil and the turpentine coating should stand for between twenty-four and forty-eight hours. Two wash coats of thin shellac are applied and the surface is sanded down until no vestige remains on the surface. The purpose of this is simply to fill the pores of the wood. The third coat of shellac is rubbed very lightly with a fine grade paper, and then cleaned with a tack rag. All that remains is three coats of paste wax. This finish can endure for several years without any attention beyond the usual dusting. Although wax finish is advocated as the best surface treatment for fine furniture, this is not intended to be dogmatic and apply in every single case. Finishes alter treatments. For instance, while an ebony simulated surface will benefit from silicone-free wax, the coarse-grained open-pored woods, such as oak and ash, will also be at their best if wax polished, whereas pine and similar woods will not look very effective unless they have been dark-stained. Natural pine may stubbornly refuse to be improved by wax, and it is best stained or

FIGURE 30. When applying the initial coat of pure beeswax polish ensure that a generous layer covers the wood, and then rub it well into the grain, using a relatively small cotton pad and using as much pressure as possible. *Photo: Andrew J. Gigg*

varnished, or given several coats of thin shellac.

Liquid wax polishes, sometimes called 'cream' polishes, are complex chemical mixes which usually contain silicones. In use, they have a multiple action, cleaning and polishing the surface in a single operation. The manufacturers appear to market these polishes while under the impression that the user will prefer a high gloss finish on furniture. It is for this reason that they promote them on their ability to create a glassy surface with what they call 'less effort'. The same applies to aerosol polishes. While part of their claim is true, it is debatable whether all the superficial and other dirt can be totally removed in the same action as polishing. More often than not, at least some of the dirt must be trapped between layers of polish, and this will cause a build-up of grime which will probably go unnoticed as the furniture grows older. This does not matter too much where modern mass-produced furniture is concerned when it looks really dreadful, because many people simply sell it and buy some more. Or else they go on living with it until it falls to pieces. Interestingly, a few furniture manufacturers have attempted to create a 'middle market' by offering furniture with a distinctive design appearance. With this has grown a range of wax polishes based on old fashioned formulae, though still with the addition of silicones for 'time-saving'. If manufacturers could get away from the idea that the mysterious silicones, which are in fact simply hardeners, and persuade users that more time spent putting wax on the wood rather than chemicals there would be more satisfaction all round.

Silicones are not at all magical. In fact, they can cut through various finishes, including lacquer and some types of varnish.

But wax has its own magic.

FIGURE 31. Cream-based wood polishes should be applied very liberally and allowing the first two applications to stand for a time to allow it to take effect on the grain. They take somewhat longer than pure beeswax and other compounds, and as many as four to six coats may be needed, working the polish well into the grain.   *Photo: Andrew J. Gigg*

9

Oil Finishes

Formulary and Application

THERE is one initial drawback to applying the very basic oil finish to hardwood and it is found in the method of application, for it demands rather more time than many craftsmen possess and it does call for a lot of energy. The oil must be applied warm or hot, and it has to be rubbed into the grain with what amounts to tremendous ferocity and undiminished enthusiasm. It has to be done thoroughly, otherwise the wood will soon begin to look very patchy and scabrous and the condition will become progressively worse. On the other hand, if oil polishing is properly done, it can be among the most effective of all finishes in its ability to impart a glowing finish.

The true oil finish which has had a few years' wear is something to charm and entrance the heart of the connoisseur, but to the person who does not know one finish from another it probably looks like nothing more than a dull-looking surface. A closer examination shows a glow which has all the richness of mature wine. As far as the craftsman is concerned, it can take several weeks or even up to a whole year to achieve a really presentable appearance, and for this reason oil finishing may not be a commercial proposition. But in the world of conservation, where authenticity is everything, it does have a special place, and it is also important to the private collector of furniture who employs only the discerning craftsman. Perhaps the most interesting aspect of the essentially humble oil finish is that it can never be said to be quite finished. It will always benefit from some additional rubbing in return for which it will give up even greater beauty. The same cannot be said of many finishes, nor do they wear as well or withstand dampness and extremes of heat.

The true rôle of oil finishing as far as the relationship between timber type and utilisation is concerned is that it should be used for fine period furniture. This process and its materials ante-dated the use of varnish, and in England practically all furniture prior to 1600 was oil finished, using the product of the poppy, various nuts and other oil-yielding plants. The use of these crude and often unrefined oils resulted after considerable periods of time in the oak furniture of that time oxidising to the typical blackness now associated with old English oak furniture. There were additional contributory factors, such as the application of paint and stain to some domestic furniture. Principally, however, the blackening was due to oil and many thousands of rubbings over a period of several centuries. In Renaissance Italy the walnut coffer chests, each surface crammed to capacity with carved surfaces and exceedingly sumptuous in appearance, were also enhanced by oil finishes, using greatly refined oils and perhaps a somewhat higher standard of workmanship.

The oil polish finish, while requiring great endurance on the part of the craftsman, still offers a great many advantages over other systems. It will not, for instance, suffer from heat blistering and it can literally be sluiced with water without in any way affecting the fibres of the wood. Nor will it wear down or suffer from bare patches. These and other faults are evident when shellac or varnish is used. So durable is the properly applied oil finish that it will rarely need to be renewed once it has impregnated the wood. There are obvious advantages in giving this type of finish to, say, a dining table. There will be no need to use heat resistant mats, and no unsightly marks or white rings will materialise if a hot casserole happens to be placed on the surface.

The frontier between oil polishing and french polishing has certainly narrowed in recent years, due to the efforts of some finishers to 'improve' the process by using additives. Basically, however, if a genuine oil polish is required, then the process must be kept as pure and as basic as possible, and this applies not only to the technique but also the materials.

Central to oil polishing is linseed oil, and it should be used in its raw form, because if boiled linseed oil is applied, the action of the driers will act as an accelerator to the detriment of the ultimate finish. On the other hand, if there is a time limit to the job, it can be governed by using a 50/50 mixture of raw and boiled linseed oil, but obviously the finish would not be as fine as a genuine raw oiled finish.

The choice of the furniture to be oil polished is crucial. The best results will be obtained on large flat areas, such as tables and sideboards. If it is applied to heavily detailed furniture the oil may accumulate in the crevices and ultimately darken them. But some modified oil mixtures can be used quite successfully on carved surfaces. The formulae are given at the end of the chapter.

The oil is heated by placing it in a container and standing it in a bowl of hot water which can be frequently renewed. Warm oil will flow much more easily. Assuming that the wood is smooth and clean, a generous film of oil is applied, using a broad brush. The rubbing is done with a piece of soft felt wrapped round a brick, and working from area to area. The first coat will rapidly soak into the wood. There may be a possibility of using a power tool with a lambswool bonnet or buffer to work the oil into the wood in the early stages. Providing the movement is constant to avoid making any friction marks on the wood, this can be an effective method of keeping the oil warm and encouraging it to penetrate the surface.

The end of each phase is marked by the disappearance of the oil. The first coat will not provide even a mere hint of polish, but if the operation is repeated some results can be expected. Depending on the condition of the wood the results will definitely appear after the fourth coat, and it will be marked by sweat points as saturation point is reached. These sweat marks should be removed with a rag soaked in methylated spirit, the use of which will not impair the final finish because it rapidly evaporates.

It is not possible to overdo oil polishing. The completion will be obvious, because the oil will no longer penetrate the wood and prolonged rubbing will do nothing for the final appearance.

An alternative method of oil polishing is to make a mixture of two-thirds raw linseed oil and one-third turpentine. This is faster acting than pure oil, and it is suitable for the finishing shop which is engaged in commercial work. It will also accept a colour tone if pigment is added in powder form to the turpentine and then well mixed with the oil. The mixture is not applied to the wood at a high temperature because the turpentine will evaporate and act as a hardener. This mixure is suitable for detailed and complicated furniture, but care must be taken to remove any residue from the crevices, otherwise it will become tacky and act as a dust trap. Orange sticks moistened in spirit are used to remove such deposits. The first coat is applied with a soft cloth and rubbed for about fifteen minutes, by which time the wood will have absorbed it.

As with other methods of surface finishing involving the use of oils and spirits, the humidity of the atmosphere has an effect on the work. If it is done in the summer months it is advisable to allow the workpiece to stand for two or three days before the second coat is applied. It is quite simple to find out whether the oil is being properly absorbed, and this is done by placing the palm of the hand on the flat surface and sliding it in several directions, then examining the skin for any traces of oil. If there is surplus oil, it means that the wood is not ready for the next coat. About four coats will, however, be sufficient if the oil and turpentine mixture is used and it can take about two months to apply them. That is not necessarily the end of it, because the furniture should be similarly treated once a month for a year and thereafter once a year.

One of the drawbacks to the prolonged surface finishing technique is that the thinner sections of the wood may begin to warp or buckle due to the action of the oil. But if there is any doubt about the risk attached to a job, then it is advisable to give the reverse side an equal treatment to create a balance of the oil content.

It is possible to accelerate the glow caused by the oil polish by applying a quantity of very fine pumice powder and mineral oil, rubbing after the final coat. An alternative is to use rottenstone instead of pumice, though the action will be much the same.

Another method of reducing the time spent on oil polishing is to close the pores of the wood with a suitable filler before any oil is applied. This effectively reduces the absorption area and provides a firmer area to be polished.

A mixture which will produce very quick results consists of spar or waterproof varnish in a quantity of one-third to one-half stirred into a mixture of two-thirds linseed oil and one-third turpentine. It should be brushed on in generous quantities and then rubbed in the usual way. This will create a shiny finish which, however, will not compare too favourably with the true oil polish, though it will pass in undiscriminating company and is quite suitable for general purpose furniture and certain types of panel finishing.

In the course of time the craftsmen-finishers have evolved a variety of recipes, including the following:

Take one pint of raw linseed oil, one pint of turpentine and one ounce of white or yellow beeswax. Melt the beeswax in the oil, using a double boiler, then add the turpentine. It is applied in the same way as oil polish and imparts a hard and lasting finish.

Take one pint of raw linseed oil, three pints of water, one pint of denatured alcohol. Stir the oil into the water and pour in the alcohol. The constituents will emulsify when the mixture is briskly stirred, and this should be done throughout the application. The surface of the workpiece is cleaned, and the emulsified mixture is applied with a cloth, briskly rubbed for a time, then allowed to stand for about one hour, after which it is again polished. At this stage a high polish should begin to appear.

Take half a pint of vinegar, half a pint of denatured alcohol, half a pint of paraffin oil. Shake together in a bottle and apply with a clean cloth. The effect will improve if the workpiece is allowed to stand for one hour before being repolished.

Take four parts of raw linseed oil, one part of turpentine, one part of vinegar and one quarter part of butter of antimony. All the ingredients with the exception of the butter of antimony are mixed together, and this is added last. The polish should not be stored in a metal can but kept in a stoneware or glass jar. The polish is sparingly applied and allowed to stand for fifteen minutes, then rubbed with a clean cloth. This particular recipe is widely used in the antiques restoration business.

Take one pint of paraffin oil, one pint of denatured alcohol, one pint of vinegar and three ounces of rottenstone. Mix the ingredients together, keeping the rottenstone until last. It should remain in suspension by vigorously shaking the mixture just before applying it. The rottenstone has an abrasive action and any rubbing should be done in the direction of the grain.

10

Plywood and Blockboard Finishes

THE plywood now in common use was the subject of an American patent of 1868, when it was introduced as a material with a much greater strength than conventional wood. Describing the method of manufacture, the patent stated that '. . . the invention consists in cementing or otherwise fastening together a number of scales or sheet, with the grain of the successive pieces, or some of them, running crosswise or diversely from that of others. . . . The crossing or diversification of the direction of the grain is of great importance to impart strength and tenacity to the material, protect against splitting, and at the same time preserve it from liability to expansion or contraction.' It was not until World War Two that plywood came into its own, when it was used for utility furniture and for aircraft and light boat construction. But by the Thirties the development of waterproof adhesives and the first synthetic resins enabled designers to explore different types of construction methods in which conventional wood was unable to find a place.

Even so, plywood remains the Cinderella of wood utilisation, and this may be due to the fact that conventional wood has been in such good supply for many years. Undervalued and often dismissed as flimsy and makeshift, plywood has often been overtaken by other products, such as blockboard, which is made as a sandwich of reconstituted wood chips and lacks the tensile strength of plywood. In the Thirties the term 'plywood furniture' was synonymous with jerrybuilding methods of contruction not only in housing but in general use as well. Yet the irony is that plywood is able to offer many different elements of visual beauty as far as the figuring is concerned, and it has a great many different applications, from bentwood furniture to panelling. Certainly, in

Scandinavia it has been very fully exploited. As early as 1901 Gustav Strengell (1875–1937), Finnish architect, expressed what was required in his essay, *New Aesthetic Values:* 'People have once again begun to realise that every material possesses its own characteristic which often calls for a special technique. . . . A chair is beautiful the moment it achieves its purpose in full. No matter if it is lacking in every form of ornament, providing it is comfortable to sit in. . . .' This might well apply to a minimal finish applied to plywood. Its basic attraction in one respect is its strength which enables the craftsman to force it into 360 degrees or a series of double and treble curves, and in fact into a helix if so desired without any sign of fracture.

Run-of-the-mill modern plywood has an external skin, invariably of fir, which lends itself to practically any finish but is often best treated very lightly for the sake of its own appearance. It should never be used as the basis of disguise or common fakery by obtrusive dark staining, bearing in mind that the grain or figuring is of the greatest importance. There may be a feeling that three-ply is thin when compared with other wooden construction, and this will perhaps inhibit any intensive surface finishing. But it is in fact far from flimsy or insubstantial. It is enormously strong and one of the most enjoyable materials as far as high quality surface finishing is concerned, for it is perfectly smooth and it is unflawed in the superior grades. While it will always benefit from the skiful enhancement of its figuring, it may also serve as a fine 'canvas' for decoupage, decorative paintings and other forms of applied decoration. It is, in short, a material for experiment.

These observations make it all the more unfortunate that much of the furniture which has been designed specifically for plywood construction has lacked visual appeal. Indeed, most of it has been so downright ugly that no amount of surface finishing would do anything to improve it. This applies even more directly to the more substantial multi-ply, which is the term applied to plywood consisting of more than the standard three layers. It appears that plywood has by its very nature inhibited the efforts of finishers. Exactly why this should be so is a question for the designers who have failed to properly exploit plywood.

In view of what has been said, it may well be that finishers will find very few opportunities for the imaginative treatment of plywood for the simple reason that it will seldon come his way. Plywood nowadays is more likely to be found in showrooms, bars, theatres and cinemas, although it has to be said that enormous scope exists for plywood wall facing in domestic settings, replacing the monotony and standardisation of painted walls and much modern wallpaper.

The most superficial examination of plywood will show that the machine-cut surface must be given a thorough sealer before any work can be done on it. Fir is open-grained, and it will absorb any amount of liquid and continue to do so until it presents a scabrous patchiness. Although commercial sealers can be used, it is better to prepare a sealer in the workshop in the form of a thin shellac which can be brushed and rubbed into the pores. First of all the figuring should be studied. If it is quite striking, then it should be exploited. There is no point in covering it with a depressingly dark stain and cloaking its beauty. When a light finish is desirable, it is advisable first of all to wipe the surface over with a rag soaked in turpentine. This will demonstrate the figuring in both light and dark contrasting tones, and suggest what it might look like when the surface finish has been applied.

Regardless of how smooth it might seem, the plywood must first be sanded, for there may well be a great many hair-like fibres standing proud of the surface. They can be quickly disposed of with fine sandpaper. It is a job to be done entirely by hand. If a power-tool is used, it can cut straight through the outer skin and break into the underlay of the ply.

The next step is to apply a single coat of resin sealer, followed by a washed-on coat of white shellac, preferably in a two-pound cut. If the resin sealer was properly applied, the shellac should dry very quickly, and when it is dry it should be lightly sanded to give it sufficient tooth in preparation for the next coat, which consists of lacquer or varnish. A fine satin finish can be achieved by rubbing with very fine steel wool and then putting on a finishing coat of wax. It is, of course, entirely a matter of personal choice, but a high gloss finish is not always entirely suitable for large areas of plywood due to its reflective qualities. A satin finish is more desirable.

There is, of course, no limit to the number of finishes which can be applied, but an alternative to the one described above is a blonde finish, the application of which is somewhat more involved and calls for more time to be spent on it. The surface is sanded smooth, followed by a coat of a material composed of one gallon of white undercoat which has been thinned with three quarts of turpentine and one pint of raw linseed oil. It should be so thin that the first coat should sink straight into the pores. It may be advantageous to speed this by taking a piece of clean hessian or sacking, and rubbing the surface very briskly and very hard while the paint is still wet. Any surplus paint should be removed. Although it may seem that it dries quickly, it will still remain wet in the pores, and so it should stand overnight. The following day it should be painted with white shellac, rubbed down with a fine sandpaper, and then painted with white shellac, or varnish, rubbed with fine steel wool and then waxed. As we have said, all this does take longer, but it gives the sort of finish which will withstand a lot of wear over a long period. Variations are possible if colour is added to the initial white undercoat. Grey flecks are easy to create, while constrasting colours can be applied in stripes or patterns, which will look effective.

While plywood can be completely painted so that the figuring is totally obscured, this is more in the sphere of decorating than wood finishing. The emphasis in this chapter is upon enhancing and preserving the figuring. One method is staining. Conventional wood stains, especially if they are applied undiluted or neat, will act rather quickly on plywood and may seem much too harsh. To avoid such a drastic reaction it is advisable to dilute, or cut, the stain to a considerable degree. Plywood is like blotting paper and it is easy to create lap marks and smears, and so stain should be reduced until it is only slightly discernible so that several coats will be needed to create any effect. This, however, creates more control over the finished result. The choice between water and spirit stains is a personal one, because while the water stains will raise the fibres and necessitate sanding before the application of varnish or shellac, the application of the fast-acting spirit stain will call for skill. If there is any choice at all, then it must be for a diluted spirit stain, applied quickly with a broad, well-charged brush.

The variety of experimental finishes is large. Two tones are possible if the base coat of tinted shellac or varnish is applied on top of a resin sealer followed by a final coat which carries a tint in the contrasting tone. The application of two-toned finishes calls for a certain amount of finesse because the colours should not be too heavy or overdone, otherwise the results will be confusing and muddy. It is an advantage to finish the toned area with a glaze of thinned varnish.

Blockboard is similar in certain respects to plywood as far as the outer surface is concerned, and it can be surface finished in the same way. It is supplied as a rule as a building material rather than for decorative purposes, and the outer skin is generally inferior and lacking any distinctive figuring. It may well lend itself to graining, as described in chapter twelve. If the surface is perfectly plain, however, all surface finishes which do not rely on the figuring for effect can be used.

One other possibility should be mentioned, and this is the sugi finish, a technique described in detail in chapter twenty-six, though in a modified form because charring might well affect the glue and make the wood buckle or bow. But if the flame is gently wafted over the surface the figuring will be darkly emphasized while the plain areas in between the veins will remain unaffected. Once the mellow tone has been created, the entire area should be sanded with medium and fine papers and then dusted down, after which a sealer can be applied. After sanding, a thinned varnish or shellac can be put on. The final appearance should be of old and well seasoned wood.

It is advisable to use methylated spirit to thin shellac when a colour is added, because the spirit will act as a carrier for the colour and ensure that it is not too heavily attracted to the darker areas. If a mature appearance is desired, put on three coats of shellac, giving the first two a thorough rubbing with fine steel wool. If coloured oil stain is wiped on with a well charged rag, the colour will naturally be intensified, but this should not be overdone.

Although we have assumed throughout that the outer skin will be fir in both plywood and blockwood, other woods are used. Oregon pine, for instance, is common enough, in which case a filler can be used to counteract the open pores. It should be used as a heavy paste, well brushed in and rubbed with a coarse cloth. This will call for a great deal of rumbustious craftsman-like energy before all the pores are totally filled. Oregon pine is a peculiar wood. While it will accept a number of finishes, it is generally advisable to stick to the following method, which gives a mahogany effect. Equal parts are mixed of stale beer and water. If possible, genuine real ale should be used, for other more chemical brews have irritating variations. Up to two ounces of burnt sienna is then dissolved in the liquid. After the first application the surface must be well sanded, and then thinned shellac or varnish applied.

Another method of treating plywood or blockboard in preparation for top finishes consists of applying a water colour coat. This is made by mixing a water colour powder with water and glue size. During the painting it may look pretty thin and uninteresting, but a solid colour can be built up with successive coats. The glue size, which is in the ratio of one ounce to one gallon of water, should sink straight into the pores and give a sound base for any finish other than wax or french polish. It can be very useful if a multi-toned finish is required.

11

Marbling Panels and Furniture

THE habit of making wood look like marble was not originally a simple desire to make common wood look like stone. It grew out of architectural decoration when it was clearly impossible to hoist and fix heavy marble panels into ceilings which would not withstand such stress. Expense was another consideration at a time when some noble patrons happily embarked on grandiose internal decoration schemes without fully appreciating what the final cost would amount to. Faced with towering costs beyond their purses, many of them compromised by agreeing to the decorator's suggestions that the more lofty and inaccessible areas could be marbled rather than moulded and gilded without any loss of opulence. What this entailed was fastening a wood fascia in position and then employing a marbling technique. It was not only ceilings and cornices that were treated, for wooden columns, pillars and architraves were similarly treated. All varieties of marble, from grey to serpentine green were cleverly imitated, and by the eighteenth century there was even a fashion and a passion for fake marble furniture. Table tops, in particular, were given the marble treatment, at first in a garish and downright unconvincing way, but gradually moving towards a refinement of appearance. It was applied not only to furniture but elsewhere in the household. In the eighteenth century the surface of earthenware was marbled, and it was used for slipware between the sixteenth and eighteenth centuries. Wedgwood's 'granite' and 'porphyr' pottery of the later eighteenth century was seen as a natural addition to marbled furniture. The boards of books were also decorated with marbling, as were the endpapers which they produced by taking a sheet of unsized paper and laying it on a trough of colour floating on size. Rivalling the surface finishers who specialised in marbling furniture and architectural features, the producers of marbled papers soon began to offer very large sheets of paper for fixing to furniture and walls. Highly polished, or glazed, it was perhaps even more effective and certainly much cheaper than other forms of decoration. One of the major manufacturers was the Le Breton family, who made marbled papers used for the endpapers of books by such famous French bookbinders as Mace Ruette, Le Gascon and others. In the seventeenth century marbled papers were highly esteemed and even collected, each sheet being entirely different. Many patrons used these sheets to show surface finishers what they wanted their furniture to look like.

Although marbling was common in eighteenth-century England and the United States, it most probably had its early origins in Iran (formerly, Persia) and reached Europe from Turkey towards the end of the sixteenth century, conveyed, in all probability, by craftsmen-monks.

Like so many other techniques, including graining, the craft of marbling became debased by misuse in Victorian times. There is little or no comparision between what was accomplished in the earlier Adam period and the abortions produced by the well-meaning but fumbling Victorians. It seems probable that marbling technique was dropped in the Victorian era due to the introduction of other methods of surface finishing in which the wood rather than its disguise became more important. However, the last few years have seen a new interest in marbling, which accounts for its presence in this book together with suggestions for its refinement. Isolated craftsmen are applying it at the present time to small furniture, though still almost as a novelty rather than a feature in its own right. This may be due to the fact that it calls for rather more artistic sensitivity and application than other surface finishing methods and techniques.

While the technique itself is simple, the variations are many. The final effect depends on size of the area. A ceiling, for instance, should be boldly done if it is to be seen from a distance, whereas a piece of furniture in daily use demands a more considered and detailed amount of work.

The basic technique is subject to a great many variations, some of which can be plainly described, while others call for improvisation. The choice of colours is limited to those of natural marble itself. As a general rule, only three colours are used, the first of which is applied and then allowed to dry. The second colour is then put on, using a broad soft brush. The third colour should be put on with a stiff brush while the second is still wet, and it is 'pulled' sideways in a wavy motion. The success of this method depends almost entirely on the relative stiffness and the softness of the brushes used, also the colour contrasts between the second and third coats of paint. The method is efficient enough when large areas have to be covered.

The second standard method involves the manipulation of the second and third colours with a worn feather. The choice of the feather is important. It must not be new and fresh, because the even edges will do no more than simply make even lines in the wet paint and this is something that is not wanted. A worn feather is a better tool. The second colour is applied with the tip of the feather, and the lining of the marble should be defined by creating uneven and jagged lines, which are carefully smeared every now and then for the sake of realism. The same applies to the third colour. The secret of this technique is in the wet working of the various colours, and to ensure that they are well blurred in certain sections. Nowhere is this form of marbling better exemplified than in the Music Room, Sun Street, Lancaster, a building erected as a garden house about 1730, and treated to 6,000 hours of restoration work by the Landmark Trust, its present owners.

FIGURE 32. The worn feather, perhaps from a gull or blackbird, is used for marbling, and the ideal combination is a length of about six inches with one side more tattered than the other in order to obtain a variety of effects, using both the tip and the sides.

Marbling cannot be executed very efficiently unless reference is made to a good colour photograph of the natural material. Mineral streaks and abberrations form many strange patterns under immense pressure which means that the various types of marble are positively unique in their markings. It is precisely this unique quality which should be simulated and notice should be taken of the vari-coloured marking which provides the strange contrasts.

There is another method of marbling which is related to the process used to marble decorative paper. Providing a container can be found which is large enough to contain the object being marbled, it is possible to achieve effects which are far beyond hand marbling unless the craftsman also happens to be an accomplished artist.

The tank is filled with cold water to about one inch of the top. Enamels which have been thinned by about one-third of their volume are then floated on the surface of the water. The object is then gently laid in the water, where it will pick up the enamels and marbleize the entire surface of the wood. The enamel and the water will not mix, and when the object is withdrawn from the water it will dry very quickly.

There are many variations of water marbleizing. As many colours as may be needed can be floated on the water. There is no limit to their number. When they are resting on the surface, they can be arranged in predetermined or random colours and patterns, using a spatula, comb or stick. The arrangement will remain quite static because the enamel is heavy and viscous until dipping takes place. Not only can this be used for conventional marbling, it can also be used for the application of various forms of wood grain, using such appropriate colours as sienna and black, the pattern in this case being laid lengthwise on the water rather than swirled round and round.

FIGURE 33.   A surface can be scumbled, or patterned, using bunched-up newspaper or a crumpled rag against a two-tone colour base. The result is very much a random pattern, but when it covers a wide area it can look extremely effective.   *Photo: Andrew J. Gigg*

Each dipping will, of course, remove the paint from the tank and so the film should be replenished between applications, otherwise a very patchy effect will result.

Areas of the workpiece where marbling is not required can easily be masked off, using a waterproof tape to create curvilinear forms or straight edges, the tape remaining in position until the enamel is completely dry and then stripped off. The 'barber's pole' effect is very simple to achieve on table and chair legs providing the tape is carefully applied and any wrinkles avoided. In a more advanced form varieties of differently coloured and patterned enamel can be put on if the process is phased and the areas which have already been treated are covered with water resistant tape. Great care should be exercised in this process, because if the enamel is not completely dry the tape may well lift areas

FIGURE 34.   Marbling can look startlingly realistic, as here, when large slabs of colour are used and then pulled out and modified with a feather-edge. Boldness rather than delicacy is required.

Photo: Andrew J. Gigg

when it is removed.

The methods used to lower bulky objects into the tank are a matter of pure and often ingenious improvisation. If a table top is to be treated with random patterns it is necessary only to lower it very gently on to the surface of the tank, and it can be lifted out again with a complete film of enamel adhering to it. But if shelving is being dipped as a complete unit, and the tank happens to be too small for the job to be done in a single operation, then it can be done in two halves or even in quarter sections. Making exact repeat patterns by this method is practically impossible and the solution when dealing with large areas or pieces is in creating a contrasting or 'continuous' pattern to form an overall complete job. If the first dipping is unsatisfactory as far as pattern and colour distribution are concerned, the pieces can be allowed to dry and then

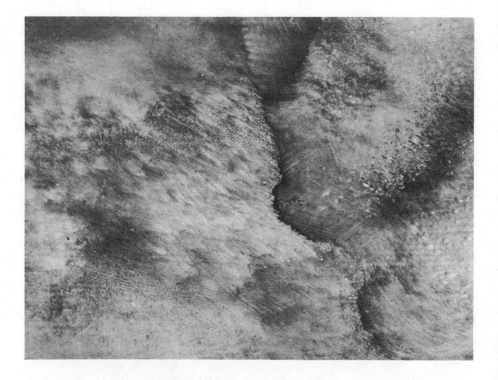

FIGURE 35. Detail of marbling showing how the dimension of successive layers can be suggested, using the technique of dragging the colour and blurring the detail. The blurring should run in one direction, and the edges of colours may be touched up with a darker tone of the same colour tints.   *Photo: Andrew J. Gigg*

re-dipped without the necessity of stripping off the first coat. Each coat will completely cover the previous one.

The final finish for a marbled effect is a glaze with thinned white shellac or varnish, the latter giving a mature effect if tinted with burnt umber. Two coats are generally necessary to provide a resilient and long-wearing coat.

Marbling is not, as many may think, a cheap, fast and gimcrack finish. Granted, it can be debased and it will then look cheap and nasty, but if it is well done and expertly finished, it will have the appearance of quality. One ideal application is children's furniture, when it can be combined with decorative stencilling and bright decoupage. Elsewhere in the house, the marbled finish will lend itself to many unusual decorative effects. An otherwise ugly and plain wooden fireplace

FIGURE 36.   A two-tone colour effect with some patterning in which the bolder dark lining is put on with a fine lining brush and then dragged with a flat brush, finally being overlaid with a contrasting opaque tint.

Photo: Andrew J. Gigg

surround can be hand marbled, using the worn-feather technique, and the pattern continued up the chimney breast and, indeed, all over the wall if so desired, or inside an alcove. This sort of job calls for a lot of patience and not a little artistry, and time needs to be spent on it. In such cases the base coat should be white oil paint which can be dulled by rubbing with fine glasspaper. To achieve a really high class finish, artist's oil paints should be used in a glazed wash composed of two parts of paint to one of white spirit. This is washed over the base coat and then dabbed with a flat sponge or crumpled tissue to create a broken surface appearance. The veining is done by using a mixture of black and raw umber, applying it with the side of an artist's brush and running the lines in a series of irregular zigzag patterns, always ensuring that they are logical and have a beginning, a middle and an end, like a well composed short story or novel. The precise amount of compression of the lines themselves depends to a great extent on the area to be marbled, but it should certainly not be overdone to the point where it looks like a series of cobwebs. While the lines are still damp, they should be dabbed with a sponge to blur any solid-looking appearance. When the paint is quite dry, some white lines can be inserted, crisscrossing the deeper hued blurred lines, using an artist's brush and then smudging them with a sponge damped with turpentine.

When the marbling is dry, it can be painted with clear polyurethane varnish and, when practically dry, it is rubbed with ordinary baking flour to impart a sheen.

Initial attempts at this advanced type of marbling may well be somewhat self-conscious and fail to reach the anticipated standard. This is due not so much to the paint itself, but to the artistic technique employed. The word 'fidget' when applied to the lining of the marble, is very apt, because the line must look like an erratic fidget, as though created by the same awesome force which creates real marble in the folds of the earth. But, like so many of the surface finishing techniques, it does call for a certain amount of practice.

In a more advanced form the effect can achieve peaks of perfection, for instance by using a base coat consisting of enamels mixed in equal proportions to a 50/50 base of oil and mineral spirits. The oil-mineral mix is put on the wood in a generous quantity so as to provide a film on which the marbling is capable of floating and can be manipulated. The thinned colours should be somewhat thicker than the oil-mineral mix. Separate brushes are used for each colour. Before being loaded with colour, they are dipped in the spirit and oil mixture to improve the running quality. The tip of the brush is dabbed on to deposit a streak of colour here and there at random. An alternative method is to load each brush with a separate colour and hold them in a bunch to apply groups of colours.

The next step is to take a piece of cheesecloth, rolled up tightly like a sausage, loaded with individual colours in patches. The sausage is then rolled across the working surface to deposit swatches of colour in a single swathe. Various improvisations can follow, such as thrusting a stiff round stencil brush loaded with one colour or the other and twisting it across the surface. The final operation consists of dripping pools of oil and turpentine across the surface, and then manipulating the colours with the edge of a feather. Patterns will then appear of their own accord. The most important factor when using this technique is to keep the surface wet enough to allow for the manipulation of the colour without totally muddying it. It should be wet enough to blot with a tissue in the final stage before it is left to dry and harden.

There are some variations. For instance, faint islands of contrasting colour are advisable to relieve a large area of plain marbling, and an eyedropper can be used to place patches of oil at various points. The pigment is mixed with spirit and dropped into the oil, then swirled round with the end of an orange stick. A feather edge is used to splay out the colour like a web thus avoiding a blob of solid colour at the centre.

FIGURE 37. The capital of a column, restored and given a surface treatment to antique it, consisting of marbling on a wood base and ensuring that the grain of the marble runs in one direction (right). Seen from a short distance, the illusion is complete. *Photo: Andrew J. Gigg*

12

Graining and Colour Combing

Technique and Application

GRAINING has acquired a very bad name, and this is due to the fact that it has usually been very badly done since the Thirties, when it was literally scraped on to both external and internal doors, many of which looked as though hot brown toffee had run down the panels and then been pawed with a broken-toothed comb. It was a vogue which painfully endured for a time and fortunately expired when it was found that a plain painted door could look so much better than a poorly grained one.

Yet, when it is expertly executed, graining can become one of the most exciting forms of surface finish for many features of a house, including the door panels, kitchen cupboards and items of furniture. There is also a wide scope for grained plywood panels to line rooms and passageways. Graining stands on a par with marbling. At best it is, of course, an elaborate fake, because it disregards any of the beauty which the base wood might offer and proceeds to replace it with an idealised interpretation of what it could look like. It is as a rule applied to inferior wood, and while it is a very basic technique, it has a number of useful variations, such as dragging, in which colour is applied over a glaze and then partially removed.

In the briefest possible terms, this is how ordinary graining is done. The cleaned wood is painted with a background colour of the chosen hue, which can be a branded paint or something concocted in the workshop. In the case of oak, for instance, one pint of white lead paint is mixed with a half a pint of golden ochre together with boiled linseed oil or raw linseed oil and driers. For birch, on the other hand, raw sienna is substitued for the ochre. Maple requires a touch of deep vermilion and lemon chrome.

The base coat is generously applied and allowed to dry, followed by a second coat. The graining is done with a mix of raw sienna and varnish, which is put on with a broad brush and then treated with a dry graining brush which is dragged lightly and without interruption in the direction of the grain. The action lifts the glaze coat in such a way as to simulate grain. When it is quite dry a varnish finish should be applied.

That is the kind of graining which started as long ago as the Middle Ages and died in the Victorian age, the motive being to make cheap and inferior wood look rather better than it was. There has, so far, been no attempt to explain that a certain amount of deft artistry is required to make the finish aesthetically acceptable. In fact, if the craftsman were to blindly follow the above technique to the letter he would find that only the final stage of lifting the glaze and using the dry graining brush would afford any real satisfaction. But one thing which would become quite evident is the importance of the first two coats of paint and the correct depth of the tint prepared specially for the job. Many interesting experiments can be carried out with colours which might seem to contrast oddly or even clash under other circumstances. For instance, a red base coat and a green glaze make good bedfellows as far as graining is concerned. Likewise, yellow and buff or ochre marry and live well together. Even gilt on black or gold on blue can be striking. The modern province of graining tends to be on smaller pieces, such as the inset panels of cupboard doors, stair panelling and even an uncarpeted staircase, which can be given a couple of coats of polyurethane varnish. Another use for graining is to ennoble battered piano cases, especially when they have to live in bright modern interiors. They lend themselves admirably to vari-coloured treatments, as do some of the Victorian furniture monstrosities, though it should be hastily added that care should be taken to avoid the sort of furniture which resembles Gothic tomb structure. Grained in the modern colour idioms, such furniture can provoke screams of horror.

On the assumption that the graining has to be applied to a very inferior wood, the following method is recommended. It makes use of at least part of the technique of marbling, described in chapter eleven. The purpose in this case is to fake the wood to resemble fruitwood. It is the essence of simplicity.

The wood is first well sanded. In this basic method the finish will be opaque, and so a base coat of paint is not required. Instead, the lines of the fruitwood grain are drawn direct on to the clean wood, using a mixture of common varnish and white spirit in equal amounts. A cupful will provide enough drawing fluid for a large expanse of wood. The pigment to use is burnt sienna, one teaspoonful of which will be quite enough to create the colour when it is dissolved in the varnish and spirit mixture. It may well be advisable to use a kitchen mixer to get the correct colour tone. The tool for drawing is the well sharpened end of a feather, cut with a razor blade or sharp knife. No matter how sharp the point, however, it will be quite impossible to draw a perfect line with it. But that is all to the good because the more wavering it happens to be, the more natural it will look. The spirit content of the drawing mixture should cause some feathering and a fuzzy appearance, which further enhances the realism. The drawing of the grain should be adapted from a photograph rather than done from memory because grain, or figuring has its own logic. Improvisation can run off the rails with a fine disregard for what might be called the natural order of things.

The drawn grain should be allowed to dry for at least twenty-four hours. If it happens to fade here and there, it can be retouched. It should be mentioned that when rendering grain in this way it is not a good idea to draw with an equally intense line throughout the entire area, but areas should be created in which there is a certain amount of artistically contrived fading. If it is all quite even, it will probably look false. Granted, graining happens to be false, but it should not look like a blatant fake.

The build-up of the effect can continue with the application of a very thin mixture made by mixing two-thirds of flat white paint with one third of mineral spirit with the addition of just enough raw sienna to create a weak-tea colour. It is essential that this is thoroughly mixed if an even coat is to be achieved. It is applied liberally to the wood and immediately wiped down with a piece of clean cotton, then permitted to dry. Exactly how much should be left on the wood can best be described as a thin film, but it should be well rubbed into the wood and then dried overnight. It is followed by two coats of thinned varnish or white shellac.

There are, of course many graduations in any form of graining. Exactly how much restrained or bold effect is required depends on the nature of the piece which is being treated. In the method just described a more restrained effect can be reached by drawing the grain rather more faintly and applying additional coats of varnish or shellac. If it is desired to create a more aged effect, this can be done by adding a quantity of burnt umber to the varnish or shellac. This will tone down the drawn grain and it can be compensated by drawing the grain more boldly. Quite obviously, it is advisable to plan the final effect beforehand. If any drastic modifications of the process are introduced during finishing, the effect will generally be disappointing and perhaps look very makeshift. Many amateur finishers tend to disregard the need for a basic plan of action before embarking on graining and proceed to gaily apply techniques which are alien to the piece being treated. This eventually leads to something which can only be called a visual uneasiness.

Graining of high quality is not quickly done. It is a precision job which calls for judgement, skill and an appreciation of the possibilities.

Some indication of the lineage of the craft is reflected in an 1830 publication, *The Cabinet-Maker's Guide* in which the author, G. A. Siddons, stated that the tools of the trade included '. . . common brushes, as used by house-painters, sash tools of various sizes, camel hair pencils with long and short hair, camel hair flat brushes in tin for softening off; graining tools which are flat brushes of a few hairs in thickness, and of different widths, fastened into wooden handles, and, lastly horn combs purpose-made for graining; and these are chiefly used for imitating oak on wainscot though they will often be found useful for other purposes; they are sometimes fixed into a wooden handle, in the same manner as a graining tool, though generally in the form of a common comb; they should be very thin and elastic in order to adapt themselves to the several mouldings they are drawn over, in order to produce the grain so peculiar to oak or wainscot.'

Wainscot is a term of Dutch origin meaning oak quarter cut. The boards were used for wagon building for which the Dutch word was *wagenschot*. By the time of Sheraton's *Cabinet Dictionary* in 1803 it was 'The wooden work which lines the walls of a room as high up as the surbase'. The latter word is an architectural term for mouldings of various types.

Siddons also provided a number of rules for the grainer, and said that '. . . these few rules, if joined with a close attention in studying from nature, will enable the ingenious mechanic soon to make himself master of an art which adds so much to the beautifying of our apartments, and which has lately become so much in vogue, that a modern room can scarcely said to be finished without these decorative embellishments'. Despite his high opinion of graining, Siddons probably saw the technique become debased in his lifetime to the extent that it was clumsily and roughly applied without any regard to its suitability for practically all cheap furniture in Victorian times. It eventually killed itself and did not revive until the 1920s and 1930s, when it appeared in a somewhat different form, but still sombre and circumscribed in a form known as colour combing.

This method used combs made from wood, metal or stiff card, which were used to break through the wet paint of the top coat to expose the dry paint of the base coat, which was done in a contrasting colour. This was not true graining, because all it consisted of was a series of scrolls and wavy lines, not unlike the ancient Essex craft of pargetting, which uses combs in wet plaster dressing of exterior cottage walls.

Modern colour combing is a simple technique which can be adapted to create an unusual looking finish on large flat areas, including wooden floors, using flat paint, tints of all colours, and white spirit. The surface should be absolutely clean, well sanded and devoid of grease and any discoloration. The base colour is thinned in the proportion of one to three of white spirit, and it is applied liberally to form a solid base colour. The colour to be combed is applied when the base coat is dry. It should not be put on too liberally, otherwise the excess will probably form puddles and pools during combing.

The comb itself should have large and bold teeth, and it can be made by cutting pointed or rounded teeth out of a strip of plywood or hardboard. Complicated patterns can be formed by using several differently-toothed tools and over-combed. If a floor is being combed, it will be necessary to decide beforehand whether geometric or random patterns are to be executed, and in this case a working drawing is a good idea. If a geometric design is required, then masking tape can be used to avoid any edge feathering and smudging. Combing lends itself very well to two colours, but more can be used. It is, however, at its best if it is kept simple.

FIGURE 38. The modern triangular graining comb with teeth of various lengths for contrasting effects. Made of rubber, it is easily used and cleaned. Combs can also be made from hardboard or cardboard with teeth of varying aperture within the same length in order to impart greater visual interest than blank uniformity in the finished result.

When the combed pattern is quite dry, it should be given two or three coats of polyurethane varnish. A floor decorated in this way will last for several years and will be enhanced by a few rugs in contrasting colours.

The effectiveness of both graining and colour combing depends to a very considerable extent upon the finishing coat, or glaze. While polyurethane has already been recommended, there may be craftsmen who want to experiment with home-made glazes. These glazes form the basis for the brushed application of the tint when grain is being simulated, or they can be used as a finishing coat. If they are used to form the grain, they must have a wet but not sticky pliability which allows the artist's brush to move smoothly and comfortably to take all the twists and turns which are necessary in certain types of grain imitation. A lot depends upon the brushes used. Graining is not done solely with conventional artist's brushes. Specialised brushes are quite expensive and only if a lot of work is to be done will it be worth investing in such items as overgrainers, floggers and mottlers, the names of which are descriptive of their various functions. If multiple spaced lines are needed in some types of graining, ordinary decorator's brushes can easily be modified by razoring out groups of bristle so that the wide brush now becomes several separate brushes in one handle. One of the most invaluable and cheapest tools in the grainer's kit is the common cork, which can be cut down with a sharp knife to make a pencil shape, a knife edge or a wedge. If this is drawn over the wet glaze, it will give satisfyingly jagged lines which can be drawn with great precision and in close proximity.

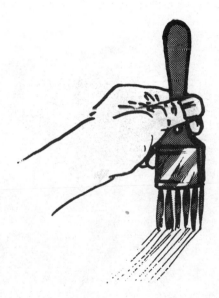

FIGURE 39. The overgrainer with multiple groups of bristles is generally used to add a second pattern to a surface which has already been grained. It gives a series of very fine lines and its most common use is in giving an interwoven effect.

It may be helpful to know something about the five main graining brushes which are available from suppliers. They are:

Dragger, otherwise known as a flogger, supplied in widths from three to six inches, the bristles being split in such a way as to produce a series of very fine lines when it is dragged through the wet glaze.

Grainer, supplied in a variety of widths with bristles which are sufficiently spaced to create more or less evenly spaced stripes. A grainer can be made from an ordinary flat decorator's brush if some of the bristles are cut away with a razor blade.

Duster, used for stippling and creating smooth glazed coats.

Overgrainer, supplied in widths from one to four inches, and looking like several brushes in one, the bristles being very soft and pliable and capable of drawing precise lines on a wet surface.

Mottler, not unlike the grainer, is available in widths of one to four inches.

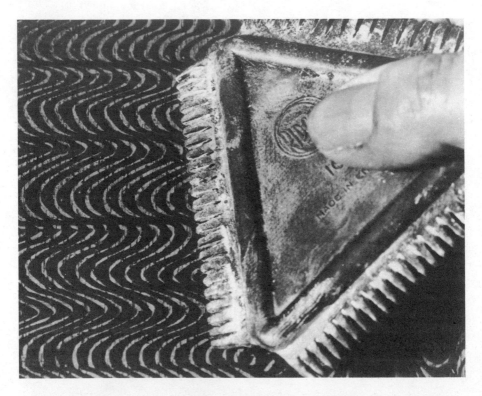

FIGURE 40.   Colour combing can be on any scale. In this example a rubber graining tool is being used to create a wavy effect in two contrasting colours, the lighter one forming the base. Combing is often best done when the paint is slightly tacky, otherwise it may run and fill in the pattern. Graduations of effect are created by holding the tool at various angles. Providing the paint texture is right, any errors can be covered by re-combing the surface.   *Photo: Andrew J. Gigg*

FIGURE 41. A traditionally grained old door in which the distinctive pine panelling has been artificially simulated, using the worn-feather technique. Balance and proportion plus an understatement of the grain is advisable to avoid visual confusion. *Photo: Andrew J. Gigg*

Here is the formula for a fine high quality glaze which can be used for both graining and colour combing purposes. Mix one part boiled linseed oil and one part of turpentine and one part of drier. Whiting should be added in the ratio of one to two teaspoonfuls to every quart of paint. This is added to provide some substance or body and has a distinct advantage when a dragged pattern is applied. If a glaze has to be tinted, this can be done by mixing artist's oil colour in white spirit, then adding a small quantity of the glaze before mixing with the main supply.

One of the working difficulties with a glaze is that it can dry fairly quickly in a warm atmosphere, but this can be retarded by adding a little boiled linseed oil. Unfortunately, this also creates a gloss which cannot be dispelled.

*   *   *

Graining is not at all the narrow conservative craft which its chequered history might suggest. It can happily be applied to all kinds of wooden surfaces, from stools and chairs, all the way through to massive bookcases, beds, shelving and floors. Whether it is suitable for exteriors is a matter of taste, of course, but it can enhance such commonplace and generally uninteresting areas as door panels and skirting boards, stairs and balustrades, especially if a wild imagination is used in the selection of colours, either in direct contrast or as single-hued tones.

13

Shading and Distressing

BOTH of these techniques are widely used in the antique restoration trade, sometimes as a method of making young furniture look old and old furniture even older. It is not necessarily employed in the high quality antique trade except when it is necessary to match-in a replacement section of wood which has to look exactly right. Both methods demand an ability to know exactly when to call a halt, not particularly because the piece may look dowdy but to make it match a particular period. In the case of distressing it should not be maltreated to a point where it is in danger of falling to pieces. But by dint of a tasteful combination of shading and distressing, even the miraculous may be achieved, given enough practice and the sweaty manipulation of colour tones.

Any comparison between a piece of old furniture and a piece of new furniture will aptly demonstrate what shading should amount to. Unless it is a piece of deliberate reproduction, the new furniture will have an even colour and it will not show any sign of wear. A piece of old furniture, on the other hand, will have a great many areas in which the colour has worn away, leaving some areas which are lighter than others. This is not a reference to the quality which is generally known as patina, caused by the attractive effects of time, but to the wider areas of panels, for instance, and the middle sections of cupboard doors and all the places where a certain sort of 'baldness' shows. It is this quality of really old furniture which is so greatly appreciated by collectors and connoisseurs, and it becomes part of the aura of a particular piece. When applied to carved wood, it is best explained by imagining the surface to be coated with paint which is immediately wiped off, leaving odd and uneven traces in all the crannies and recessed sections. Something of the same can be done with perfectly flat surfaces, for grains of paint will lodge in the pores and remain there if the coat is rubbed in with a piece of rough cloth. It is rather more than simply smearing the area because the pigment is encouraged to leave traces in the pores. The method by which it is achieved has several different names, including glazing, highlighting and antiquing. There are other trade synonyms, but all of them mean precisely the same as far as technique and application are concerned.

The most common way of creating shading is by using ivory paint. The entire surface is first painted with it and it is then allowed to dry, after which raw umber is wiped over it. Described in this somewhat bald manner, it sounds so simple as to be probably ineffective, but the secret lies in the art of imparting the effect, which is accomplished by wiping off the type of surface which is being treated. To take a gross example, supposing a piece of chip carving is treated in this fashion, the burnt umber will sink into the deeper cut sections while the upper sections are wiped more or less clean in direct imitation of what happens through years of direct wear. The finishing coat can be either thin shellac or varnish put on in two or three coats. Perhaps a more sophisticated method of shading is by working direct on to the bare wood, first applying a light shade followed by a darker one. The trade trick here is to achieve not so much a direct as an indirect contrast, using the stronger shade to create the highlights. This works best on larger pieces of furniture rather than on small objects. The art is not so much in completely covering the surface to a uniform shade as varying the depths of tone and making sure that the lightness of the wood shows through in areas where wear would naturally occur.

One of the variations of this form of shading is achieved by applying a fairly strong stain on to the bare wood in an even film and, when it is dry, rubbing in the highlights with fine steel wool. This is more effective if the wood has not first been treated with a filler compound.

Some craftsmen prefer to use a spray gun for creating highlights. This is not strictly necessary, because just as much and probably more can be achieved with delicate brushwork and imaginative applications of steel wool. Certainly, brushwork is to be preferred to a spray gun when a piece is composed of different woods. Patched-up motley-looking rubbish is a case in point. In such cases it is advantageous to work very boldly, giving the workpiece a uniform coat of light to medium stain, followed by the dabbing on of walnut stain to emphasize the highlights. If a tinted varnish utilising raw umber is applied the end result will be one of highlighting. But to be really effective, this must be done selectively, not simply at random all over the workpiece.

It has to said that highlighting is at best a technique which supplements other methods, most notably the aptly named distressing or antiquing. Some misinformed craftsmen think that distressing is the physical maltreatment of a piece of furniture, using bruising and rasping of the edges, denting by hammering of the surfaces, and chain-banging of flat surfaces, and in general an attempt to suggest hard use. In a more purist sense, antiquing is a dimensional mellowing of the furniture, and it is here that the antique glaze plays a considerable part. Every craftsman has his personal preference as far as the glaze is concerned.

While antique glaze can be made with many subtle variations, all of them are based on a standard formula consisting of three tablespoons of turpentine mixed with one and a half tablespoons of boiled linseed oil and one tablespoon of raw umber. A slightly different effect is caused by substituting raw sienna, which imparts a warmer tone. Black gives the appearance of great age, but it is very difficult to work satisfactorily simply because in anything other than skilled hands there always seems to be either too little or too much of it. Black is one of those unfortunate colours which is difficult to diminish but seems to intensify once it is on the wood.

When it is thoroughly mixed, the glaze is painted on to sections of the workpiece and then wiped off before it can dry. Cheesecloth is absorbent but it sometimes leaves filaments behind. Washed cotton sheeting is better. If it is desired to work the glaze deeply into an old-looking surface, then it can be massaged rather than scrubbed into the surface with a stiff brush which may inflict scratches. Just how dark the tone should be in one place or the other is purely a matter of personal preference or sheer instinct, which will become apparent during the process. As a rule the centre of any flat areas are lighter than the edges and corners. Indeed, a moment's thought about the action of dirt, dust and wear over a period of time will, or should, suggest the kind of colouring to follow. Some of the most interesting antiquing can be done on bare carved or gessoed picture frames and mirrors. The mixture of whiting and parchment size from which gesso is made seems to favour the treatment. The more deeply incised the detail, the better, because the glaze can be applied very generously so that the deeper portions are dramatically darkened. Any surplus which lodges and forms little pools can be soaked up with an orange stick or a dry brush. When treating carved and moulded frames, the highlights are quickly lifted to prominence if the higher portions are wiped down with a turpentine-soaked rag while the glaze is still wet.

What has been described up to now is a very basic method of antiquing, but there are many variations, including the use of green undercoat and ordinary gold paint rubbed into the carved sections so that only traces and mere hints are seen. Alternatively, green and silver make an interesting contrast with a touch here and there of raw sienna or umber. Another method of applying colouring is by the use of stage greasepaint, which can be rubbed into the wood and mixed in the same way that an artist uses pastels.

Some pieces of furniture which are already stained can have their top polish removed without detriment to the stain and then antiqued quite effectively if the following method is used. Many amateurs who lack experience believe that stain alone will create the impression of age. This is quite untrue. All the stain does is to colour the wood. Just like a woman who uses lipstick and fails to attend to her hair and the rest of her appearance, she looks half finished, and so does the piece of furniture which is merely stained and left. Assuming that the workpiece possesses some carved features, the first move is to wipe it over with an ivory paint to which a small quantity of brown lacquer has been added. Regardless of how acceptable the staining might be, charge a broad brush and apply the ivory paint to the surface, then use a pad of bunched cotton cloth to wipe off the surplus. The purpose is to remove as much paint as possible, but give some of it a chance to sink in. If the wood is close-grained the paint will pass into the pores and a flecked appearance will result. Having decided in advance where the highlights should fall, a turpentine-soaked rag is used to remove areas of flecking. It is necessary to work quickly to achieve this effect before the paint dries and hardens. This does not mean that alterations cannot be made. An area can quite easily be modified providing turpentine is flooded on and a hard cloth is used to scrub off the flecking.

What has been explained above applies only to close-grained woods. Open-grained woods call for a somewhat different treatment if they are to be successfully antiqued. Such woods as walnut, mahogany and oak are in this category. As before, it is assumed that the workpiece is satisfactorily stained. The next step is to mix a grey paste filler to a creamy consistency, using a cloth to wipe it across, rather than with, the grain. It is not always possible to create highlights when using this sort of filler, because the silica content is difficult to detach from the pores of the wood once it has settled in. However, if the coat of filler is applied more sparingly in some places than others, then a highlighting effect should result. The process is completed by painting the workpiece with shellac and then, when it is dry, polishing with yellow beeswax.

A great deal of successful antiquing is done not by following a textbook to the letter but by experiment. At least one antique faker does not hesitate to mix cigar and cigarette ash with workshop dust and linseed oil, and then rub it into carvings which are executed in the South German fifteenth-century idiom. Elsewhere, roaring blow torches are taken to pieces of furniture and the surfaces are then scarified with rasps and chains. This is only one small part of a long process, for each individual bruise must be later treated to age and darken it. Most effects, however are best achieved by gentler and less time consuming means, many of which involve the use of waxy substances in which some form of pigment is suspended. For instance, an ordinary liquid furniture wax, not cream, can be used as the base for such colours as Vandyke brown and raw sienna. The colours will not mix very well with the liquid wax, and it is necessary to keep the fluid well stirred throughout application, but once on the wood they will disperse and look effective enough. Some improvement can be made by the addition of a quantity of rottenstone, which gives body and substance without scratching the wood. The actual proportion of rottenstone to fluid and colour cannot be specified because the density of colour varies, but it is sufficient to say that about five ounces of pigment and rottenstone can be added to every two pints of liquid wax as a starting point. The mixture happens to be turpentine-soluble and a well-soaked rag should be kept handy for use as soon as the mixture is brushed on to the wood. Wipe away any coating of the smooth areas but allow the liquid wax to rest in the curved sections, thereby creating the highlighting. It will take a certain amount of attention before it is ready for a final coat of varnish or shellac, and it may in the meantime be necessary to use an orange stick to dry up any surplus patches in the hollows and crevices.

The enthusiasm for knotty pine furniture clearly demonstrates that some surface finishers and the commercial manufacturers themselves have a great deal to learn about antiquing, for a lot of this present-day furniture is emerging from factories with a pristine look which is unacceptable to those looking for a more mature appearance as no amount of waxing will make pine look any older; it is an awkward and difficult wood, and apart from its soapy appearance it does tend to have a monotonous look to it. The art of the finisher being what it is, however, at least part of a miracle can be achieved if it is liberally doused with water and then washed down with a corrosive mixture of one part of sulphuric acid and three parts of water. Once the acid has done its swift work, the surface should be washed down with dilute ammonia to neutralise the acid. The wood should by now look like mature double Gloucester cheese.

WARNING: acid should be added to water, not vice versa. Goggles, strong rubber gloves and protective clothing must be worn, including a long apron and gumboots, when treating the pine. If the eyes are splashed, wash and irrigate them at once with cold water and seek immediate treatment.

When the wood has dried out, it will be found that the acid has bitten into all the soft portions of the pine, leaving intact the harder knotty sections. After sanding to get rid of any upstanding fibres, the piece can be lightly stained and then varnished. The acid treatment does not work very well on other woods, although it does have a marginal use with Japanese oak and will impart an antique appearance.

One of the commonest methods of creating the age stains on domestic furniture, which some buyers find so attractive, is by pouring vinegar or acetic acid on the unpolished tops of kitchen tables, which are generally pine. Deliberate staining of this sort of furniture is philistine, because it was originally scrubbed clean every day, but certain types of cottage furniture look out of place if they are over-immaculate, hence the vinegar treatment. To complement acetic acid staining some surface finishers and outright fakers will add clumps of fly specks. This is done by using a thick brown lacquer into which is dipped a very stiff brush and then running a piece of wood or a pencil over the bristles while holding the brush over the table in order to flick convincing specks here and there. The marks are lightly sanded and then, after lacquer or finishing varnish or shellac, is applied, they will look completely authentic. The same applies to the dents which are applied as a rule with a ball pein hammer or the edge of an adze or axe, and then lightly tinted with raw umber, making sure that they are darkest at their deepest point. If multiple coats of glaze are painted over such areas, the results will quickly look aged, but to complete the total effect a thickened lacquer can be applied. When it has hardened to the extent of having formed a skin, a crumpled tissue or rag can be pressed down on it to wrinkle the surface. Lacquer will thicken if poured into a shallow vessel and left to stand for an hour or two.

A method of creating an antique Oriental appearance is by wiping the surface with gold paint and then taking a six-inch nail soaked to dripping point in blue or red paint. An aerosol of compressed air of the type used by photographers to clean their lenses is used to direct the jet along the length of the nail so that flecks of the blue or red paint are air-flicked on to the gold paint. When dry the surface can be mellowed and aged with a coat of burnt umber mixed with clear thinned varnish. This method is used in a more sophisticated form by interior decorators who are commissioned to create luxurious-looking panels when the client wants the job done as cheaply as possible. The most costly part of this operation is gold paint, which should be of such quality that it will be thick enough to adhere to the base surface and remain liquid enough to wrinkle when hit by the compressed air. Gold paint will thicken if left exposed to the air for a few days, but the oil base will remain.

The basic materials of the antiquer's kit differ from those to be found in the surface finisher's workshop. They include such basic ingredients as aniline powder colours, orange and white shellac, flat paint of various kinds, japan colours, paint remover, caustic substances, varnish, liquid wax, turpentine, paste wax and a selection of brushes, such as the 2″ oxhair, a 2″ stiff bristle, a 2″ shellac brush, orange sticks, a selection of sandpaper and steel wool in the finer grades and the invaluable felt polishing cloths, a roll of cheesecloth and washed cotton. Unless a lot of antiquing of pine has to be done, it is not very wise to store large quantities of sulphuric acid, which is a very dangerous substance to have in any workshop. At least some of the work of the antiquer is such that protective clothing is essential, and a rubber apron and gumboots can save a lot of wear and tear on working clothes.

Many people are always inordinately curious about the methods of the antiquer, who is often regarded as a faker, but it depends who he is working for. It should be said that antiquing methods are intensely personal to the craftsman himself, and although a number of methods have been described in this chapter, there are literally hundreds of others. Most of them have been devised by the craftsmen themselves, but never described or written down. Much of the most effective antiquing is done by the use of very elementary methods, some of the worst antiquing being over elaborate. Quite often Nature herself will do most of the job if the workpiece is left to weather in the garden. Perhaps the most essential ingredient of antiquing is personal taste. This is something which the individual craftsman must develop for himself, often over a long period with the constant examination of genuine antiques.

14

Fuming and Patina

THE passion for fumed wood started in the 1890s. For some years no furniture was considered properly finished unless it had either a grey tinge or was almost black. Another finish of the time was limed oak in which the wood was treated with lime to create an unpolished and speckled appearance. This was part of the Edwardian partiality for cottage type furniture which consisted of scaled-down versions of the larger items to be found in opulent country houses and mansions. In the 1920s and 1930s it was found that oak could be artificially and quickly darkened after it had been made into furniture, and so fumed oak became the rage. Many pieces were indiscriminately fumed, taking them right out of character. Some manufacturers of Jacobean reproduction furniture still use this same method of fuming, but it has been largely superseded by faster and synthetic methods of darkening the wood. The heyday of fumed wood in England occurred in the late 1890s when it formed part of what was termed New Art and became a subject for discussion in the trade journal, *Furniture and Decoration and the Furniture Gazette:* '. . . that new style called "Quaint", which seems to be the carcase without the new style promulgated by the Arts and Crafts and other societies'. It was described by cynical commentators as having a decoration of writhing trees and explosive foliage with the excessive use of heart-shaped holes in the backs of chairs and cupboard door panels. Most of the products were given a fumed finish, although a cheaper version was produced made from the then plentiful birch and, rather surprisingly, finished in a green tint.

In our own day the fuming of oak is practised mainly by restoration craftsmen who need to create a section of wood to match the older surrounding section. Fuming is a process which is easily controlled and has the virtue of being very inexpensive to operate, and it calls for remarkably little equipment. What it does demand is vigilance and a constant checking of the oak to ensure that it does not over-darken, because once the hue has been reached, it may be difficult to lighten it again, though this is not entirely impossible. Most types of oak respond more or less readily to it, and it is preferable to apply it to the complete workpiece. For instance, if a rosette is required to match older rosettes, then a new one should be fully carved but not waxed or varnished before fuming, because this will only form a barrier and prevent the ammonia fumes from reaching the wood.

Depending on the amount of fuming to be done, it may be as well to look at two methods, the first for large workpieces and the second for the smaller ones.

It would seem that English and Baltic oak are best for fuming. Certain types of American oak, including the red variety, will fume only patchily, but Japanese oak seems to react very usefully even if it does not reach the dense blackness of English oak.

For large pieces of furniture, figure carvings and other sections of any bulk, it is advisable to use a fumigation chamber. This should be about nine feet long and four feet high. It is essential to incorporate several glass windows so that the fuming can be inspected from all angles without opening the door and permitting the fumes to escape, thereby retarding the process. There should also be a good light inside to cast adequate illumination all over the piece which is being treated. The problem of making the fumigation chamber as airtight as possible is solved by the use of draughtsman's tape which can be stuck all over the joints and the door.

The operation of the fumigation chamber is very simple. Once the workpiece, with any brass fittings removed, has been positioned inside the chamber, between six and twelve saucers are placed on the floor at more or less equal distances, and into them spirits of ammonia, or 'point eight-eighty', as it is called in the trade, is poured. Exactly how much ammonia is put in the saucers does not matter, because the purpose is simply to create a density of fuming.

WARNING: avoid inhaling ammonia fumes and wear a mask while pouring it into the saucers and on opening the fumigation chamber. Fuming begins as soon as the door is shut and sealed. Depending on the cubic capacity of the chamber and the number of saucers in use, some change should be noticed within twenty-four hours, but in the summer months, when the air is warm, this will occur more rapidly. In winter it will take longer. As a general rule five hours fuming should be enough to produce a colour difference. It should be inspected at regular intervals.

As soon as the workpiece is removed from the fuming chamber, the darkening will begin to fade. If it is left too long, it will eventually revert to its original colour, at least to some extent. This means that the wood must be oiled and polished without delay to seal in the colour. If by any chance some sections are too dark, then they should be left un-oiled until the colour fades to match, and then similary treated. The actual surface finish is a matter of personal choice, but french polish is a very effective seal and will prevent the fumed colour from fading.

The second method of fuming oak is suitable for smaller articles, such as boxes and flat sections of carving. The workpiece is laid on a piece of thick felt and a single saucer of ammonia is placed next to it. A large cupboard-like cardboard box is then placed on top and all the edges sealed. The drawback to this method is that when it becomes necessary

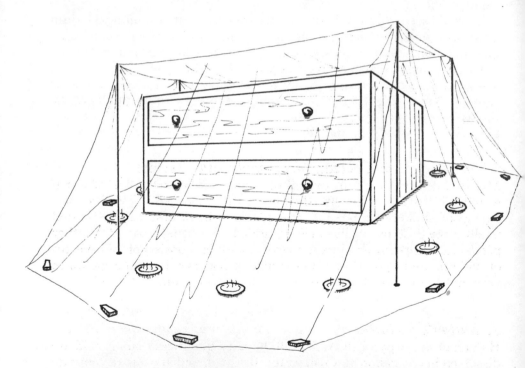

FIGURE 42.   The construction of a polythene tent to totally enclose a piece of oak furniture to be darkened with the vessels containing ammonia at strategic places to ensure an even build-up of fumes. The edges of the polythene should be weighted down to prevent any seepage of fumes. The fuming area should be spacious enough to permit overall circulation and even effect on the surfaces of the wood. (N.B. Drawers in the sketch would, in practice, be removed from the chest, and are shown in place only for pictorial effect)

to inspect the progress of the fuming, the box has to be lifted clear and this disperses the concentration of fumes. But it is certainly good enough for processing small items.

A third method, which makes use of modern materials, is to construct a 'tent' of transparent polythene and place the workpiece inside, then follow the instructions for the fumigation chamber as far as the number of ammonia saucers is concerned. Sheets of polythene can be stuck together with adhesive tape and will be secure long enough for fuming. This method has the advantage of enabling the craftsman to see exactly what is happening inside the tent.

Oak fuming is a matter of taste and personal preference. If the wood is fumed to the point where it becomes densely black, any carved or delicate features may well be lost in the general darkness of the wood. On the other hand, if it is only half-fumed and leaves patches of lighter or darker blackness, the final appearance may well be unsatisfactory. The ideal colour is reached when the overall features can still be seen and the patina of age is obvious.

Fuming need not necessarily be done with ammonia. Certain chemical solutions can be applied in such a way that the effects can be controlled, resulting in a somewhat more restrained effect. Here are the formulae for the solutions:

1. Suitable for oak, poplar, pine, maple, ash, chestnut

Mix between two and four ounces of tannic acid in one gallon of warm water. This is mixed and brushed on to the wood and allowed to dry. The wood should then be sandpapered. A red-brown tint can be created if one ounce of pyrogallic acid is added. A second coat of another preparation is required to fix the colour, and this consists of four ounces of bichromate of potash and one ounce of potash mixed in a gallon of very hot water. It should be brushed on while still hot.

2. Suitable for birch

Half an ounce of pyrogallic acid and the same quantity of tannic acid are dissolved in one gallon of warm water. Brush on and allow to dry, but do not sandpaper. Prepare and apply the following solution: two ounces of carbonate of soda, and one ounce of bichromate of potash are dissolved in one gallon of hot water. Now prepare and add a mixture of copper sulphate dissolved in eight ounces of water. Add ammonia until precipitation occurs, resulting in the crystals settling on the bottom. Continue adding ammonia until the crystals redissolve. The solution should be brushed on to the wood after the first coat has been completely dried and the surface has been sandpapered. The surface is finished with two coats of orange shellac, then rubbed dull with fine sandpaper. Alternatively, it can be waxed.

3. Suitable for oak, ash, chestnut
Six ounces of permanganate of potash is dissolved in rain water, if available, otherwise use ordinary tap water. It is then brushed on in a liberal quantity and it will dry lighter than anticipated. Now apply a light wash of iron acetate which will darken it. When it is dry, apply three or four coats of a mixture of two ounces of raw linseed oil, one ounce of japan drier, and rub well in with a cloth, finishing it with two coats of shellac or thinned varnish. It should be rubbed dull and waxed.

4. Suitable for oak, ash, chestnut
Make a saturated solution of chrome alum or manganese sulphate, using one gallon of warm water, and brush it on to the wood. Finish with shellac or varnish, sandpaper dull and then wax.

5. Suitable for walnut
It is necessary to use a silica filler darkened with Vandyke crystals and a quantity of black. Dissolve up to six ounces of permanganate of potash in one gallon of rainwater, or tap water. When dry, sandpaper smooth.

6. Suitable for birch, maple, beech
Dissolve one ounce of logwood extract in two quarts of hot water. When it is thoroughly dissolved, brush it on to the wood while warm. Two coats may be necessary, in which case ample time should be allowed for drying. Now dissolve one ounce of green copperas in one quart of very hot water. This should be brushed on in liberal quantities and allowed to dry. The final finish should consist of a mixture of raw linseed oil, two ounces of which should be mixed with one ounce of japan drier and five ounces of benzine, which is rubbed into the wood, followed when dry by two coats of orange shellac. A day later it can be rubbed dull with pumice powder, using mineral oil as a lubricant. It may be advisable to add a little nigrosine black to the shellac to achieve the desired hue and create a silky appearance.

7. Suitable for oak, chestnut, ash
Dissolve four ounces of carbonate of soda in half a gallon of water, then add half a gallon of aqua ammonia. This should be sponged, not

brushed, onto the wood until the surface is well soaked, allowed to dry, then sandpapered smooth. Mix one ounce of sulphate of iron in one gallon of water and brush on if a darker colour is required. When dry, finish with shellac or varnish, rub dull and wax.

8. Suitable for oak, ash, chestnut, maple

Dissolve one ounce of nitrate of silver in three pints of water, and brush on, then sandpaper smooth. Make a solution of hydrochloric acid and water and apply to the wood. When dry, apply a wash of aqua ammonia, followed when dry by a coat of thin shellac. If a filler is required, use zinc oxide mixed with oil and thin with boiled linseed oil, one ounce of japan drier and six ounces of benzine. Paraffin wax mixed with 50/50 turpentine and benzine provides a suitable finishing polish.

All these formulae should be used with some discretion, because the majority have an immediate action, and once the wood has been darkened it will be difficult to lighten it again. There are other hazards. Oak, in particular, can be a temperamental wood, and it is impossible to predict with any accuracy how it might react to one formula or the other.

One of the familiar features of old furniture is its patina, which occurs not only on edges, as many people seem to think, but also on flat surfaces. It is, in effect, the trademark of age and it is caused by constant handling, wear and tear, and the layers of polish, some being of indifferent quality. But once seen, patina is unmistakable. A false, but quite convincing, patina can be applied to suitable wood by stripping off the old polish and then applying boiled linseed oil to which artist's sienna or Vandyke crystals have been added in a spirit solution. It may also be necessary to add a little spirit stain which will deep-colour any scratches or dents. Once the colouring has been done, the linseed oil is painted on, after which the area should be covered with brown paper or a felt pad and several layers of blanket, the purpose being to maintain a constant temperature which helps the oil to penetrate. If the blanket covering is removed after a couple of days it will be found that the oil has penetrated the wood pores, and any surplus should then be rubbed in, and a generous coating of yellow beeswax dissolved in turpentine pasted on. The piece can now be left in a dust free atmosphere until the final treatment, an energetic rubbing with a cotton pad and linseed oil.

A patina to oak may be 'created' by rubbing or burnishing with a piece of the same wood, when it will quickly develop a sheen which will be improved by waxing. Special burnishing tools are obtainable of agate, polished steel, ivory or boxwood. If an intricate carving has to be burnished, a tool with a rounded end is used; flat surfaces can be done with the end of a toothbrush. Burnishing will also remove any scratches left by sandpaper and will result in a perfectly smooth surface.

15

Polychroming

THE word 'polychrome' simply means many-coloured. When applied to wood finishing it obviously has a great many applications, from varieties of tinted french polish to vari-coloured staining, straightforward painting and the imaginative decoration of all kinds of woodwork.

In recent years there has been a considerable revival of interest in painted furniture in which the main theme has been the painting itself rather than the intrinsic value of the furniture. This means that ordinary 'rubbish' furniture can sometimes be made beautiful. Quite common utilitarian wardrobes with plywood panels can have copies of classical flower studies painted on their doors, small cupboards have been embellished with a tondo, or circular painting, suggesting an unrolled scroll or an inscription tablet, and even a classical cartouche. In America the timbers of modern houses have been embellished by skilled artists working in *trompe-l'oeil*, depicting in meticulous detail the perspective and shadows and lights of objects or drapes calculated to craftily deceive the eye. In Britain the styles of floral pattern originated in the nineteenth century by William Morris and extended by famous firms like Liberty, started in 1875, have been painted on furniture. In brief, there has been a very energetic resurgence of the desire for old ideas made new, and some bold experiments have been carried out, notably in house decoration. But we have to admit that it does call for some courage to embark on a programme which includes hand-executed decoration inside a house, especially if a non-professional artist undertakes what may well be a considerable task.

The historical roots of polychroming are as old as building itself. The tombs of ancient Egypt are full of examples of intricately painted woodwork and stonework. In the medieval period the woodwork in churches and practically all the furnishings therein were brightly coloured to such an extent that if we were able to see them today we might well imagine ourselves to be in some kind of ecclesiastical Disneyland. Whether these edifices were 'tasteful' in the modern sense is quite another question. We would most probably consider them garish and over bright, but in their own time they provided a visual stimulus for people who lived rather drab and colourless lives. The outmoded combination of gilt and coloured paint is now thought tawdry, yet in its own time it was considered to be in fine taste. Nowadays we are considerably restrained and we pussyfoot when it comes to any large scale commitment to bold colour. While many people favour what are termed 'autumnal' colours, relatively few prefer the hotter colours of the spectrum, such as red and yellow. Our taste for colour has been seriously stultified to such an extent that we have all become much too conservative. In the last decade or two there has been great amazement when old master paintings have been thoroughly cleaned to expose the works in veritable riots of colour. At the present time we are probably at some sort of crossroads as far as colour is concerned. We live in ignorance of its true qualities and feel only faintly that it probably has something to offer.

But how does all this relate to the craft of wood finishing? In truth, little enough, because while the professional craftsman is forced to follow the dictates of the market rather than himself setting new criteria and influencing and even changing public taste, the amateur remains inhibited. If he is working on a piece of furniture for the house then he is more likely to try and please his nearest and dearest rather than himself.

The range of conventional wood stains is sufficient for ordinary everyday use, ranging from mahogany to walnut, and they are all, so to speak, much of a brownness. But wood can certainly be treated in other ways as far as the basic business of staining is concerned. It can, for instance, be dyed in the same way as cloth can be dyed, because precisely the same cold water stains are used, and they are readily obtainable from any chemist. They are very easy to mix and equally easy to apply providing the wood is very clean and free of grease, and they can be finished with varnish, wax or shellac. Dyes provide a very wide scope. For instance, a brilliant yellow can be brushed on to the wood in a strong concentration followed by a dilute crimson or red. This can be done by predamping the wood in such a way that it will be practically impossible to discern the point at which the red ends and the yellow begins. Using varieties of colour effects enables the craftsman to depart from convention and yet avoid affronting the senses since they can be suitably mellowed by the application of finishing coats of varnish or shellac to which burnt sienna, umber or darker pigments are added.

Another method is to use a two-colour scheme similar to the one just suggested, and then rub gold wax into it. Gold wax is a fairly expensive item, but very little of it goes a long way. It is necessary to apply it only here and there to impart a mere suggestion of gold before using a spirit-based varnish as a finishing coat.

Historical methods varied from one area to the other. In East Anglia, for instance, a tempera, mysterious in its composition, was used in medieval times. Made from fish glue, it was applied in a series of coats of white paint as the ground on which the thin colour was painted to create a surface entirely free of brush marks and usually in two coats to avoid obscuring the lines of the carved wood to which it gave an added glory.

What has been considered so far is the application of different colours to the surface of the wood while still retaining the nature of the wood itself. But we can now consider the wood as a carrier of painted decoration, revealing an entirely new field. Painted decoration with its many different styles can employ traditional motifs and there is also pictorial art and figurative art, which may mean naïve painting or much more accomplished work in the classical tradition. On the other hand, it is not impossible to adapt the work of many twentieth-century painters, such as Leger, Picasso and Braque and render pastiches or 'gentle forgeries'. The source books for the contemporary artists are many.

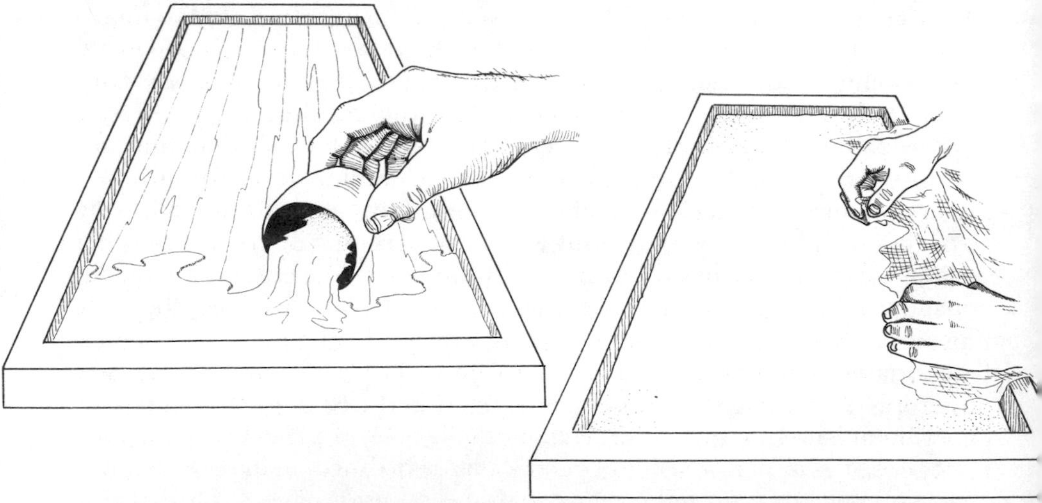

FIGURE 43.   To form a firm ground, or base, the first layer of plaster is poured into the recessed panel to about half its depth, and a sheet of linen is laid down and allowed to dry and harden. The top half is then poured and a second piece of good quality linen or canvas is placed on it while still wet. When dry and hard the panel will be strong and firm, providing an excellent base for pastiche painting.

Literally thousands of illustrated books on modern art have been published, as a result of which there is no lack of material to copy or adapt. Another idea for adaptation is Russian icon art, although some readers might feel inclined to point out that all icon art is religious and associated with the Eastern church and to adapt or imitate it is by its very nature sacrilegious and perhaps even blasphemous. The point is taken, and it is up to the individual craftsman to make up his own mind whether this is an avenue to be explored if not exploited. Yet icon painting has something to teach us as a technique, for it can be applied very effectively to the sunken panels of doors, cupboards and chests. In order to prepare the ground for such a panel, it is first lined with linen, which is glued into position with rabbitskin glue, available in sheet or granule form and melted in warm water When it is dry and hard, a quantity of fine white dental plaster is mixed and then poured into the recess. Alternatively, a mixture of gesso and glue is mixed to a creamy consistency and poured into the panel. The panel is only half filled and, when it is set a second layer of linen is laid down for reinforcement and pasted over with glue. A final layer of plaster is now poured, and the surface is perfectly smoothed. In some techniques a top layer of linen is laid down and sized to form a ground for the painting, but some artists prefer to work directly on to the plaster in much the same way as the muralists, working while it is still wet. But this is a highly specialised technique and it does call for experience. For present purposes, however, the surface of the dry plaster is given two coats of glue size and the painting is executed in gouache and finally varnished. Such a panel in a cupboard door or a full sized door is likely to become heavy in relation to its size, and for this reason it may crack if jarred. It is advisable to use this method for only the smallest panels which will withstand the stress of hanging and constant movement.

Working directly on to the wood itself is simple enough, using conventional oil, tempera or acrylic paints. The best and most receptive woods include oak, pine, mahogany and walnut, but any well seasoned wood will prove quite satisfactory. When panels are prepared for painted decoration, they should be sized on both back and front in order to equalise the moisture content and avoid future warping. This is best done by applying several coats of oil paint. The most reliable wood for painted decoration is, in fact a good quality plywood between 1/4" and 3/4" thick. If the plywood is anything other than best quality, the adhesives which hold the layers together may separate.

Apart from painting pastiches on furniture, the more traditional medallions, flowers, swags and ribbands can be executed and made to look antique by crackling, or crazing, the surface. It is a process which calls for a fine judgement, because the thin shellac is applied while the painting decoration is still wet, and it may be an advantage to use a spray gun. The action of the shellac should make the paint crack as it dries. An alternative and perhaps a better method is to put on the final coat of shellac mixed with turpentine which is fast drying, followed by a coating of starch, which locks in the paint. After a couple of hours the paint will begin to craze. By a careful application of the starch, starting in the centre of the panel and thinning out towards the edges, the appearance of the crazing will look as though it has happened by age rather than design. Genuine cracking generally begins in the middle and works outwards until it finally expires to a few hair lines. There are available from artist's suppliers patent varnishes which are formulated to give a crackle appearance.

Painted decoration is a matter of taste. Traditionalists dislike any radical decoration of wood, and echo what Ruskin wrote in his *Seven Lamps of Architecture* in 1849: 'The laws of Art are best learnt from the observance of Nature; and though architectural ornament is not to be a congeries of imitated objects, it is to be treated as Nature would treat it. Now the colour of Nature does not emphasize the form; it ornaments the animal, or the flower, or the mountain, by partial confusion and concealment of structure. And, in good architecture the colouring should not bring out the forms, but cross and dapple them. As in Nature the colour should play about the surface, interchanging and complicating the forms'. The Great Exhibition of 1851 endorsed Ruskin's views for practically all the furniture on show was heavily embellished with naturalistic forms, most notably in the upholstery materials which depicted coarse and large flowers, such as dahlias, roses, hollyhocks and hydrangeas. It would seem that any painted decoration of furniture is more likely to curry commercial favour if it adheres to strictly naturalistic forms. Practically all other experimentation is still regarded as dangerous to the senses simply because the majority of people do not understand it or even want to understand it. Naturalistic forms are in the Morris tradition and this explains the continued success of apparently traditional firms like Liberty, and, around 1896, the somewhat less successful Glasgow School, led by the Scottish architect, painter and furniture designer, Charles Rennie Mackintosh (1866–1928). It was Mackintosh who adapted the Celtic school of design and was innovative in the use of bold colour. But by 1908 it was all over apart from Mackintosh's continued influence on the Continent.

It would be foolish to be dogmatic about the form which the painted decoration of furniture, should take, for this is a highly individual field and it is, above all, always experimental. If it happens to be blatantly decorative every now and then, it is none the worse for that. One attractive example is the charm of English and American naïve art which features city street or village scenes, character portraits and, invariably, a cuddle of fat cats. In particular, vernacular architecture

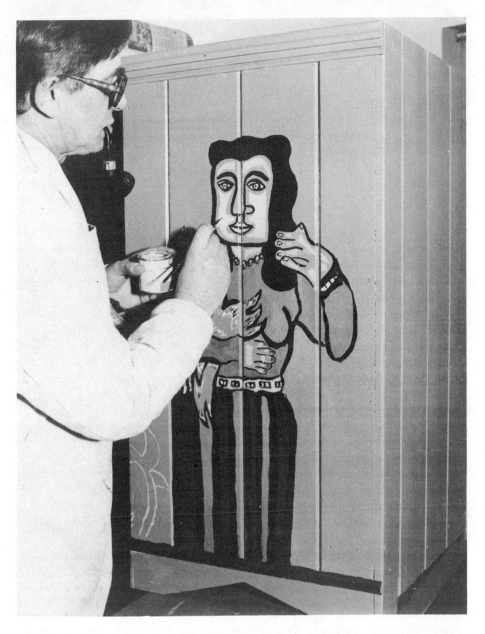

FIGURE 44. Preliminary work for the polychroming of a piece of painted furniture – in this case a common kitchen cupboard embellished with a pastiche based on the art of the French painter, Fernand Leger (1881–1955). The beginner is advised to select bold subjects in which bold enamel colours can have full play. Finicky designs with a multiple of detail are liable to result in visual confusion. *Photo: Andrew J. Gigg*

lends itself to this form of treatment, and it is possible to depict entire streets on the sides of wardrobes and across doors. Another possibility is English canal boat art in which luscious flowers act as a counterpoint to romantic castles and fairytale landscapes.

American folk art provides rich inspiration and is best exemplified in the decorated furniture of the Pennsylvannia Dutch. Motifs like the tulip echo the tulipomania of seventeenth-century Holland. But there are also the mermaids, the lions, griffins, the crowns of medieval heraldry and that long-standing symbol of virginity, the unicorn. American methods of construction seem to have encouraged decoration. Overmantels, for instance, were generally constructed of one or two boards, which gave a wide area for the painting of landscapes surrounded as a rule by fanciful cartouches. In the summer months many fireplaces were blocked up with fireboards consisting of planks battened together at the back with the front painted to portray a large and fearsome animal, a lion for instance.

Thomas G. Matteson, who was active in 1825 as a maker and decorator of chests in South Shaftesbury, Vermont, was an original craftsman who used brilliant colours on a dry surface, using very inferior brushes by today's standards, crumpled newspaper and sponges. He also finger and hand painted many of his chests, using yellow as the base colour. Another of Matteson's methods was to coat a surface with one or two colours and then drag a crumpled newspaper across it to form random effects. He was also in the habit of forming putty into a patterned stamp which was 'walked' across a wet surface to form a repeat pattern. Corn cobs were used to make fan patterns by twisting them round on wet painted surfaces. Another method, which might be adapted, was to waft a smokey candle over the wet paint in such a way as to impart trails of sootiness which became part of the pattern. Yet another method was to apply a final coat of paint, solvents and linseed oil, the individual components being incompatible. They separated in unpredictable patterns and dried. It may be possible to adopt the methods of the now much collected Matteson and his contemporaries for modern use. The precise nature of naïve art need not be discussed in the present context except to state that it is a form of painting done by non-academic and generally self-taught artists. Much of it displays a remarkable amount of talent and it should not be regarded as 'childish', although it has often been called childlike.

The day of polychromed furniture is over, but it could very easily return and create a new vogue. Even experienced craftsmen remain unaware of its possibilities, yet it is an aspect of wood finishing which enables the craftsman to show off his artistic abilities in addition to creating items which are in all respects truly unique.

FIGURE 45. Marine polychroming in the late 17th century was often elaborate to draw attention to imaginative carving. This is a quarter-board from a sailing vessel, done in red, blue and gilt, all traditional colours. It is at the Chatham Dockyard.

16

Papier-Mâché

IN origin papier-mâché is Chinese, but, like many Oriental processes, it was taken up by the West and considerably changed and modified, and used in applications which the Chinese originators had never considered. Some authorities believe that it originated in Florence in the sixteenth century, but it was certainly used by the Graeco-Egyptians to make sarcophagi composed of layers of pressed paper made from papyrus reeds. Today papier-mâché is employed in the manufacture of small trinket boxes in Kashmir and marketed as Kali-z Kalundari ware. In England it was the process chosen to start what amounted to a minor industry which produced bowls, trays and other utilitarian items, to be finished by lacquering and gilding. But in Europe its initial use was for architectural ornamentation, and in the later eighteenth century it was modified for coach panel manufacture under the name of *Carton pierre,* consisting of paper pulp mixed with whiting and glue, which was also used in architecture. Lighter and harder than plaster of paris, it was a French process used in London by the firm of Jackson and Sons. The heyday of papier-mâché in the West was from 1770 to 1870, when it was japanned and splendidly gilded by such firms as Spiers and Son of Oxford. They mass produced large quantities of blanks which were decorated with views of Oxford. In the furniture industry chairs and tables were made by a process which involved an inner reinforcement of iron or exposed japanned wood. In 1795 Henry Clay of Birmingham started a business and called himself 'Japanner in Ordinary to His Majesty and HRH Prince of Wales', specialising in coach doors and furniture. There were at the time many different compounds, including one which rivalled the clay formula of glue and potash, and it consisted of pulp, glue and resin, which was very light and would not warp.

By 1832 pulp was being shaped in metal dies, and the finished products were surface decorated with bronze powder in 1812 and mother-of-pearl as early as 1825, both included in the original decoration of the House of Lords. In 1840 it was discovered that papier-mâché could be shaped with acid. In Birmingham the firm of Jennens and Bettridge and Alderman and Illidge of Wolverhampton marketed all kinds of furniture with either decorated panelling or formed around a wooden or metal core. The Victorians created papier-mâché furniture which looked as though it was extruded, rather than made in a conventional fashion, with so many curves and decorations that it looked as though it was on the point of melting. In America at about the same time chairs were decorated in black and gold and inlaid with mother-of-pearl, and they were copies of Oriental lacquer items which were, in turn, copies of late seventeenth-century English designs. There was no limit to the applications to which the material could be put. In 1853 C. E. Beilfield, a Birmingham entrepreneur, made ten full-sized cottages and a ten-roomed villa out of papier-mâché and shipped his village all the way to Australia.

There is another somewhat hidden history of papier-mâché and it comes from inside the industry. In 1760 a gilder and woodcarver called Duffour, perhaps of French extraction or an emigre, was in business at the Golden Head, Berwick Street, Soho, London. He issued a trade card which stated that he was the 'Original Maker of Papier Machie', but by 1762 a Peter Babel, in business near St. James's Street, Long Acre, London, proclaimed that he was a 'Papier Mâché maker of frames and Ornaments Maker.' Behind these two announcements by rivals was an industry doomed to destruction by the introduction of stamped tinware, but for several years the papier mâché craftsmen grappled for business, including Duffour, and Babel and many others who rumoured that there were some special trade secrets which enabled them to produce a product which was in every respect superior to the rest. The secret is that there is no secret whatever in the making of a material which can be hardened to the point where it can be turned on a lathe, formed into the most intricate designs, used as a sculptural medium, sawn and shaped with a file, and finally given practically any waterproof or other surface finish which will endure for many years. It is nothing more than a basic paper pulp with a few additives, all of which are common enough to be found in any decorator's supply store. As to the basic material, practically anything from common tissue to newsprint or Kraft paper is suitable. The difference is in the application of the material.

There are two methods, the first and most traditional consisting of pasting layers of paper on to the base. The second involves breaking down the paper to a pulp which will accept almost any detail and gradually harden to the point where it can be surface finished. A simple formula for the pulp manufacture is as follows: tear up the paper and leave it to soak in water until it breaks up into fibres. A small amount of liquid soap will hasten the process. From time to time shred it between the fingers. If necessary, use a food grinder to make a fine gruel-like mash. Expel all the water from the mash and to each ounce add three ounces of clean water, four ounces of dry plaster of paris and one pint of dissolved cold water glue size. Mix together to a sticky paste. Plaster should be sprinkled into it until it stiffens up, and then the balance of the glue size can be poured in. All this may sound somewhat rough and ready in comparison with other formulae, but the texture depends on the work to be done. It is possible that the pulp will absorb a considerable quantity of glue size, which should be added gradually, all the time fingering the substance to test its stickiness. The material is now ready for use. It can also be stored for some time if a few drops of glycerine are added during the mixing. Before use it should be smeared on the fingers. If it leaves a coating, it is suitable for use. Similarly, if it sticks to a pane of glass and cannot be removed after three hours, then it is ready for application. If it is rolled out, it should dry in about half an hour. In use as a surface finish in a thickness of about half an inch, it should be ready for painting or waxing in as little as six to ten hours.

The durability and strength of well-made papier-mâché is remarkable. While it is relatively light in weight, it nevertheless possesses the wearing qualities of stone itself. This is borne out by the uses to which it has been put over the centuries. In 1800 Isaac Weld, author of *Weld's Travels*, which described his travels in North America, built a papier-mâché boat and sailed it on the lakes of Killarney. In our own time a group of icon painters near Moscow suffered a certain fall in demand due to the Revolution and the suppression of religion, and turned to the production of a type of papier-mâché known as Palekh or Mystera, many of which now appear in antique dealer's shops in the West. They are more durable than water resistant, but it is their decoration, adapted from the luminous icon colours with gold and silver stippling that makes them much sought after.

While papier-mâché has many uses as a plastic modelling medium, we should confine ourselves for the present to one main example in which a plain chest of drawers is used as a base, the purpose being to enhance it to a point where it is transformed into something akin to a collector's piece.

The wood is first of all completely cleaned, perhaps by washing it down with hot caustic soda to remove all paint and grease.

WARNING: when using caustic soda observe all the usual precautions and wear protective clothing and eye goggles. Wash any splashes off the skin without delay. If the eyes are splashed, irrigate them with clean water and seek immediate medical help.

The second and more traditional method of papier-mâché is by layering or laminating the paper. The most important aspect is the paste. Common paper-hanging paste is generally suitable, while flour and water can fail miserably. The paste should be mixed to the consistency of a half-set table jelly. Glue size is added to create adhesion, also a small quantity of boric acid which will prevent the growth of fungus. Ideally, the paper should be an absorbent 150 gsm Kraft. The texture is important, and it can be tested by dipping a piece in water to see whether it becomes leathery and pliable without actually falling to pieces. The stock of paper is torn up into pieces about 5″ × 5″ for convenient handling and glue is poured into a shallow tray. The pieces of paper are sunk separately, piece by piece, into the glue to ensure that they are all well soaked, and then removed after about ten minutes to drain off all the excess liquid.

It is essential to lay down an even film of the wallpaper paste on to the wood. Some finishers may recommend painting the wood first of all, but this seldom provides sufficient tooth for the papier-mâché, and it may at a later date begin to peel. The unsanded bare wood is ideal, and it is a good idea to go over the surface with a nail punch, making many indentations into which the paste will sink and act as an anchor.

When the paste is tacky, the sheets of size-impregnated paper are laid down to an equal thickness all over the wood. It is advisable to work systematically, and not simply lay them on at random, otherwise this can result in an uneven bumpy surface which will create difficulties when the surface is ready for finishing. A careful check on the number of sheets which make up the layers should be kept to avoid peaks and troughs. If Kraft paper is used, as earlier recommended, only three and certainly no more than four pieces will be needed to form a substantial layer.

The thoroughly saturated Kraft paper can easily be moulded round corners and formed into angles. Corners should have the paper carefully folded round them and pinched into position. If the consistency of the paper is just about right, they will firmly hold the edge and dry and harden into sharp angles. The same applies to any moulded, rounded or carved surfaces, including handles and knobs. Any slight roughness in the surface when hard can be removed with a file or sandpaper.

It is a good idea when the laminating is completed to lay a cloth pad down on it and exert a downward pressure to drive out any air bubbles and at the same time soak up any excess paste.

If the mixture of adhesive and glue size is correct, the drying time should not be very much longer than the time taken for wallpaper to dry on a wall, although it will take several days to harden completely. It can be hastened, if necessary, by the application of artificial heat, but this should not be at too high a temperature, otherwise the top layer will curl. On average, there should be definite signs of drying within eight hours, first in small patches and then all across the entire surface. Within forty-eight hours the surface should be completely dried out, leaving a perfectly smooth finish apart from one or two curled corners of paper which can be trimmed off with a razor blade.

The workpiece should be left for several days to allow the interior of the paper layers to dry and harden, after which it can be given a coat of varnish or shellac as a preliminary to whatever final finishing has been decided upon.

What papier-mâché really provides is a surface which can be treated and hardened in one of many ways, from paint to lacquer and inlays, but it will not satisfactorily take wood stain or french polish. It does offer many opportunities for all kinds of painted decoration in whatever style is desired, and it can also be wax polished with success.

Furniture can be embellished with paper pulp, which is a further development of papier-mâché. The pulp used for the coating is made from paper reduced to a fibrous mass to which is added a small quantity of plaster of paris, a limited quantity of modelling clay, which is first broken down to a creamy slurry, and some whiting to provide body. The consistency should be fairly stiff. As with lamination, the wood should have a perfectly clean surface and a good tooth to which the pulp can adhere. It is advisable to coat the surface first of all with glue size. The pulp is then smeared on and well distributed with a spatula to build up a firm foundation before any modelling is carried out.

Paper pulp is an incredibly versatile material. It can be modelled in the rococo style or fashioned into Adamesque garlands without any difficulty, using modelling tools. Provided that the consistency is correct, it should easily support its own weight, but for large sections a wire armature is advisable, anchored into the base bed. Simple straight-planed furniture can be elaborately decorated by this and other improvised means, and later decorated with oil-based paint or stain and spirit dyes, using varnish or shellac for the final two coats of waterproof material.

It is also possible to make papier-mâché moulds of festoons or badges or even heraldic arms, using the pulp for both mould and cast, working on the basis of a clay model. But this is somewhat beyond the scope of the present book.

17

Pickle Pine

WHEN the term 'pickle' is used in wood finishing it can be taken to refer to a number of widely differing effects, from a silver grey on a brown ground to a faint green on an ashen ground. It was heavily exploited in the Thirties, when restaurant decorators used it for chic types of internal decor. Public houses applied it to impart what they thought would be a positively luxurious effect, although quite the opposite was usually achieved. It was a case of mutton dressed up like lamb, and it showed. After the Second World War the paint manufacturers brought out a special paint which was intended to convey an antique weathered and pickled effect, but this, too, failed to find a market and was withdrawn. Mercifully.

The pickle finish can be applied by one or other of several techniques, not only on pine, which is a traditional medium, but also on oak, plywood and other woods. It is possible to pickle finish the best quality plywood and create exceptionally striking panels for wall facing. Seen in certain types of environments and accompanying other forms of surface finish, pickle boards are equal to the most expensive interior decor, and yet they cost a fraction of other materials.

In its earliest form pickle pine relied for its effect on nitric acid, and it has to be said that the process was quite dangerous to health. Today it can be accomplished in the following rather safer manner. If the wood is fairly light, is should be stained darker. A grey flat paint is now applied, and then wiped off with clean hessian, leaving certain traces. When dry, it is given two coats of water-white lacquer and the surface is then covered with beeswax. Finally, rottenstone and wax mixture is rubbed on to complete the surfacing. It should by now look aged and fake-dusty, which is all part of the general deception.

There is an alternative to this process, and it is more suited to furniture which has some carved features. Because it has more stages, it takes somewhat longer and perhaps calls for greater patience. If the wood is light, it should be spirit-stained and allowed to dry. It is then painted all over with a sealer made from thinned shellac. The next step is to apply a glaze of white lacquer and wipe with a clean cotton pad so that deposits of the lacquer are left in all the recesses; avoid any accumulation. The glaze is an important factor. If it is not dense enough, it will simply look very dirty. The following formula will provide the best glaze for a quality job. White lead is thinned with turpentine to which a small amount of boiled linseed oil and japan drier has been added, the ingredients being thoroughly mixed before application. The glaze should be allowed to dry, and then painted over with white shellac. The total effect can be improved by melting a few spots of brown or black (or both) wax shoe polish and adding it to the shellac. Alternatively, black or brown polish can be added to the spirit-based shellac, and this will create a further impression of age, because the pigment will sink into all the recesses. The precise point at which the pigmented polish should be applied is a matter for experiment. In some treatments it is best to apply it directly after the stain has been put on and then it can be lightly sanded to bring out any highlights. This type of colouring, or tinting, should be used in a subtle rather than bull-at-a-gate manner, and it is perhaps best used as a retouching material rather than a total surface colouring.

It was earlier said that pickle effects can be achieved by the use of various techniques. For instance, oxalic acid can be applied in a solution of about twelve ounces to one gallon of very hot water, and mixed with hyposulphite of soda. The fluid is washed on to the wood in generous quantities. Provided that the water is hot, the required effect is reached quickly, when the acid should be immediately neutralised by sluicing with clean water or a solution of water and borax. The latter is more sure. The wood should be left to dry completely before the next stage which consists of a wash of very thin shellac and it should be brushed on in an even film. When it is dry apply a light stain of whatever colour is required and then a sealer, followed by three coats of dull or flat lacquer, applying fine sandpaper to the first two coats. A suitable stain can be made by taking one pint of turpentine and thoroughly mixing into it aproximately $\frac{1}{4}$ lb of raw sienna, $\frac{1}{2}$ ounce of yellow ochre and $\frac{1}{4}$ pint of japan drier. The proportions can be varied to make a greater or lesser strength, but those given will produce a distinct colour which is at least a good starting point. In fact, the essence of a good pickle finish is to avoid using too noticeable and blatant a stain. Restraint should be influenced by a consideration of whether the wood is close or open pored.

Open grained wood is treated in the following fashion: the surface is sanded, using a fine paper; it is then bleached, using a commercial two-stage bleach or oxalic acid and hyposulphite of soda, as described above, and it is then neutralised. The surface should again be lightly sanded when it is dry, because the bleach may create some whiskery fuzz here and there. A wash of white shellac is then applied to act as a sealer, and a filler paste thinned with turpentine is applied. If it is allowed to stand for about half an hour and then wiped off before it completely sets, the paste should have the opportunity of penetrating the grain, or pores. Wiping the paste should be done vigorously both across and with the grain, using a coarse cloth and then a fine one to remove all surface residues. A further coat of white shellac is now applied, allowed to dry and then sanded. Two further coats are applied, after which the surface is rubbed with fine steel wool, followed by beeswaxing.

Close grained woods are similarly treated, except that a much more intensive application of filler paste is required, and, instead of sanding, some fine pumice powder and mineral oil is used to polish the surface.

It will be useful to consider the effect of colour on pickle finish. Many tints are available, and it does not always follow that a 'natural' colour, such as dull brown on oak, will be completely satisfying. It is necessary to make the fullest use of colour if pickle finish is to work at all.

For the effect of grey limed oak a stain can be made from ½ ounce of black water-soluble aniline dissolved in a quart of hot water. A somewhat more superior effect can be obtained by using ½ ounce of silver-grey water-soluble aniline in one quart of hot water. The final effect is necessarily variable, depending on the wood itself, but these stains are at their best when used on oak, ash or chestnut. Staining is followed by sealing with a thin shellac, and, when dry, sandpapered.

The next step is the most important one of all. It consists of painting the wood with a white undercoat which has been well thinned with turpentine and then, while it is still wet, a piece of washed hessian sacking is wiped over the surface, forcing the paint into the pores, but not leaving any gross trace anywhere. It should take about twelve hours to dry, after which a coat of thin shellac can be applied. The final coat should be of thin varnish, followed by fine sandpapering. If total perfection is desired, then a further coat of varnish can be applied followed by a rub down with fine steel wool, used dry. The surface is then finished with yellow beeswax melted in turpentine.

There are one or two shortcuts in these methods. For instance, some of the intermediate coats can be cut down. Where two coats of shellac or varnish are called for, only one is used. So long as all the steps are observed at least singly, then a presentable finish will be achieved. But if the full treatment is followed, then the finish will endure for twenty years or more. There are no real shortcuts, however, and perhaps the only drawback to this is that regardless of whether the entire process is followed, or an abbreviated one adopted, it will demand a great deal of time. The finished result, however, will be visually worthwhile.

To impart a pink colour, which is not quite as garish as might at first be imagined, the wood is bleached in the usual way, and a stain is made from ¼ ounce of red mahogany water-soluble aniline in one quart of hot water. The amount is varied to give either a lighter or a deeper shade. Red mahogany aniline does tend to dry a lighter shade and some allowance should be made for this.

To look effective, the wood must first be limed. This is done by putting on a coat of flat white paint which has been thinned to a creamy consistency. If it looks somewhat stark and cold, this can be alleviated by adding enough chrome yellow to break down the whiteness. The paint is thoroughly brushed on and then wiped off with a clean hessian pad, ensuring that it is allowed to sink into the pores. When it is fully dry, a coat of thin shellac is applied, followed a few hours later by sanding with a fine paper. The finishing coat should be a clear white shellac which is rubbed down with a fine steel wool, after which it can be besswaxed.

Mahogany is not, in fact, the best of woods for liming, due to its naturally red hue, and it cannot as a rule be satisfactorily bleached to a perfect lightness before pickling. But it was at one time in widespread use in house internal decor, and it may occasionally be necessary for the craftsman to tackle it in situ.

In contrast to mahogany, pine should always be mellowed. The quickest way of doing this is by painting it with flat white paint into which a little raw umber or black has been mixed. It is probably easier to actually demonstrate precisely how much paint should be left on the surface after wiping, but sufficient to say that it should look like a layer of dust rather than a coat of paint, and the addition of umber or black will add to the effect. As a rule, paint takes longer to dry on pine than on other woods, due to the soft and absorbent surface and, in the case of pine, the resinous content. As much as twenty-four hours should pass before a coat of thin shellac is applied. When dry, sand it, with a very fine paper, followed by a second coat. When it is quite dry, rub it down with fine steel wool, after which it can be wax polished, using either white or yellow beeswax and turpentine.

Up to this point the pickling effect has been achieved by clever use of paint and pigment, shellac, varnish and wax coupled with techniques which require a certain amount of skill, such as the wiping of the wet paint in such a way as to leave minuscule traces in the pores of the wood and the carved features of furniture. The modern craftsman will use these same techniques extensively because they are not, in fact, difficult once the technique has been mastered. In commercial surface finishing they are accepted as pickle. In truth, they are nothing of the kind. While high prices are charged and usually paid for furniture which has been tricked out in this way, it seems deceitful to make fat profits out of such minor efforts. But this is an unfortunate feature of the trade nowadays. Dodges, short cuts and often cheap tricks of the trade enable them to keep going and they generally flourish all the more at a time when the traditional craftsmen is forced to put up his shutters because he cannot spend as much time as he should on quality jobs in the hope of making enough profit to keep going. Despite such thoughts, there is, however, nothing desperately wrong in utilising these cheap and cheerful finishes provided that the craftsman is honest enough to point out to the customer that they are mere substitutes and not the real thing. Pickle finish can look spectacular and expensively pleasant in the right setting.

It would be wrong to end the chapter on this or any other note without providing the basic information necessary to create an authentic pickle finish. If we start with the idea that pickle means ageing, then it follows that the treatment must inflict upon the wood a kind of stress effect which will be obvious to the eye. When this true pickle is combined with distressing effects, such as bruising and retouching the wood with darker colours, the final effect can look very convincing indeed.

This is how it is done: half a bucketful of unslaked lime is covered with water. Those who have handled lime will know that it can create quite a rumpus once water is added, but this eventually subsides. When it has quietened down, the water is gently poured into another bucket, taking care to avoid any spillage of the lime into the second bucket. About ¼ lb of caustic soda is added to the water, followed by four pints of water and four ounces of chloride of lime or half-a-pint of ammonia. This is a lethal mixture and the greatest care should be taken while mixing and handling it. The usual protective clothing and goggles should be worn, and the work should be done in the open air. If it is carried out in a closed room without any ventilation, the fumes will gather and become concentrated, and the craftsman will probably wind up in hospital. Always ensure that there is plenty of ventilation, keeping the face away from the solution during mixture. Above all, ban children from the area, no matter how inquisitive they may be about what is going on. In any case, children should not be allowed inside finishing workshops because they have curious and often sticky fingers.

When the mixture is liberally sloshed on to the wood there will be an immediate effect. It will bite straight into the softer parts of the wood while leaving any harder parts virtually untouched. The action is easily controlled if a hosepipe is kept handy to direct a jet of clean water over the surface to neutralise and halt the pickling process. The overall tone will now be light brown, which is usually best left as it is as the wood dries out. Bichromate of potash solution can be used to deepen and enrich the colour of lighter coloured woods.

There is now only one further stage after sanding and dusting off, and this is the wax polishing. Do not use just any old wax polish. Mix as much lamp black as may be required with yellow beeswax melted down in a double boiler with turpentine until it becomes cheesey in texture after cooling. The turpentine will simply assist penetration, but it will in no way aid the final sheen. It is the beeswax which does that. What happens during the lavish application of the cheesy wax is that the turpentine evaporates with friction and carries the wax into the wood. A soft boot brush can be used to some advantage on any intricately carved sections, followed by a dry brush for burnishing. Creating a good old fashioned wax polish by this means is not a matter of a few minutes or even an hour. Some woods demand up to six or seven coats of beeswax before any appreciable results begin to appear, but if the wood has been well pickled and sanded smooth when dry, there is no reason why the polish should not have an effect after two or three coats.

One of the areas in which failure occurs is when the caustic solution has not been properly neutralised. If wax is applied to such areas it will create a patchiness. Short of wearily starting all over again, there is no quick solution to the problem and the only remedy is to strip the bleached area and vainly attempt some touching-in with a solution of Vandyke crystals or some other darkening stain.

A final word about partial pickle. In some cases it may be desired to treat only one part of an area in which case melted candle wax is used to mask off the section which is to be unpickled in much the same way as wax is used in batik.

18

Two-Tone Finishing

BECAUSE wood finishing is a craft with long historical roots and a somewhat conservative tradition, the tendency is to apply the majority of finishes for an overall and restrained effect, using compatible tints which seem pleasing to the eye. It is, of course, true that certain techniques use other materials, such as papier mâché, découpage and even the addition of porcelain medallions, gilded metal fittings and ormolu. Yet there is, in fact, no reason why a somewhat different and non-traditional finish should not be applied to a chest of drawers or a dining table in which both colour and contrast are exploited. Whether a multi-hued piece of furniture is acceptable to the majority of people is quite another matter, although it has to be hurriedly added that the multi-hued effect can be achieved in a very subtle way so as not to offend the senses.

Two-tone finishing has no particular history. It is the outcome of experiments carried out by finishers in Britain, France and America, but most notably on the Continent where many other radical contrasts have been attempted, including gold and silver flecking, and the use of diametrically opposed colours, such as black and white. In Britain such experiments have naturally been much more restrained and somewhat in keeping with the national character. They have included the application of two tones of the same stain or two entirely different stains, either water or spirit based. It must be admitted that this has never gained a commercial foothold. People seem to want furniture to look like furniture. The exception to the range of furniture which has to be treated in a conservative way is the bedroom, where some degree of whimsicality is often permissible. Beds, which have an ample amount of woodwork, are the most likely candidates for two-tone finishing. It is possible to treat headboards with this method. Wardrobes, too, are possible targets, including those persistent and often nondescript Victorian models which are ornamented with badly carved features. This, then, is the most promising area of domestic furniture to embellish and even enhance with a striking contrast of tones, if only to detract from the hideous character of the design, shape and other negative aspects.

The final appearance is governed largely by the materials used. The basic choice is between lacquer enamel, which provides dense and solid colours, or the various wood stains, which share a sameness of red to brown. Alternatively, stains can be made to yield wider contrasts in the workshop, and they can vary from very light to very dark and incorporate colour. Certain types of common paint can also be modified if the final finish is intended to be shellac, varnish or a clear lacquer. No firm rules can be applied.

Take enamels first of all. If a white base is used, it can be sprayed on, using a method of either applying complete covering in certain areas or by simply putting it on with a dispersed spray which will give a speckled effect. But if the wood has first been stripped, cleaned and sanded, then it will be necessary to apply a base coat of a very light stain to tone down any rawness. If the enamel is sprayed on to the bare wood, it will sink straight in and its colourful quality will be lost. The choice of exactly how to apply the first coat of enamel is a personal one and it will be governed to a great extent by the design of the furniture.

If panelling is old and in poor condition, it can be prepared by the use of thinned fillers to fill the pores, and then treated to a coat of clear lacquer, followed by the application of the two-tone. Certain nondescript woods were used in the Victorian era for panelling staircases and hallways. To remove them leads as a rule to the need to refinish an entire wall surface. Two-tone finishing offers a very useful solution to this. It is certainly a good deal less expensive than simply ripping out the wood and then having the wall rendered in preparation for mundane wallpaper or paint.

The sprayed colour is not the only method of starting the two-tone finish. It can also be speckled, using a stiff and well-charged brush and simply flicking enamel on from a distance of several inches. Alternatively, by distancing the brush a wider distribution can be achieved.

We come now to stage two. The actual two-tone contours must be a matter of personal decision, and they are formed not by a freehand application but by the use of masking tape, which is used to completely cover the first stage areas, making allowances for the overlaps. When the design seems correct, then the second stage can be applied by either spraying or painting. And that is all there is to it apart from the careful removal of the tape and the application of a protective top coat.

Apart from water or spirit stain, which can be applied in much the same way, it should be said that the wood should always be well prepared before any real work is done. Red mahogany and brown walnut are relatively close to one another within the colour spectrum, but if red and black stains are selected, then it will be advisable to bleach the sections where the red stain is to be applied if it is to have any effect at all.

One of the often overlooked possibilities is the use of a two-tone made up of bleached and unbleached areas, providing the wood is clean to start with. A bleach can be tempered to merge gently into non-bleached areas, and the entire area can then be either varnished or wax polished. One example of the application of this type of 'natural' finish might be a chest of drawers in which the drawers are left unbleached while the frame is bleached.

Elementary though two-tone finishes might at first appear, they can have a wealth of application, the effective use of which demands a craftsman's imagination. Conventional kitchen stools, for instance, can have their legs and cross-stays two-toned, leaving the seat itself bleached. Old fashioned sash window frames are another possibility if there happens to be enough wood on which to work. Extending the idea even more, the old-fashioned upright piano with its often indifferent wooden case can be two-toned by creating a striped or geometric effect. If the craftsman is blessed with sufficient time, the two-tone can be extended to another dimension by, say, french polishing certain areas of a workpiece and using lacquer or enamel on the other areas. The art of all this is in the placing of the masking tape prior to the second phase. The skill is in the way the materials are applied. Historically, it may be nothing more than a modern extension of the art of inlay.

19

The Imitation of Ebony

AMATEUR finishers are often under the misapprehension that
ebony can be convincingly imitated by simply painting the
surface of the wood matt black or simply staining it with a
branded preparation which is labelled 'Ebony Effect'. Comparison with true ebony will quickly demonstrate how wrong they are,
for the wood (genus *Diospyrus*) happens to be blessed with a particular
appearance, and it has a blackness with a depth which cannot be faked
in any facile way.

There are two essential ingredients if a perfect ebony appearance is to
be obtained. The first is a close-grained wood, such as mahogany or oak.
The second is a blackness which is rather more than skin deep. In fact,
the dense colour must permeate to an appreciable depth before it can
begin to look like the real thing, and the final surface finish must be
immaculate.

Ebonising wood is nowadays done by workshops in which modern
furniture is made. In recent years there has been a fashion for black
matching chairs and tables for the dining areas of kitchens, but it has
also been applied to fitted kitchen cupboards, facing surfaces of work
areas on doors. In fact, a door which is ebonised on one side and treated
with a contrasting finish on the other can prove extremely attractive. But
apart from furniture, shelving can be ebonised to good effect, also certain
types of furniture. If it has been properly done, the distinctive black
colour will not stain or show blemishes and while it may be left in a
natural state it may also be waxed or lacquered. If lacquer is applied,
then it must be dulled by rubbing with fine steel wool. Alternatively, it
can be polished to a dull sheen, using beeswax and turpentine.

To create professional ebonising the first move should be to completely clean the surface, making sure that any greasy residues or earlier polishes are removed. Much can be done by bleaching when the piece has few surface faults, but if there are dents and scratches they will need to be attended to.

A basic ebony stain is made by taking one ounce of logwood extract and adding about two quarts of boiling water. The mixture is made by dissolving one dram of potassium chromate in a small amount of hot water and then adding it to the logwood extract. This is a very powerful stain and it should be kept away from clothing because it is extremely difficult to remove by ordinary drycleaning methods.

The stain works best if it is applied hot to the wood, and it should be put on with a soft brush which is capable of carrying a large charge. The brushing action should be both against and along the grain. It is a useful idea to bring into use a coarse hard brush which will not, however, scratch the wood. This is used to thoroughly scour the colour well into the wood fibres. One coat should completely blacken the surface, but on drying it may be found that some areas are slightly lighter than others, and it is therefore necessary to apply a second coat. One of the oddities of this particular stain is that it will not necessarily blacken the wood any more if a large quantity is applied in the first coat.

It is entirely a matter of personal preference whether the finish is lightly sanded and left at that or is now given a coat of shellac. Much depends on the use to which the furniture is put. There is always the matter of dust to be considered, and it is noticeable that the un-shellacked ebonised surface will have a tendency to show dust deposits. But if it has a coat of shellac, it can always be wiped down with a slightly dampened cloth. The application of shellac does not, of course, make it waterproof. If too much dampness is applied, it may well develop an opacity or milkiness or a white streakiness caused by water penetrating the surface.

One other form of finishing which is both economical and speedy is black boot polish, which should be vigorously brushed into the surface, and then polished with a lambswool bonnet on a power tool, taking care to maintain a steady movement. If the polisher remains in one place for too long, it may overheat the wax and cause charring.

Some customers have a preference for a highly glossy black finish. While this cannot be called ebonising within the strict sense of the word, it nevertheless warrants inclusion at this point because it does have a similar appearance and is much more glossy and mirror-like.

The wood should first be well sanded. It is then darkened with a black spirit stain. After it is dry, apply a black well-thinned paste filler and let it stand for up to twenty-four hours. Finally, apply two or three coats of black lacquer and follow it, when dry, with two coats of water white lacquer. This can be wax polished, resulting in a very high gloss.

FIGURE 46.   The fully ebonised case of the concert grand piano with its nine-foot length represents one hundred hours' or more labour by a single craftsman to achieve a bright polish finish.
Photo by courtesy of Whelpdale Maxwell and Codd Ltd., London

A quickly made and applied black stain which will pass for ebony even though it is in reality a mild fake can be made by taking a quantity of aniline spirit black and dissolving it in methylated spirit to the required density, then adding one spoonful of french polish to give body.

The traditional wood for good quality simulation is mahogany, which has at least some of the characteristics of the original wood. It is quite capable of yeilding the typical ebonised appearance which we admire on concert piano cases. The mahogany is cleaned and sanded, and it is then stained with black oil stain, although some craftsmen prefer to use a water-soluble dye to which a little ammonia has been added to aid penetration. The filler is made by mixing the dye with black pigmented dental plaster to a thin but still creamy consistency, and then forcing it into the pores by the usual method of rubbing with a hessian pad. It may be difficult to know whether the filler is actually entering the pores because it is, of course, dense black, but the action can be checked by frequently examining the surface in an oblique light if the work is done by a window. The white shellac french polish is mixed with pigment to the required density. It is, of course, not possible to exceed the ultimate blackness, and so it is impossible to overload the french polish. Although there are several ebony polishes on the market, it is possible to make the substance very cheaply by dissolving ½ ounce or more of black spirit aniline dye in a pint of white french polish with the addition of a small amount of washing-blue to intensify the black. To avoid any specks of shellac in the polish, it should be strained through a piece of silk or nylon before using.

The polish is applied in exactly the same way as french polish, described in chapter four. After two applications it should come up to a fine sheen, which should be cut down to resemble true ebony by rubbing with fine pumice powder. This is not done by rubbing with a pad but by using a soft brush and sprinkling a fine layer of powder over the surface. The brush should be stroked, not forced down, and moved in a series of straight lines through the pumice. It should result in the formation of a series of almost microscopic lines, which are one of the hallmarks of true ebony. When brushing is completed, the pumice is blown off, the best tool for this part of the job being a domestic vacuum cleaner with an extension tube which blows rather than sucks. Care should be taken to avoid any contact with the surface. On no account should a feather duster be used to remove the powder, nor should it be flicked away with a cloth, because this will probably cause pitting, scarring and a general disfigurement of what will, hopefully, be a perfect surface. The direction of the lines on any particular piece of furniture is a matter of discretion and it is not possible to particularise about them, because all workpieces are different. A perfectly even and logical pattern should be followed, and where the lines converge on a corner they should be made to meet. This is done by placing a piece of card on the surface and taking the lines up to the edge of it, then working the same way from the opposite direction to form the lines into a right angle.

Ebony is a finish which is attractive in small amounts at a time. One would not, for instance, have an entire room full of furniture of all shapes and sizes in this style of surface finish because it would be funereal in the extreme. The occasional piece can look very attractive. Reintroduced into Europe in the seventeenth century, it was popular in the veneering and furniture industries. In his *Cabinet Dictionary* of 1803 Sheraton noted 'pear tree and other close grained woods have sometimes passed for ebony, by staining them black. This some do by a few washes of a decoction of galls, and, when dry, adding writing ink, polishing it with a stiff brush, and a little hot wax.'

The Victorians favoured all kinds of ebonised furniture and, as usual, they overdid it, but in the ensuing years the Scandinavians adopted the style and made a success of it.

In conclusion, here are three further formulae for general ebonised effects:

For use on any wood

1. Take three lbs of extract of logwood, one lb of lye, or caustic soda, and boil in one gallon of water. The fluid should be strained and then brushed on to the wood while still hot. When it is dry, brush on hot table vinegar to which four ounces of sulphite of iron has been added.

2. Mix together four ounces of water-soluble nigrosine, four ounces of acetic acid and one gallon of hot water. This should be brushed on in a generous quantity and, when dry, the surface is sanded with a fine paper. Certain woods, such as oak and chestnut, require a silica based filler, which should be mixed with some drop black mixed with oil. Now mix together two ounces of hot boiled linseed oil, one ounce of japan drier and five ounces of benzine; rub into the wood while still hot, and remove any surplus. After the wood has stood overnight, apply a wax finish, varnish or orange shellac, then rub dull with fine steel wool.

For use on beech and birch

3. Dissolve one ounce of logwood extract in two quarts of hot water and brush it on to the wood, allow to dry, and then apply a second coat. Ensure that it is quite dry before sanding. Now mix one ounce of sulphate of iron in one quart of water. Apply to the wood and allow to dry. A suitable final finish consists of a mixture of two ounces of raw linseed oil, one ounce of japan drier and five ounces of benzine. This should be rubbed into the wood while still hot and any excess wiped off. When it is completely dry, paint on two or three coats of orange shellac to which a small amount of spirit-soluble nigrosine has been added. Finally, rub down with fine pumice powder and oil.

20

Imitation Leather

THE custom of covering wooden furniture with animal hides and skins dates back to the Egypt of 2980–2475 BC and probably much earlier than that. In medieval times in England the trade of the cofferer was recognised, for he covered wooden boxes with leather. The name of his trade was derived from old French, *cofre* or *coffre* and *coffre-fort*, the latter meaning a safe. Another branch of the trade specialised in the manufacture of trussing coffers, which were the travelling chests of the fourteenth and fifteenth centuries. They were covered with leather and sometimes ornamented with metal and paint to protect them against the rigours of travel. They were the forerunners of the modern suitcase. By the sixteenth and seventeenth centuries the leather covered coffers were being ornamented with highly elaborate patterns and gilded and painted. By the eighteenth century leather was in common use for the backs of chairs and seats, and it was also used in the cabinet-making trade. The trade has its own specialities. For instance, some tradesmen used fine quality leather made from goatskin, a product of the Moorish kingdom of Cordova in Spain during the Middle Ages. The tradesman who used the goatskin in England became known as a cordwainer. There is a reference to the cordwainer in 1272. Henry VI granted a charter to the Cordwainer's Company in 1439.

As time went on the varieties of leather used for the embellishment of furniture became more refined. Morocco leather, made initally by the Moors in Spain and Morocco, was a goatskin, fine in texture, very flexible and with a distinctive grain. It was at the heart of a large industry which later spread to the Levant and Turkey, where it was known as Maroquin and Turkey leather. Dyed red, blue and green, it was greatly favoured by bookbinders from the sixteenth century onwards. By the eighteenth century it was being utilised by cabinet makers for desk tops, chair backs and seats. Its popularity continued into the nineteenth century, and in 1883 *Practical Upholstery* commended it as 'by far the best leather used for covering purposes, its durability and fastness of colour being qualities not common to any other material'.

In the America of the mid-seventeenth century the plain Puritan furniture often incorporated leather fixed with decorative brass-headed nails and some restrained carving. At about the same time the furniture makers used the substantial Russia leather, manufactured from hides and treated with an oil made from birch bark. It was widely used in the American Colonies, and a document of 1703 records: 'Seven doz. of Russia leather Chairs' for 'furnishing the rooms above-stairs', intended for the first Capitol at Williamsburg, Virginia.

Leather has a long history in the decoration and the utilitarian aspect of furniture making, but it has now fallen out of general use for anything except the finest quality reproduction work.

While the technique of leather upholstery is beyond the province of the present book, it it nevertheless worth describing a method of surface finishing by which a leather effect can be created. Experiments show that it is possible to create the look of leather which will withstand scrutiny from a close distance, although it does not, of course, have anything like the distinctive touch of real leather. It can, however, be used for decorative purposes in areas where it is not in contact with the human body. Certainly, inset panels are quite suitable, as are parts of pieces of furniture. It is by no means claimed that authentic Morocco or Russia leather effects can be done, though appropriate colours such as red, green or brown, can be introduced to a good effect.

The basic material for the leather effect is white lacquer or enamel, which is applied to the clean wood and allowed to dry, after which it is rubbed with a fine waterproof abrasive. Wipe over the surface to get rid of dust and debris, using a tack rag, and then paint it with a coat of appropriately coloured glaze in such a way as to leave a generous film. The exact thickness of the film is a matter for experiment, but it will be necessary to wipe it over with a clean cloth when almost firm.

The next stage is critical. A well washed cotton cloth is taken and crumpled into a pad, ensuring that the working surface is well wrinkled. Alternatively, a crumpled newspaper can be used. It is lightly laid down on the glaze at the stage when the skin is about to form. A patting motion is used to produce the appearance of leather, complete with all the lines and the faintly crackled look. The artistry is in how the patting and pressure is carried out. By gentle pressure the glaze can be eased in any direction to make an irregular surface. The glaze should be left to dry for one or two days, and it can then be finished with varnish, using two thin coats and ensuring that it does not accumulate in the wrinkles.

21

Crackle or Crazed Finishes

IN SOME of its varieties the crackle finish is closely akin to the simulated leather finish described in chapter twenty, but it also has many more possibilities which can form the basis of individual experiment. Almost any item of furniture can be crackle finished and look aesthetically satisfying, especially when large areas have to be covered, although this particular technique can also be used on more detailed surfaces, such as mouldings.

The basic mechanics of the crackle finish are simple, because all it consists of is the use of two materials, one of which is slow-drying and the other fast-drying. This creates a sort of push-pull effect in which one of the materials is stretched to the extent that it breaks under stress, giving rise to the crackle appearance. The element of experiment is in the fact that either, or both, of the materials can be modified to the point where the push-pull can be extended or shortened. When combined with colour, the final effect can be quite striking despite the fact that it is entirely accidental and beyond the control of the craftsman.

Crackle finish can be applied to practically any wood surface providing it is given a coat of a material which forms the catalyst. If crackle is attempted on bare wood, it will not work because there will be no elasticity in the base material. The initial coat is, therefore, at least two coats of lacquer which will create the bed for the second material. But before the lacquer is applied, the wood must be totally sealed off. If the wood is open-pored, two coats of ordinary lacquer will be sufficient, and this will also form an adequate cushion for the top coat. The base lacquer can be any colour whatever, bearing in mind that it will play an important part in the final appearance. It must, moreover, be of a colour which is compatible with the top coat, although it can be as neutral as grey, black or white providing it is going to be counterbalanced with a top coat of, say, red, green or yellow. The choice of colours is an important consideration at the outset. One of the more obvious choices is, of course, red over black or black over red, because we are all influenced by the traditional lacquer schemes. But there are many other possibilities, such as green on gold, blue and red, white and silver. The combinations are virtually endless.

It is essential that the lacquer is sprayed on to the wood. To date a good and reliable brushing crackle enamel has not been forthcoming, although some lacquers are now available in aerosol form and it is not, therefore, necessary to use an expensive spray gun. The lacquer is sprayed on in a to-and-fro motion in such a way as to create a perfectly even film. Almost as soon as the covering coat has been formed, it should begin to crackle, revealing the colour of the undercoat in a series of weblike lines in a crazed pattern. Exactly why the pattern forms in this way is governed by the consistency of the lacquer.

Experiment is necessary to discover the consistency of lacquer which reacts slowly or quickly. If an aerosol mix is being used, the craftsman will have no control over that particular aspect. But if a spray gun is employed, the lacquer can be cut with lacquer thinners to achieve radically different effects. Whereas a thin film will start to crackle almost as soon as it settles, a thick one may take somewhat longer.

Because the process is beyond the operator's control as far as the actual pattern of the crackle is concerned, this forms part of the interest. The random patterns which appear are generally very complicated and beyond the scope of the human imagination.

There is one other 'home-made' method of creating a crackle finish. It is done by making a saturated solution of magnesium sulphate in water to which dextrine is added until the solution becomes as sticky as varnish. Water stain is used for colouring.

The wood is now glue-sized to form a non-absorbent base, and then allowed to dry. If the magnesium sulphate mixture is brushed or sprayed on, an identical crackle will occur.

A leather effect using the crackle finish looks just as convincing as the method described in chapter twenty. Colour selection is unnecessary in view of the fact that the top coat will consist of a brown lacquer enamel and a dark brown japan which is wiped over the surface in such a way as to deposit colour evenly over the crazed surface. A finishing coat of clear lacquer completes the job. It may be advisable to experiment with this method because a leather-like appearance should consist of compact formations of very fine lines and a fairly thin mix will perhaps react more suitably than a thicker one.

22

Pearl Lacquering

LACQUER is a versatile and a striking material which is capable of acting as a carrier not only of pigment but also certain other materials, including very small fish scales. While this is known as pearl lacquering, it has little or nothing to do with the pearl except for a superficial resemblance which it bears to crushed mother-of-pearl shell. It may well be that in its original form it did utilise crushed mother-of-pearl, but there are no records to confirm this.

What pearl lacquer does is impart a sparkling and irridescent appearance to the surface when it is applied and properly finished. To work efficiently it needs a substantial base, and it is not considered suitable for large objects, such as furniture, although it can be used to give a special look to small occasional furniture which would otherwise look mundane and very ordinary or to woodware such as jewellery boxes or picture frames. If it is applied to large areas in an indiscriminating way it can look somewhat cheap and glittery, and in the end defeat its purpose. But used with taste on small areas it remains acceptable. The craftsman would not, for instance, cover a full size table or a sideboard with it, although a child's chair or a stool may well be considerably enhanced by its application. The ultimate horror would be to see a fine antique piece coated with pearl lacquer.

Unlike many finishing materials pearl lacquer cannot be made, it has to be bought, and if it is good quality it will be expensive. It is composed of very small fish scales in colourless lacquer. This enables the craftsman to tint it to the required hue. Because it is supplied in a heavily concentrated form, a little can go a long way providing it is evenly distributed over the surface, otherwise the final dissatisfying effect will be one of lustre streaking, which is not what is required. The pearl lacquer should consist of a perfectly even coating so that an overall lustre is attained which catches the reflected light. If the tiny fish scales are too spaced out by inferior brushwork, the result will look very feeble indeed and the desired effect will be totally lost, in which case there is no alternative but to strip the surface and start all over again.

The application of pearl lacquer, or lustre as it is sometimes called in the trade, calls for a certain amount of practice with a soft and pliable brush, the bristles of which should be slightly bent as it passes over the surface to avoid smearing and streaking. The brush should be only moderately charged and a careful eye kept on the supply of fish scales as they flow from the bristles.

The surface of the workpiece is first thoroughly cleaned in the usual way, and an intial two coats of thinned clear lacquer then applied. It is necessary at this early stage to decide which colour is required, because this will influence the appearance of the final coat. The depth of the colour should be suitably restrained and not too strong, otherwise the final effect will be overpowered. What should be aimed at is a transparent luminous quality, which is not always easy when using primary colours. The keynote is restraint; a tint is preferable to a full-bodied colour in view of the need for the fish scales to impart their lustre.

When the two base coats are quite dry, the pearl lacquer should be similarly tinted to match the two base coats. It is a good idea to examine the dry lacquer for a colour match when it is dry rather than in fluid form, which can be deceptive. Enough colour should be mixed at the outset in order to make the match, although a greater density of the pearl lacquer can lead the eye astray. First make tests on a piece of wood of a similar nature to the object on which the work will be done.

The pearl lacquer is brushed on in the manner previously described. A first coat is allowed to dry, and it is then rubbed down with a fine grade of paper in order to provide tooth for the second coat, which is then applied in a somewhat thinner film. This, too, is rubbed down, and then cleansed of all dust and debris. A coat of lacquer thinner is either sprayed or brushed on to seal the surface, and it can then be polished in precisely the same way as any other lacquer finish.

Some variations are possible in pearl lacquering. They are concerned with colour. For instance, two faint yellow tinted undercoats and an equally faint scarlet pearl coat will give a very unusual effect, while blue and red will be equally attractive. But, as has already been said, any over-enthusiasm with colour will probably look disappointingly garish. The total effect should be one in which the pearl lacquer is allowed to play a dominant part. Colour is almost secondary.

If there is any criticism of pearl lacquering it is that the wood has no part to play, any inherent beauty being completely obscured. However, it is certainly a finish which can be used on inferior wood and may beautify it.

23

Wrinkle Finish

THE previous chapter mentioned the versatility of lacquer, and there are many special effects which can be arrived at, some by haphazard experiment, others by calculated design. If it is applied in a thin film, a glasslike finish will result. When it is coloured it can look positively gemlike. If several tints are swirled around in it before it starts to set, a mildly marbled look can be created. Equally, it will act as a carrier for alien materials, such as the fish scales used in pearl lacquering. It has been known for Oriental craftsmen to crush semi-precious stones to a powdery dust, using the garnet and the amethyst to make jewelled surfaces. The trick of how this is done has not as yet reached the West, and so it follows that while there are secrets there must be research.

Wrinkle finish does not happen to be the most attractive of all the finishes in which lacquer is used. Indeed, some seasoned craftsmen believe that it resembles the hide of an aged and very tired elephant. For all that, it does have its uses, especially when novelty or fantasy furniture is being created and there is scope for special effects. Its sole use may be in this particular sphere, because there has for some years been an eccentric school of cabinet making in which the innovative designers have moved towards the sculptural rather than the utilitarian and purely decorative. It is not all that 'modern', because the tomb furniture of Ancient Egypt provided fabulous beasts in the shape of tables, chairs and cupboards.

When an upholstered appearance is desired, wrinkle finish is the technique to provide it. There are a few minor limitations, such as the size of the piece which can be treated. To achieve the distinctive wrinkled effect, the workpiece has to be literally baked or treated with direct heat. Granted, this may be difficult when a full-sized wardrobe has to be covered with wrinkle finish, and no doubt some ingenuity is called for.

The basic material is known, obviously enough, as wrinkle lacquer. It cannot be made in the workshop, and it must be purchased from a supplier. It is dense and very thick. A gallon of it goes nowhere at all, because it must be practically plastered on. This happens to be a technique which does not call for any of the fine and delicate brushwork used in other forms of lacquering. It is coarse finishing and it is slapped on with a wide thick brush. The quality of the wood is unimportant, because it becomes covered. Wrinkle lacquer cannot be sprayed on very effectively, because it is much too thick to be forced through even the widest nozzle.

If the lacquer is almost too thick to brush on to the wood, this means that it has probably been in stock for a considerable period of time; it can be thinned to a manageable consistency by using a dash or two of naphtha and mixing well. Stirring wrinkle lacquer is an exhausting job, but it has to be done because the naphtha must be completely absorbed before any brushing can be attempted.

Every endeavour should be made to cover the wood in a single coat; the lacquer should stick to the wood like chewing gum, hanging like a wet skin and looking utterly repulsive. No attempt should be made to smoothe it down, because it will even out of its own accord when the heat gets at it before it starts to develop its wrinkles.

When the area is well and truly covered, the piece should stand for 30 to 45 minutes to permit the naphtha to evaporate and reduce the threat of fire during the heat treatment. It has been found that a common hair-drier can be used to achieve good results providing the nozzle is wafted in short and graceful passes across the surface. If at all possible, however, and the piece is sufficiently portable, it should be baked in an electric oven for one hour at 180 degrees Farenheit. In this time the wrinkles should materialise in some profusion. Once this has occurred, the wrinkle finish is, in fact, complete, although it is still necessary to extend the curing time by applying a heat of 250 degrees Farenheit for up to two more hours. This makes the lacquer become rock hard, after which the piece is removed from the oven and allowed to cool.

It is appreciated that not all pieces of furniture can be inserted in ovens, especially domestic ones, because they will probably be too unwieldy. In this event the hair-drier can be used or, alternatively, an electric fire can be placed in such a position as to provide constant heat. When this method is adopted it is advisable to keep a fire extinguisher handy, although an outbreak is unlikely providing the fire is far enough away to avoid making the lacquer bubble and start crisping. From time to time the workpiece can be repositioned until the entire area has been well baked.

During the baking, wrinkles will form into haphazard patterns which are not entirely unattractive. If an additional colour decoration is desired, lacquers of contrasting colours can be applied when mixed with naphtha and will take admirably.

And that is all there is to wrinkle lacquering. No final coat is required because the lacquer forms itself into a very hard and quite impenetrable coat which will show no sign of wear for many a year.

24

Spatter Finishes

SPATTER finish has unfortunately acquired a bad name for itself, harking back to the often Ugly Thirties when it was invariably done in a very clumsy and blotchy manner, consisting as a rule of nothing more than haphazard splashes of paint on nursery walls, landings and staircases, and looking like nothing so much as the accident of a drunken decorator. For many years spatter was neglected for the altogether logical reason that surface finishers could not see any particular application for it. Most of them classified it as a form of home decorating having nothing to do with the craft of wood finishing. But in recent years a more adventurous spirit has asserted itself, and a great deal of twentieth-century furniture has been improved by the now refined spatter. Significantly, the application has turned half cycle because it has now passed out of fashion for floors and walls, although there is no reason why the refined technique should not make a comeback in interiors where wood has a major role to play.

Spatter is not as a rule applied to bare wood, although it can be if the surface is prepared with a coat of matt varnish or clear gloss polyurethane paint to preserve any distinctive figuring. Alternatively, if the wood is inferior and downright ugly, the best course is to cover it with a ground colour. The choice of the ground happens to be very important in view of what follows. If the spatter is to consist of a combination of fairly bright colours, then a low-key ground, such as brown, olive green or even battleship grey can be used. Indeed, that workhouse colour of ill repute, chocolate brown, can often form an ideal ground if the spatter colours are well chosen. It would be a mistake to suggest that matching colours should be selected, and it must be said that a firm and dogmatic adherence to a rigid 'colour scheme' will in all probability lead to a very conservative-looking finish which is devoid of surprises. A good spatter finish should have at least some surprises in it, and they will be caused not only by variations of colour but also in the degree of spatter, ranging from almost microscopic to coarse, dictated by the dimensions of the piece which is being treated.

The material to use for spatter is lacquer. Ordinary domestic paint will not do because it lacks the consistency and often winds up in a sort of scabby smudge and much visual confusion. Lacquer, at least, has the good grace to stay exactly where it is put and it remains predictable as far as the finished colour is concerned.

Jackson Pollock (1912–1956), the American artist, initially created a furious hullabaloo when he produced canvases by simply dribbling household paint all over them. Yet his seemingly erratic way of working enabled America, in the words of one critic, to 'free itself for the first time from European dominance'. His pictures became a network of lines of varying thicknesses, dictated by accident rather than logical design. It is much the same with spatter. The flying paint spots can be directed only to a very limited extent, after which they will fall as they wish. There is little point, therefore, in attempting to create any tightly conceived designs, and the main purpose must be to ensure that the colours do not fall into total confusion. Yet even the most riotous spatter can have something to offer to the eye.

All the colours are prepared beforehand and laid out in separate pans or dishes, and a separate brush should be allocated to each container. The technique of creating spatter is as follows: only the tip of the brush is dipped into the lacquer. The bristles should not be overloaded, nor should the brush be fully charged to the point where it drips surplus lacquer. The craftsman stands at a distance from the workpiece, holding the brush in one hand and a screwdriver or a wooden spoon in the other. By striking the brush handle sharply it is possible to discharge the paint in speckles straight on to the surface. Experiment will show that distance lends variety. At a distance of about six inches the spatter will be closely packed, while at eighteen inches it will be much more widely spaced.

The initial colour is now spattered, always allowing space for the second or third colours. Some beginners become very enthusiastic and apply far too much of the first spatter only to find that the second and third coats of different colours obscure the effect entirely or partially. The motto is to exercise restraint.

The first spatter coat is allowed to dry. If it is still wet when the second spatter is applied, there will be some globulating and the lacquer will probably start weeping down the surface.

The second coat is now applied in much the same way. At this point there are possibilities of variation. For instance, masking-shields of irregular or regular shapes can be cut out of cardboard and laid on the

FIGURE 47. By tapping the loaded brush on a block of wood, it is possible to make multi-coloured spatter patterns which are more controlled than by fingering the bristles.

surface in such a way as to create areas for the third colour. By adept masking it should be possible to create an effect in which the spatter colours merge imperceptibly from one to another, presenting an effect of coloured clouds or shapes. This sort of thing is suitable for giving some enhancement to otherwise austere nursery furniture.

When the second colour dries, it can be followed by a third one. It is, of course, possible to use many different lacquers, but three has been found to be an acceptable number without muddying the final effect. A lot must depend upon the initial choice, but it is almost impossible to make a serious mistake, and such combinations as, say, purple and yellow and black, and white and red can be used to good effect.

One other basic fault should be mentioned. Many beginners doggedly continue to apply the spatter coats without occasionally taking time off to inspect the job. Like other artists, he should study what is happening to the colours. Red and green, for instance, react to one another, and they have a rather strange vibrancy. If black and white are being used, some account should be taken of the effect of the white, because it may make the workpiece much too stark, and so there may be a necessity to introduce a third colour to break it down. A mature look can be created by applying a final coat of varnish tinted with burnt sienna, but if brightness is required a coat of clear varnish is advisable.

Spatter calls for a taste for colour. It demands some discretion. It requires an urge to explore and excite. Like the finished effect itself, it requires a craftsman who is a mixture of all these qualities.

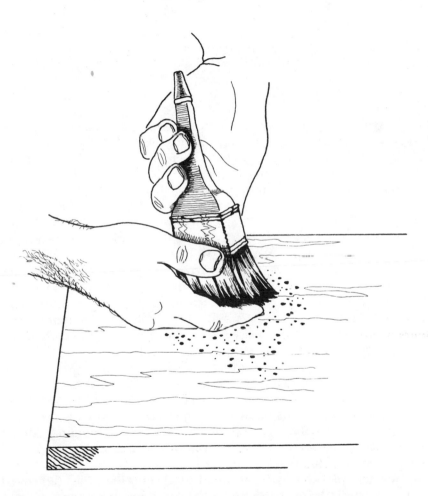

FIGURE 48.   Concentrated spatter effects can be achieved by loading the brush and then riffling through the well soaked bristles with the fingers, always keeping the brush on the move to create an even effect.

25

Stencilling

WE can go back to the Egyptians of 2500 B.C. for a rather uncertain trace of stencilling, because it was used to decorate mummy cases. There is a possibility that the Chinese used stencils prior to 3000 B.C., and the most substantial evidence was found in 1907 when Sir Aurel Stein, the Orientalist, explored the *Cave of the Thousand Buddhas* at Tunhang in western China. They were dated sometime between 500 and 1000 B.C., and contained silks on which the figure of the Buddha was stencilled. The stencil patterns themselves were also found, and while they did not exactly resemble the stencil plates which we now know and use, they were, nevertheless as distinct a tool. Some time later the Chinese introduced Derma printing, using an acid-ink which was painted on to the parchment and allowed time in which to eat its way through in such a way as to create a stencil. By A.D. 600 the Chinese were exporting not only stencilled silks but also mass produced cottons.

Other countries, including Iran and Thailand (formerly Persia and Siam), adopted the craft, but it was Japan which became the leader. They used processed mulberry fibres which were protected with varnish, some of which had human hairs incorporated in the surface as a reinforcement, and used a second plate for further strengthening. All the motifs of this period were drawn from flora and fauna and a series of intricate geometric figures.

The various techniques later reached the West along the traditional trade routes, and the method was used for other purposes, such as stencilling the name of Justinian the Roman Emperor (A.D. 483–565), on official documents. By the Middle Ages the French were beginning to excel at stencilling, and in the fifteenth and sixteenth centuries the bookbinders of Venice and Paris used the craft to decorate the embossed spines of volumes. From 1620 in Rouen a new industry began to produce sheets, known as 'dominoes', measuring about 12½″ × 16½″, applying stencils in such a way that the separate pieces could be matched up when decorating a room. From the late seventeenth century to the early nineteenth century in Germany and France stencilling was used to decorate the woodwork of mansions and churches, all kinds of furniture, wall coverings and fine fabrics.

In North America the settlers adopted it to decorate their often rough houses, and the stencilled parlour or bedroom floor became a hallmark of domestic artistic endeavour and social status. Apart from working straight on to the bleached wooden floor, they also produced stencilled canvasses which were laid down in lieu of carpets, decorating them with flowers, stars, a huge variety of birds and the symbol of hospitality, the pineapple.

Stencilling found so much favour that it quickly became an acknowledged trade as the settlements developed, and a common sight of the time was the craftsman with his horse-drawn cart piled up with patterns, stencil plates, brushes and paints. As other nationalities arrived in North America the various styles began to emerge.

Amongst the American furniture makers who used stencils extensively was Lambert Hitchcock, mentioned in chapter 1. His Barkhamstead, Connecticut, factories produced thousands of cheap chairs with the seat and the slats stencilled in colourful designs. But it was Louis Comfort Tiffany (1848–1933) the New York jeweller's son, who really advanced stencilling and laid upon it the distinction of good taste. When he opened his interior decoration business in 1879 under the title, The Associated Artists, he used stencilling to decorate the White House for the President, Chester A. Arthur, and the home of the more memorable Mark Twain in Hartford.

Meanwhile, wallpaper remained a luxury for country people and in such areas of New England, Kentucky, Texas and Ohio it became the economical fashion to stencil designs to cover large areas of plastered wall. The complicated city wallpaper designs were simplified, taking the favoured motifs of leaves, flowers, swags of fruit and geometrical patterns done in black, green, yellow and red to contrast with the pink, yellow, grey and blue plaster. There was, in fact, a limit to the colour range because the travelling craftsmen generally made their own from various colours of clay, dried to dust and then diluted with skim milk.

Over the centuries the technique of stencilling has changed very little and the principles are easy to understand, although the materials are radically different. All it consists of nowadays is a plate of paper or acetate in which the design is cut, brushes, such as the cabinet-maker's glue brush or a rubbing brush, and the paint itself. The paint is known as japan colour of the type used by signwriters, and turpentine is used as thinner or solvent. Such paints are very quick drying. Alternatively, acrylic paint can be used. It is water based, but it dries very quickly to a hard film or skin.

What we are concerned with here is the use of stencilled patterns on furniture or woodwork rather than the decoration of entire walls or floors. For this reason it is probably better to use transparent acetate sheet for the stencil plate rather than paper, because it is more easily cleaned and it will store more conveniently without deteriorating.

The first decision is whether the stencilled pattern is going to be in more than one colour. If it is multi-coloured, then a separate plate will, of course, be required for each colour. In every case it is necessary to

FIGURE 49. Cutting the stencil with a scalpel, working towards the body rather than away from it. It is essential that the acetate sheet is firmly pinned down over the master drawing in such a way that any visual aberration is avoided.

make a master drawing of the design, or else take one from a book of stencil patterns. The essential aspect of cutting multiple plates is to ensure that a correct and accurate registration is made so that a design motif, such as a spray of flowers or a geometric pattern, will not go askew. This is done by making locating, or registration, marks on each of the plates at the outset. The key drawing is placed flat and the sheet of acetate is placed on top of it. The design is then traced, using a wax pencil or a draughtsman's pen with Indian ink to draw on the acetate. It is advisable to securely pin down the master drawing and the acetate sheet overlay to avoid any faults in the registration by slippage. Presuming this to be a three-colour set, then the first colour stencil is drawn and the colour shaded in as a later guide, using a few dabs of paint at a strategic point. The second sheet of acetate is now placed on top and fastened down, and the shape is traced and the colour dabs made, followed by the third. This makes a kind of sandwich which, when held up to the light, will show the appearance of the finished stencil. It is absolutely essential to put a colour key on each of the stencils as a guide to later working, because when applying more than two colours it is very easy to become confused. There is, in fact, no limit to the number of colours which can be used, but it is advisable to keep early attempts fairly simple.

When the acetate stencil is being executed, the knife should always cut towards the craftsman, not away. This ensures a fine and even severance, particularly when the blade moves round a curve. The stencil knife is very much a personal choice, and it can be a surgical scalpel, a craftsman's knife with interchangeable blades or, indeed, any instrument which is capable of cutting cleanly through the material and remaining directly on the line of the design and not just inside or outside it. The cutting has to be decisive if it is to give a good print. When the drawing has been made on the acetate, it should be laid down on a white sheet of paper to increase visibility, and the cutting should be done in a good light which is devoid of shadows.

It may be helpful here to mention the matter of bridges. These are the narrow and even hairlike 'pathways' which are necessary between the various segments of some complicated designs to hold the acetate together and avoid total disintegration. Exactly where the bridges should be located is up to the stencil cutter. In some designs, where wide spaces may occur, it is often necessary to create a veritable network, especially if the stencil is likely to be in frequent use. When the paint is applied this will result in some blank spaces, which must be touched up afterwards. Bridges should not, therefore, be too broad. It is better to have several narrow ones within a space rather than one broad one because it will be all that much easier to touch up afterwards.

It has to be said that cutting stencils does call for a great deal of hard practice. Regardless of how sharp the blade may happen to be, the constant pressure needed to cut cleanly through the acetate will quickly tire the muscles of the fingers. This, coupled with the need to make a continuous cut rather than a series of short and often erratic ones, can cause some weariness. Like all other techniques, it is something to be mastered. Beginners often complain of pain in the shoulder muscles, the remedy for which is a more relaxed posture with the workpiece at the right height. Obviously, crouching over it, particularly in a bad light, can cause tiredness, whereas natural light and the correct height with a good sharp knife will aid the operation.

FIGURE 50.   Stencil designs from about 1850, which can be adapted for the decoration of furniture, either in several colours or a single one. From the stencil cutting point of view, these will be advanced for the amateur, but can be cut with some practice, using a scapel for the more delicate areas and using bridges to link the isolated sections.

On the assumption that the stencil will be applied to a piece of furniture, the surface of the wood can be varnished or left in a bare state or it can be lacquered. Bare wood should be sealed with lacquer, which can be clear or in a tone which contrasts with the colour scheme of the stencil. If japan paint is being used for the stencilling, the working consistency should be that of melted butter, and the turpentine thinner should be well absorbed. This paint dries practically as soon as it is applied, and it will probably start to form a crust in the saucer once it has been mixed. Take up only a small amount on the brush, simply wetting the tips of the bristles. One of the great advantages of stencilling is that it uses so little paint, and so comparatively little needs to be mixed at a time. It can always be freshened up with a few drops of turpentine if it should start to harden.

The most obvious fault experienced by most beginners is that paint runs under the lip of the stencil and seems to ruin the possibility of making a perfect print. This is overcome by a very light loading of the brush. However, there is more to it than that, and it can be summed up in two words: 'build up'. This means that if only a very light application of paint is made in the first operation, more can be added until the solid colour character which typifies good stencilling is finally reached. If the brush is moved in a circular motion, always pointing straight down on to the stencil plate, the result should be a completely even distribution of colour. But if the paint should happen to run under the lip of the stencil, stop work at once and remove the plate, damp a cloth in turpentine and carefully wipe away the excess. At best, this is simply a trivial fault which can be remedied, and it is nothing to get bothered about. But it is a mistake to doggedly continue, hoping that it will somehow come out right. Much depends, of course, on the base colour, or the stain, on which the stencil is located. If it is painted, then it may well be necessary to retouch here and there after the stencilling is completed. If it is varnished or shellacked, then care should be taken not to use a solvent which is likely to affect the finish.

One of the drawbacks to stencilling on furniture is that it is quite impossible to use a gloss base coat, because the japan colour or acrylic colour will not take at all. All that happens is a sort of globulation with the pigment clumping together and not achieving anything like an even distribution. But there are many other alternatives, including applying the stencil on gesso, the application of which is described in chapter 6. A distinctive appearance can be achieved if it is distressed and given an antique appearance by applying tints to suggest age, such as burnt sienna or umber with a touch or two of yellow ochre. If the gesso is distressed by inflicting ridges, nicks and chips before it finally dries and hardens, all the darker colours should comfortably settle into the marks when it is wiped down with a cloth, and then the stencilling can be

FIGURE 51. How the master design for the stencil is first drawn, using a linear treatment which is placed underneath the acetate sheet and traced with india ink or wax pencil. A good stencil pattern is compact and logical, as here. Both designs date from the mid-1800s.

FIGURE 52. Designs for borders which can be used for furniture decoration, some based on near-abstract motifs, others more figurative. All of these can be executed in one or more colours.

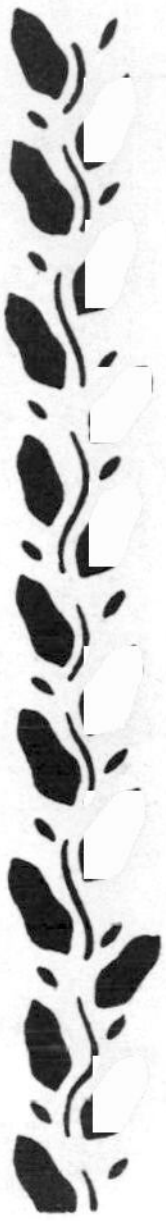
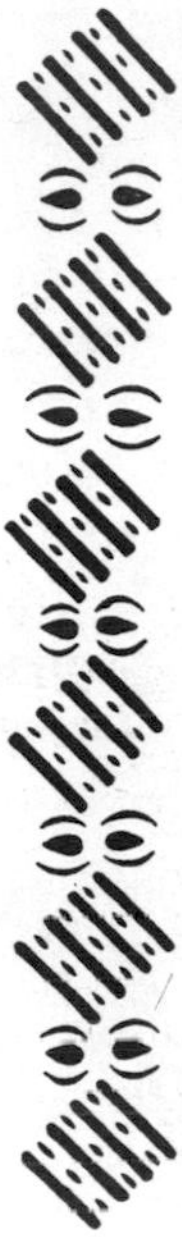
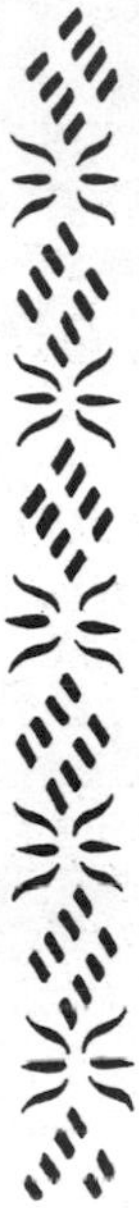
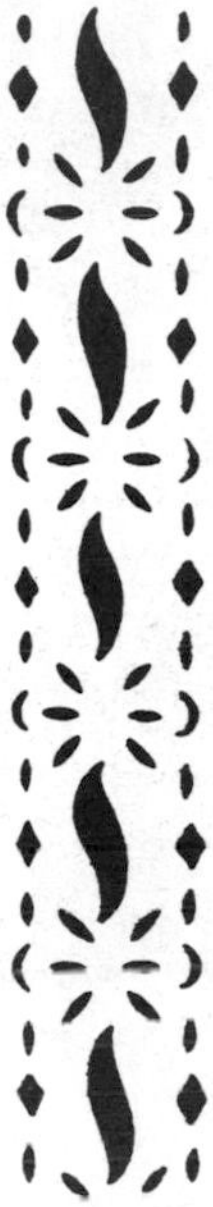
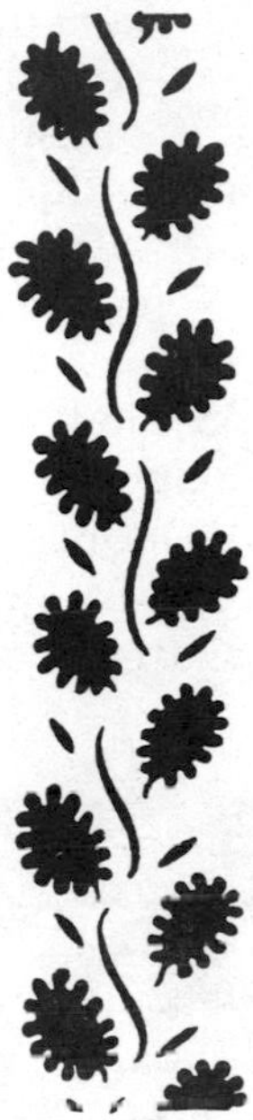

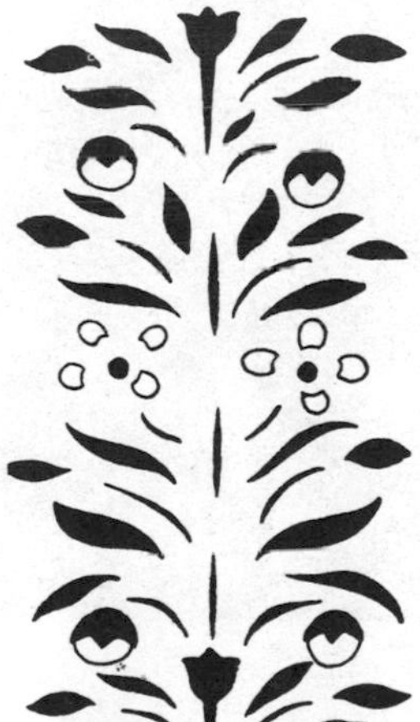
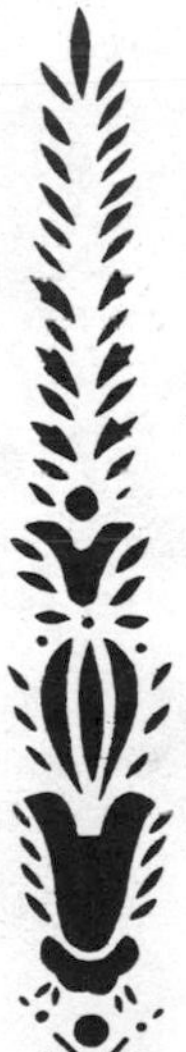
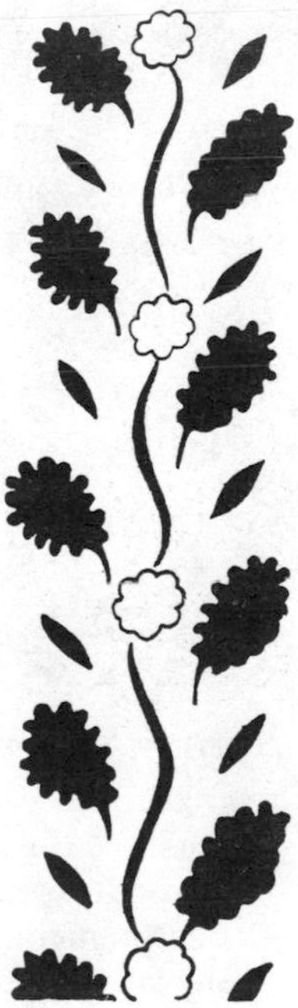

carried out. Obviously, if the surface happens to be deliberately uneven, the stencil paint will not take quite as well as it would on a perfectly smooth surface, but this can probably be accepted as a contribution to the antique appearance. Another possibility is to glaze the surface before stencilling. This is done by applying a mixture composed of equal parts of flat varnish and turpentine with about 15% japan colour. It is brushed on as quickly as possible to ensure that it starts to dry evenly. While it is still sticky, the brush is forcibly dragged along the grain to achieve the typical glazed appearance. There may be times when it is desirable to glaze over the stencils, in which case a single coat of flat varnish should be applied to protect the paint of the stencilled design. As with any other form of distressing, when age has to be suggested and the

FIGURE 53. The more delicately cut a stencil happens to be, the greater the care demanded when applying pigment with the short-bristled brush. A long-bristled brush with too much give would not enable the pigment to penetrate to the corners and edges, resulting in a fuzzy line. The pigment being applied here is water based and fairly thick to prevent any running under the stencil sections.   *Photo: Andrew J. Gigg*

stencil colour is pretty solid and forcible, it can be lightly, very lightly, rubbed with fine grade steel wool to convey the idea of wear and tear.

The commercial surface finisher may well find himself in a position in which the client wants to buy more than one object stencilled in exactly the same way. This means that the best and most economical way of working must be devised. One item which is obviously indispensible to the job is the stencil plate itself. In fact, a best selling stencil is potentially worth a lot of money. However, it is possible to discard the brush and use instead a wool or mohair roller. If, for instance, a series of doors have to be decorated, then the stencil plates should be cut to the exact size of the panels or, in the case of a plain door in halves or quarters, using the corners of the door as the registration points. A home-decorating seven-inch roller is the best choice, and draughtsman's tape is used to hold the plate in place by strapping it over the top or around the edges. The roller is very absorbent and will take up a large amount of paint. Some practice may be needed when using japan colour, which should be mixed to a watery consistency and most of it must be expelled by squeezing it on the paint-pan and the remainder by rolling on sheets of newspaper. The purpose is to leave only just enough paint to leave a trace rather than create a firm coating in one rolling. When the roller passes over the stencil plate there will eventually be a build up of paint and it will be necessary to remove the plate and clean it properly from time to time, otherwise it may run. Acrylic paint is unsuitable for this type of large-scale repetition stencilling because of the skin which forms to clog the roller and interfere with efficient operation.

*   *   *

There is a vogue for stencilled furniture, scarcely a piece of which will not benefit from this form of decoration, though it is ill-advised to apply it to genuine and valuable antiques. Plain whitewood furniture is the best medium or cleaned-up old kitchen furniture, particularly if the craftsman is in a postion to supply traditional and nostalgic designs. But that is not to say there is no room for experiment in design and colour. Who knows, stencilling might well eventually sound the death knell of all that stripped pine and bleached wood which chokes the market.

26

Sugi in the Oriental Style

SUGI, pronounced *sooji*, is nothing more or less than a charring of the wood and, like so many wood finishes, it has its origins in the Orient, where it was used by craftsmen of the fifteenth century to mellow and age wood in order to impart an appearance which is unique to the process. In essence, all it means is charring or burning.

Different woods naturally char in different ways due to their molecular structure and chemical content. One of the most suitable for this particular treatment is pine, in fact, and by a skilful application of the flame the softer parts of it will burn away, leaving the harder parts more prominent and upstanding. Oak, on the other hand, will char more evenly and change its superficial colour more gradually than pine.

The most interesting part of the process for the craftsman is that it will impart a variety of tones, from black to honey amber, and it is not unlike heating and tempering a metal, for while the spectrum is wide, it can be halted at any stage and then fixed.

Up to the present time the tendency has been to use sugi for the treatment of certain types of wood sculpture, mainly abstract, but it can also be applied to furniture. It is also useful for an unusual handling of pine panelling and stripped pine furniture. If it is used on new pine furniture which has been factory finished, it will be necessary first of all to remove the cellulose or waxed finish before any heat is used, otherwise the results will be nothing short of disastrous.

The essential tool is a reliable gas torch or blowlamp which is equipped with a variety of nozzles, from the needlepoint to the fish tail. It is necessary to have as many as possible in order to produce different kinds of burn or charred marks and ensure that the heat can be accurately directed to where it is needed.

When held close to the surface, a needlepoint flame will fan out and create a more or less circular char mark. A practised craftsman should be able to create many striking patterns by this method, but he should also be able to alternate the circular chars with deft touches from a needlepoint flame to create patterns. Another method is to use a long and floppy sort of flame which, when wafted across the surface of the wood, will create an even mellowness with a few ripples and tidemarks, depending very much upon the wood, its age and condition.

What happens when the flame first encounters the wood is that it begins to char and then, if the heat remains, the wood will of course catch fire. At the first sight of the tell-tale orange flame, the torch should at once be removed and the wood damped down with a wet cloth. One of the things to be very careful about is any build-up of heat in the wood fibres, otherwise a conflagration can start without warning. But, if the flame is kept moving in between making the darker char marks, there will be very little danger.

One other risk is excessive burning along any ledges and edges, for it is here that the wood is thinnest and most likely to catch fire. However, even if there is slightly more burning here than elsewhere, the final finishing should make the damage practically unnoticeable.

When the sugi is complete, a very stiff wire brush is used to remove any over-charred wood. In the treatment of wood sculpture some artists have deliberately left the burned wood and fixed it permanently by the injection of synthetic resins. But in the case of furniture it is advisable to use the wire brush, after which it can be sanded to a velvety smoothness. When wood has been softened by heat it is likely to show the marks of abrasives, and so a thorough sanding is recommended.

Sugi is completed by the final application of a variety of materials, including boiled linseed oil, which should be allowed to soak in and deepen the colour. Oriental craftsmen used poppy oil but this is practically unobtainable in the West. Shellac is another useful finish because it can be applied in several coats, and if it is tinted a great many effects become possible. Beeswax and turpentine can also be used, provided that a base coat of clear lacquer has first been applied.

The basic attraction of sugi is that it demands a particular type of skill in the handling of the often nebulous fire factor in relation to the nature of wood which is being treated. There is also some scope in the choice of tools. In the Orient the craftsman makes use of a blowpipe fitted with a very narrow nozzle, by which means it is possible to direct the flame in extemely precise patterns. This in no way resembles conventional pyrography or pokerwork which is outside the scope of this book, because the blowpipe can create effects of feathering or shade tapering when used almost like a pencil to draw portraits, landscapes and traditional designs. Another Oriental method, now little used, was to hold metal trays of hot coals over which a bellows was operated, directing a billowing blanket of heat over large areas of the wood and creating a series of colour changes. Craftsmen have also been known to combine sugi with forms of lacquer-work, which carries the final effect into an area approaching fine art.

27

Cellulose Lacquering

MODERN mass produced furniture is generally cellulose lacquer finished. Cellulose lacquer is a form of polish, composed of nitrocellulose, a resin, a plasticiser and, finally, the volatile element itself. The plasticisers react on the brittle quality of the nitrocellulose so that the end result is that all the elements become bonded together to form a tough film. The principal advantage of clothing wood in what amounts to a hard and durable skin is that it will wear far longer than any other form of finish and still maintain a lasting lustre. The commercial furniture manufacturer also uses plastic veneering composed of much the same material because it is both heat and water resistant and will give a polished surface which requires no special polish and can simply be wiped over with a damp cloth. The disadvantage is that if the veneer happens to become chipped or badly scarred or scratched, it will not respond to the branded domestic polishes. Unlike other polished surfaces, it cannot be satisfactorily touched up.

Plastic veneer or cellulose lacquer is applied with a spray, by simple dipping or by brushing. One of the major advantages of spraying is that the mixture of cellulose can be varied in such a way that the film can be applied equally and quickly to the wood surface and closely controlled in its drying time, which represents an obvious gain as far as standardisation is concerned. The commercial manufacturer will wish to guarantee to his wholesale customers that the quality of manufacture and finish is consistent throughout.

There is nothing very complicated about the spray itself. It is as conventional as any spray which uses compressed air for its power to atomise the fluid. In cellulose lacquer spraying, however, the degree of atomisation can be very precisely controlled.

Spray cellulosing requires a flow of compressed air, which must be totally devoid of all foreign material, such as dust and oil, the compression being of the order of about 100lbs per square inch, which is reduced for general spraying purposes to 60lbs per square inch. The amount of compression happens to be crucial for certain types of cellulose lacquer. Too fine a spray backed by too high a compression will not efficiently disperse or build up the required thickness of film on the wood.

For general purposes a cup gun is used in which the container of cellulose lacquer rests on top of the gun and is fed by gravity to the atomiser head of the spray. An alternative form of spray gun has a

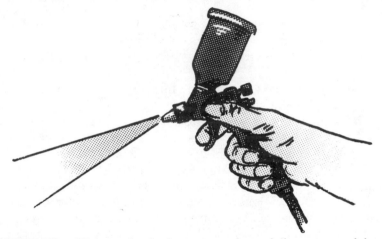

FIGURE 54.   The gravity-feed spraygun depends in some models on a form of internal air-cushion to create an unbroken stream of minute droplets. It should always be held with the forefinger on the fluid control.

container underneath the atomiser so that the lacquer has to be pumped through to the nozzle.

For mass production work the factory installation will have a system of bulk supply of cellulose lacquer from a tank, which may feed several sprays. Some manufacturers prefer the individual pressure-feed tank which can hold up to fifty gallons of cellulose lacquer. The advantages of this system is that the tank can be fitted with its own pressure gauge, inlet and outlet attachments and an agitating apparatus, such as a paddle, to ensure that the consistency of supply is standardised. Because they are portable, these pressure-feed tanks are favoured in plants where the furniture for finishing has to be moved from one section to another.

Furniture is always sprayed in special compartments, or booths, which are three-sided constructions, and with surfaces with specially treated materials to enable them to be washed down and avoid any accumulation of stray lacquer and contamination when different finishing materials are employed. There is, too, an ever-present risk of fire when cellulose deposits build up on a surface. In the well-equipped factory the sides of the spraying compartment are constantly washed with flowing water which carries airborn cellulose lacquer straight back into the recycling tanks, where it can be separated and cleaned, and then returned to the supply tank. The spraying installations are kept as clean as hospital operating theatres.

The skilled sprayer makes the job look very simple, but it is, in fact, quite difficult to finally master the art. Among beginners it is common to erratically waft the nozzle about in several directions and sometimes

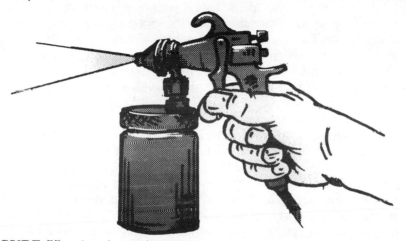

FIGURE 55. An alternative spraygun with a pump action is perhaps somewhat cumbersome to use but more dependable over long periods of operation.

even in the general direction of the furniture to be covered only to find rivulets forming and causing a sagging of the coat.

An important aspect of spraying is concerned principally with distance in relation to the composition of the cellulose lacquer. Ideally, the spraygun is held at an angle of about 90 degrees and at a distance of about six to seven inches from the surface to be coated. It is not possible to be entirely specific about this because it happens to be governed by the general dimensions of the workpiece. Beginners often create a series of rising ridges of lacquer on all flat surfaces, caused by several momentary hesitations during the operation. This is avoided by keeping the spraygun in constant motion. Even at the moment of shutting off the air pressure, care must be taken to taper off the flow of cellulose so that an excess is not built up. It is not always possible to discern the excess because of the very fine mistlike spray which is emitted from the nozzle, taking into account the fact that the operator stands directly behind it.

Spraying should be done in even lines with slight overlaps, and the spraygun is shut down at the end of each sweep. In the case of a large table or any other flat surface, the spray area should end several inches in from the ends, and this margin is done separately.

The control of the pressure is important. These tools have two separate pressures, one for the air and the other for the cellulose lacquer. This means that a diffuse spray can be applied by simply increasing the air pressure and a more concentrated one by reducing the air flow, depending in each case on the composition of the cellulose lacquer.

The range of faults in bad spraying is not great, but any one of them can be serious if it happens to go unnoticed and the workpiece is completely sprayed before the error is noticed. The most common fault is an orange-peel effect, caused by too little cellulose and too great a flow of air. The surface is rippled by the gush of air. Another fault, which is known in the trade as 'cissing', manifests itself in the shape of a multitude of minute pinhole depressions which may have white craters or haloes. The reason for this is the passage through the nozzle of water or oil carried from contaminated feeder tanks. When this occurs, the spraying should cease immediately and the spraygun dismantled and the pipes thoroughly washed with solvent. Far more serious is chilling, which is due to the quality of the solvent mixture in the cellulose. When the solvent leaves the nozzle, it tends to create a phenomenon in which the immediate area takes on a lowered temperature and picks up moisture or humidity. This means that the moisture is virtually slammed on to the surface of the wood, where it merges with the lacquer, causing a white and rather milky appearance. Where spraying is done in an environment which cannot be very well controlled, chilling can be avoided by modifying the solvent. There is available an anti-chill thinners. If a volume of about ten per cent of this is added to the cellulose, it will probably cure the fault.

After the cellulose has been sprayed, it may be found that there is a sort of softness which is not exactly tacky but will still accept a fingerprint. This means that too much cellulose is being deposited at any one time. It is possible that several layers will build up without enough time being allowed for drying and hardening of each coat. The softness is caused by the solvent part of the mixture which has had no time to act. To prevent softening spray the cellulose in much thinner coats and allow a little longer than usual for each coat to dry and harden.

Lacquer is notorious for its habit of developing a dull bloom in which the mirror sheen disappears or does not even appear at all. Even when the bloom is hand-polished away, it still returns with great and irritating persistence. Clearly, the fault must be in the cellulose itself and the way in which is is constituted, but it is certainly accelerated by the presence of dampness. If a piece of furniture is afflicted with bloom, the only solution is to strip it completely and start again, this time ensuring that the humidity of the workshop is as close to zero as possible.

It is somewhat unlikely that the craftsman finisher who specialises in hand finishes in a commercial workshop will proceed at once to instal a full-scale spraying booth unless there is a definite call for it and some profit can be made. However, there is a demand for small-batch cellulose finishing. In such cases it may be possible to instal a tank in which the pieces can be dipped. The dimensions of the tank are naturally governed by the dimensions of work to be undertaken. The process is one of the greatest simplicity, for the workpieces are lowered, either singly or in multiples, into the cellulose, using an arrangement of pulleys and hooks, which hold the workpieces. The only difference between spraying and dipping is that the tank cellulose must have a much more viscous quality, although it must be said that this has the drawback of trapping some air bubbles and often transferring them to the surface of the wood. However, by the addition of thinners, it is possible to considerably cut down the bubble faults, although the addition of an increased quantity of thinners will dictate more than one dipping. From the commercial point of view the dipping technique is much less costly than spraying and it has fewer working difficulties. What it does call for, however, is a considerable investment in cellulose and thinners to initally charge the tank, and attention has to be paid to the rate at which dipping is done.

There is really very little to be said about brushing cellulose lacquer. It is obviously a very basic process, differing little in principle to ordinary varnishing and lacquering. Brushing is rendered easier by the use of the special thinners which is made specifically for brushing and containing a volatile material which is much slower to evaporate, giving the craftsman ample time in which to create an even film.

Just as important as the application of cellulose is the area in which it dries and hardens. If the temperature is comfortably warm and air gently circulated around the piece, this will encourage the process and the cellulose should then harden fairly rapidly. While it is not possible to be specific about the time needed for hardening, the solvent component should evaporate in a matter of two or three hours while the cellulose will take several hours before it becomes hard and typically mirrorlike. Drying and hardening times are governed by the composition of the cellulose.

Lacquer finishes are applied over plain or stained surfaces, and the stains are applied in the same way as any other colouring material. In commercial production they are generally spirit based for the sake of speed of production.

28

Restoring and Refinishing Antique Furniture

THIS happens to be one of the most contentious aspects of the surface finishing trade. One school of thought, headed by collectors who are nothing if not discriminating, believes that as little as possible should be done to freshen up antique furniture providing it is in a more or less presentable condition to begin with. Other schools will claim that a fine piece of furniture deserves all the skilled attention it can get and must at any cost be in a thoroughly pristine condition when it is put on sale in the showroom. The result is that many otherwise good pieces of antique furniture suffer from being over-restored to the point where the buyer may feel rather suspicious when he is considering a purchase. The surface may shine as though almost new, the patina can be all too perfect, and while it is perfectly obvious that the furniture has received skilled attention, there is still something slightly wrong. An indefinable but certain something detracts from its value, because it looks much too fine.

The attitude towards restoration has to be established very early on in the craftsman's mind, because it is something which will influence him for the rest of his career. It is difficult to improve on the injunction of Henry Francis Du Pont, founder of the Winterthur Museum, opened in October 1951 at Winterthur, Delaware, the greatest private collection of American antique furniture in the world. Du Pont rightly said: 'Don't doll things up', and for many years he campaigned steadfastly against the excessive refinishing of historic pieces of furniture, starting in 1919 and continuing up to his death. The results can be seen at Winterthur, which consists of a mansion containing many wholly original period rooms on five floors, the contents collected personally by Du Pont or his agents. The powerful and often dogmatic American collector often found himself at odds with the museum establishment not only in America but elsewhere in the world, when many curators and directors seemed to believe that every single piece on show to the public must be restored to the level at which it was manufactured. The Du Pont philosophy, on the other hand, was to select excellence of workmanship and simply display it, warts and all. This resulted in the Winterthur showplace becoming a leader as far as the assembly of objects was concerned, even to the point of incorporating panelled woodwork seasoned with sunshine, stains and woodsmoke.

Very few true craftsmen finishers will of their own volition entirely strip off what may well be the accumulation of a century or more of varnish, shellac and polish, and then deliberately refinish a piece of fine furniture. It is most definitely preferable to leave the piece much as it is, disregarding the protestations of the client who has the audacity to demand what amounts to a new reproduction finish. Some clients even sidle up to the craftsman and infer that a 'faked up' finish will be quite acceptable. Such a replacement finish will fool very few people, no matter how well executed. The dull sheen may well be a little too bright, the tint of the stain could be a little bit off, or else the general patina is too harsh and obvious. One or all of these things will betray it immediately to the discerning eye. The paint on the face of a tart could not be more obvious.

This does not set out to be a book of ethics, nor does it purport to give advice on what kind of a business code should be observed. Such matters are up to the individual craftsman. But it must be said that the shady dealer who arrives on the workshop doorstep with a piece of furniture and asks for it to be distressed and generally fudged up as an antique should be sent packing. What he is asking for is downright forgery. In the event of such a piece being sold for a fine fat figure under a subterfuge, it could mean that the finisher may also be implicated in the event of a legal action brought by the customer. No tradesman or craftsman will possibly relish being labelled a crook, even though he might protest that he was only following orders. A craftsman should be intimately interested in antiques restoration to the extent of quizzing any dealer as to whether the piece on which he is working will eventually be sold to a buyer who will be told that the piece has, in fact, been restored. The buyer should always be told what the extent of the restoration amounts to. In the present atmosphere, the finisher may not know that the cabinet-maker has perhaps replaced various sections. If the work has been done by a skilled cabinet-maker/restorer it is quite possible that a single piece of furniture may have been remade to the extent of about 45 per cent of its whole, using a selection of antique timbers taken from other pieces. If the surface finish is well done, the piece will finally appear to be wholly in period. Worse, it may be sold as 'genuine'. No craftsman can feel very satisfied about this state of affairs if he is true to his trade.

It should now be appreciated that the craftsman must move very warily in a trade in which a few unscrupulous dealers will not hesitate to make use of the craftsman to the extent of converting him into a forger and an unwitting accomplice to crime. It is noticeable that in periods when money is in plentiful supply, there is always a new generation of collectors who know very little about antiques but have been told, or have read, that they represent a jolly good investment. Consequently, every last piece of even vaguely antique furniture is quickly hauled out of the unscrupulous dealer's store, rapidly done up and then sold at inflated prices. At such times the restorer and the surface finisher often have more business than they can cope with. The opportunities for making a lot of money are so plentiful that they are hard to resist, and it is then that morals tend to be chucked out of the window at the moment when the battered furniture is rolled in through the door and the craftsman begins to puff cigars rather than hand-rolled cigarettes. But this warning has gone on long enough. . . . Before we go on it is possible to get some idea of the atmosphere of this strange and exotic trade from a review by A. J. Penty, published as long ago as 1930 and now reproduced by kind permission of The Architectural Review (Vol. 67, 1930, pp 34–35):

'In the early days of my career I spent a year or so in the employ of a firm of antique fakers. It was an accident of circumstance that got me there, but it was great fun and I decided to stay for the experience. The firm I was with faked furniture. But they did not belong to the order of super-fakers who prey upon collectors and literally live by fraud. They were the ordinary respectable fakers who give the public what they want, and value for money. True, they sold as old, pieces of furniture that were really new, but I am of the opinion that generally speaking the public wanted to be deceived. They had come to the conclusion that to furnish with antiques was "the thing" and they were only too ready to accept anything as old on a salesman's responsibility.

'My experience of the antique trade was not in this country, but in New York. I was employed as a designer. Why should a firm of antique fakers employ designers? For two reasons. The first is that the models were not generally available to copy from, but only photographs, often very small ones taken from illustrated papers. The designer took these photographs, improvised the details, and prepared working drawings; and only a designer familiar with the styles could do this. The other reason is peculiar to America. Designers were needed to adapt the old styles to American ideas of accommodation. The accommodation of old English furniture is different from that of American furniture. In consequence, if the average American were shown a piece of genuine Chippendale, he would not buy it because it would not give the accommodation he demands. But he has read in the papers that Chippendale furniture is *the* thing and he demands Chippendale. To overcome this difficulty Chippendale has to be re-designed to adapt it to American ideas of accommodation. Sometimes this makes exceptional demands on the ingenuity of the designer as, for instance, when he is required to design a Chippendale table with a centre leg, no precedent for which exists. For in America dining tables are mostly round. This kind of design was known among us as "Chippelwhite" – one of the firm's clients having one day asked to see specimens of that distinctive style.

'In this establishment there was no separate drawing-office. The designers worked in one of the showrooms on an upper floor. The shoppers who came in every day little suspected that the drawings upon which we were engaged would in due course make their appearance as furniture in rooms two or three hundred years old. Yet such was the case and at times even the elect were deceived. On one occasion a Queen Anne cabinet made its appearance in the showroom. It was, within the limits of the style, an original design, and it was so skillfully faked that the manager was deceived, mistaking it for a genuine antique, and called in one of the designers to admire it, when to his amusement the designer told him that he had designed it himself. (The antique trade is full of amusement, and it is recommended as a vocation for anyone who finds life rather dull). In the showroom in which we worked lengths of oak panelling occupied the wall space. They were supposed to be parts of panelled rooms that were stored away in the warehouse, though as a matter of fact the remaining pieces did not exist. Clients who desired oak-panelled rooms were shown these specimens. When any one of them expressed an admiration for a particular piece the salesman would address himself to one of my colleagues. "Wilkinson," he would say, "how many feet have we got of such and such panelling?" Wilkinson would refer to a book he kept in a drawer and discover it had not been entered up, and then he would make his way to the telephone. "Is that the store-house?" he would ask. "How many feet of panelling 37d have you got?" After waiting a moment he would inform the salesman in the presence of the client that there were seventy-eight feet of it. And when the client had gone, we all joined in a good laugh.

'This ruse was very effective. When a client took the bait, the dimensions of the room were secured and a design prepared to show how the panelling could be adapted to fit the room. This, of course, always involved piecing out of the "old work" by a piece "faked to match", and care was taken that the "match" was not too good. Fortunately for this procedure clients rarely asked to see the remainder of the panelling which was supposed to be in stock. When they did, one excuse after another was trumped up until sufficient time elapsed for it to be made. On one occasion when a client was very insistent, the salesmen had to feign illness and actually had to keep away from the business until the room was made.'

Refinishing and restoring call for a great and wide knowledge of the various woods. The craftsman should know as much and more than the cabinet-maker. The latter appreciates their working qualities while the former will know all about their properties as a 'canvas' for the multitude of colour and polish effects which are possible.

The cabinet-maker/restorer works quite apart from the surface finisher, but there are still a number of traditional establishments in which the two are in partnership, generally under the same roof. From the business point of view this can be a great advantage, because restoration can then be considered as a single operation rather than two separate jobs, one of which must be sub-contracted by one or other of the craftsmen. Then again, there are very few craftsmen with dual skills who work as both cabinet-maker and restorer. Needless to say, such people are much sought after by the antique dealing fraternity. More often than not, it is the highly skilled and perfectionist amateur who combines both trades, or skills, even if he does not necessarily do it for a living. One of the comforting thoughts is that such an amateur has in his hand a pearl beyond price, because he will always be able to make a living out of it if he has to. Every man should have more than one trade to which he can turn. And every trade has its own byways, such as the ability to model replacement sections of antique furniture.

One of the most common methods of restoring carved sections is by making a compound and using it to create the missing section, using a technique which is closely akin to casting. This is commonly used by the wood finisher who runs a combined workshop, but lacks the skill to copy intricately the carved sections. The compound will accept practically any form of surface finish, for the simple reason that it is manufactured from wood. There are various ways of making it, and most of them were perfected in the 1880s, and while they are still used in a few workshops, the actual method of manufacture is not generally known.

To make artificial wood a quantity of sawdust is required. In earlier years is was usual to powder coconut shell and use it as an additive. Another additive was dry coffee grounds. In fact, almost any natural fibre which can be reduced to a dust can be used. To make a strong artificial wood a piece of pine is cut with the grain into lengths the size of large matchsticks, soaked in water for as long as it takes to soften the fibres. It is then pounded and added to a binding agent. The result is suitable for large scale work, because the wood fibres act in much the same way as old-fashioned horsehair in plasterwork. An alternative use for it is as a firm foundation for much finer work, such as replacement carving.

The binding agent referred to above is ordinary carpenter's glue, which is sold in cake or sheet form. It is broken down by pounding with a hammer and then softened overnight in cold water, after which it is heated in a double boiler until it melts into a solution. Powdered glue size can be used as an easy alternative, and some guide as to the right quantity is gained by filling a warm jam jar with size to a depth of one-third and then filling it up with boiling water, stirring until the solution reaches the consistency of treacle.

The glue solution should be put in a saucepan and left to simmer with frequent stirring. If it is reheated it will continue to lose an appreciable amount of its power, and it is necessary to use it almost immediately.

Prior to using the glue, add about one ounce of bichromate of potash. This will create waterproofing yet still accept surface finishes of all kinds. Alternatively, a bichromate of potash solution can be painted on the artifical wood when it has set hard, and this will provide a waterproof barrier.

Mixing the glue with the sawdust calls for experiment, some judgement and experience of making pudding-like substances. Mixing should go on until the paste becomes stiff. This is the right working consistency. When it finally hardens it will be like a piece of wood which can be sawn or chiselled in either direction without chipping or fragmenting. Everything depends on the amount of sawdust used. Whereas softwood sawdust will mix readily and set hard, depending on the amount of glue used, the hardwoods naturally take longer but require less glue. One of the best ways of ensuring that the finished artificial wood is quite even in texture is to sieve the sawust before the mixing starts.

The working consistency of the paste will be governed to a great extent by the nature of the work to be done. If, for instance, a papier mâché mould has been taken of the piece to be replaced, and it has a great deal of intricate detail, then the artificial wood should be malleable and capable of being pushed into all the recessed areas of detail. It is always advisable to liberally oil a mould or original before the paste is applied, otherwise the two will stick together and it will be necessary to fracture the mould during the separation. If it is oiled, the cast should come away cleanly.

Artificial wood can also be used to take an imprint of a section of carved wood providing the original is oiled or greased to assist separation. Once the slab of artificial wood has been placed on the section, it is gently pressed against the master surface, allowed to harden and then carefully lifted away, to be used as a mould for the casting of

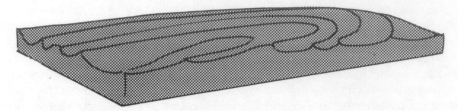

FIGURE 56. The papier mâché mould should be made in such a way that it has an ample base which makes it easy to handle and manipulate.

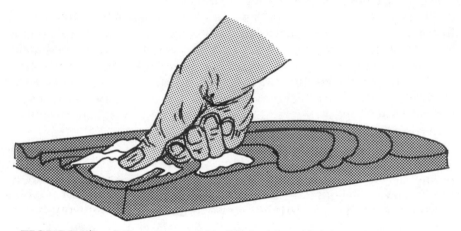

FIGURE 57. When the mould is filled with artificial wood the material should be forced into the carved detail with the thumb, ensuring that all trapped air is expelled and building up sufficient thickness to create stability and tolerance for cutting and shaping when fitting in place.

artificial wood, using the same working method.

But most of all, artificial wood is a really excellent susbstance for filling holes and modelling broken and missing edges of furniture, because it works very cleanly and sticks firmly to almost any surface. While it is being worked it will naturally have a certain amount of stickiness, depending on how it was mixed, and it will probably adhere to the fingers. For this reason any modelling should be done with clay modelling tools, and they should be dipped frequently into hot water to help the separation of tool and material. Like synthetic plastic wood, artificial wood is subject to a certain amount of shrinkage, though not as much as the plastic material, and due allowance should be made for this. When holes are filled, the amount used should be just a little bit more so that it stands proud of the surface and can be sanded away when hard and dry to make a flush surface.

Another use for artifical wood is the filling of any loose joints which cannot be remade. As far as the restoration of antiques is concerned, there is an obvious advantage in being able to stabilise joints rather than having a cabinet-maker recut them or, worse, entirely remake the section, using a wood which may match only approximately. It is also better to use artificial wood rather than pack the joint with glue and slivers of wood, which are unreliable after only a short period of wear.

As far as surface finishing is concerned, any colouring can be safely added to the artificial wood at the mixing stage. Alternatively a surface finish can be successfully applied after the material has hardened *in situ*. Much depends upon the location. As a rule water-based stains are better than spirit stains.

Artificial wood can also be used as a very sensitive and responsive modelling compound in cases where it is impractical to make a cast. In such instances a concealed fine-mesh wire cage is placed over the surface or a series of metal rods are driven into the surface, and the artificial wood is applied to form a block which, when dry and hard, can be carefully carved. If the area is likely to be very delicate and suffer from any vibration during carving, then it is advisable to use extra sharp tools, rifflers and files to create the required shape. An alternative base, or armature, can be made with dowelling pegs which are driven into the base area with the artificial wood modelling around and over them. The precise number of dowels per square inch cannot be specified because every job happens to be different. It may, however, be useful to know that more rather than less dowels should be used to create a firm base bed for the compound.

Some hand-moulded or modelled sections will require an ultra-fine material. The following is suggested.

Use limewood sawdust, which should be thoroughly dried in a wide pan over a very gentle heat. It is then pounded to a fine dust. Equal quantities of gum tragacanth and gum arabic are mixed in solution and then stirred into the sawdust, after which the mixture is placed in a low oven to dry out. Water-based colour may be added if required.

Yet another compound for very delicate work can be made by using fish glue as a binding agent, but it is likely to let out a pungent odour during mixing.

Artificial wood can be used quite effectively for the repair of marquetry. It is used in the same way as putty to fill in the areas where the pieces have been broken beyond repair or lost. Here again, the material can be either body coloured or else stained *in situ* as soon as it is hard. Allowances should be made for shrinkage, although this is likely to be minimal in small shallow spaces.

The restoration of curved surfaces can pose a number of problems, for artificial wood may crack as it dries, requiring patching with a further amount of the material. A great deal depends upon the amount of material in relation to, say, a curved section, and here it may be necessary to adopt other methods, perhaps by the use of wood shavings.

The thickness of the shavings used in restoration work is crucial, and they should be as thin as possible, perhaps almost transparent, and made by planing along the grain. The longer the shaving the better. The shavings are soaked in warm water and then laid flat and saturated with flour paste, making them very flexible and removing the tendency to form curves.

To fashion the wet shavings it is necessary to use something on which a base layer can be put down. This is best provided by a sheet of thick drawing paper or brown wrapping paper. It should be thickly coated with flour paste followed by a layer of shavings, all laid in the same direction. When it is completely covered, a second coat of shavings is added, always ensuring that a generous quantity of paste has been laid down beforehand. Before this second layer has hardened, a rolling pin is used to make a compact layer. One further coat of shavings is applied, and, when hard, the result should be a flexible piece of wood composition. When the piece is quite hard, it can be tested for flexibility by bending it. This material is easily shaped by cutting with scissors, and it can then be located with a strong adhesive or it can be pinned into place.

Most commercial wood finishing workshops receive frequent visits from local antique dealers who simply want their recent acquisitions and warehouse stock freshened up as far as the surface finish is concerned, and there may be relatively little call for expensive cabinet-maker restoration. In such a case the answer is the use of a general utility polish which can be applied without any danger of hazard to the majority of surfaces. Practically any surface can be freshened by the application of a solution of shellac and denatured alcohol consisting of about one part of shellac in thirty parts of alcohol. This is rubbed over the surface in an even film, followed by prolonged hard rubbing to the point where the shellac begins to bite and bind, making it harder to move the cotton cloth with any smoothness. At this point there should be a quite dramatic change, when the rubber suddenly starts to glide more easily. The surface will begin to show signs of polish. The point at which the rubbing should cease is at the discretion of the craftsman, but prolonged rubbing will result in a mirror finish, while an early halt will provide a dull sheen, which is preferably for certain types of furniture. This is where experience and knowledge begin to count. Oak, for instance, should not be so treated. It is best freshened by simple washing with ordinary soap and water after a preliminary wipe down with very weak ammonia. Any carved sections are also cleaned with weak ammonia, using a soft brush to get into all the detail. Some finishers apply their own special preparations to oak in order to heighten its beauty, and one of these is made by putting 70 parts of linseed oil into a wide vessel, and adding 20 parts of litharge, 20 parts of powdered minim and 10 parts of lead acetate. These should be boiled together until the linseed oil turns brown. The mixture is then taken from the heat and supplemented with 160 parts of oil of turpentine. The ingredients are generally available from industrial chemical suppliers. As a standard preparation this is probably one of the best not only for oak surface finishing but many other types of wood and the treatment of rare wood carvings on account of its preservative qualities.

The commercial craftsman will not always be able to work in his own workshop. Many clients will not move their prized pieces of furniture. In such cases the craftsman must work on the premises. This means that a 'travelling workshop' is required and, unlike the plumber of legend who usually leaves some important tools at home, he will have to carry all the necessities about with him. Composing a kit which is suitable for all jobs is a difficult task, calling for a mixture of experience, prophecy and sheer instinct, and it may be useful to note the following composition of what should be regarded as the basics to meet practically all eventualities.

8 four-ounce glass bottles with cork stoppers.
1 small and 1 large camel hair brush.
8 aniline colours consisting of spirit-soluble black, orange, yellow, Bismark brown, walnut, oak, green, methylene blue – say one ounce of each.
1 quart denatured alcohol.
6 sticks of various coloured shellac, including light, dark and medium oak, transparent, ebony, walnut and mahogany.
1 spirit lamp for melting shellac stick and a table knife for applying it.
1 pocket knife for shredding shellac.
Selection of sandpaper from coarse to fine.
1 ounce of fine pumice powder.
1 pint white bleached shellac.
1 pint liquid polishing wax.
1 lb paraffin wax.
1 pint turpentine.
And, of course, a plentiful supply of clean cotton rags.

The aniline colours are prepared by filling each of the eight bottles with denatured alcohol and then adding one teaspoon of each of the colours. These are the stock stains which will meet the needs of the majority of jobs. They will be very strong if mixed in the suggested proportions, but are diluted as required. There is an additional advantage in the fact that they can be mixed with other colours, one example of which is Bismark brown and walnut brown, which is compatible with red mahogany. Black and orange will yield a deep brown. Hues mixed in this way need only an equal quantity of white shellac added to give quick and accurate matching colours. Such stains are not simply padded on with a wad of cloth but applied much more delicately, using one of the camel hair brushes to put on the first coat and allowing it to dry, then checking for depth of colour penetration before proceeding. Any number of successive coats can be applied to achieve an exact match. This is followed by applying a light coat of paraffin oil, which is rubbed into the pores of the wood. Too much rubbing may well dislodge the colour if it has not had enough time to settle, and this means that any applied friction should be restrained. If the overall finish is dull, then all that is necessary is a touch of paraffin wax and a light rub with a piece of flannel or cotton.

When shellac is used as a filler for any dents and bruises, it should not be made smooth or mirror-like, because antique furniture has noticeable pores, scratches and innumerable other marks. Any repair which looks perfectly immaculate will probably stand out and look far too glossy. The solution, whether using a wax filler or shellac, is to use a sharp needle to make false pores and other marks, sometimes working across the grain in the interests of realism. There is no point in claiming that this can be a very quick and effective repair job. On the contrary, it calls for a great deal of patience if it is to look entirely realistic, and there may well be some cases in which an entire area has to be refinished to match in with a relatively small repair. It is always advisable to do this, otherwise the eye of the owner will in future always be drawn to the repair. To be absolutely effective, it should be very difficult and almost impossible to locate the area of the repair.

When a cabinet-maker has replaced a broken section or a joint it should fit snugly and, like the finisher's skill, be quite unnoticeable. But there may be instances of either very poor restoration or sections of the furniture where a convincing joint just cannot be made. There will be hairline gaps which have to be disguised. One instance is the turned pillar which is fitted into the base, leaving as much as 1/16th of an inch gap. Some cabinet-makers believe that this sort of defect makes for greater realism and a suggestion of age and handicraft, but a lot of collectors do not subscribe to this view, and they appeal to the finisher to help them. It is not at all difficult to fill such gaps, using a mixture of paraffin wax mixed with the appropriate colour or the artificial wood which was discussed earlier in this chapter. Once again, it is wise to embellish such repairs with artificial faults by making dents in the soft wax or artificial wood or by scribing some scratches. The extent to which this should go depends entirely on the condition of the surrounding original wood.

*   *   *

We began this chapter with a discussion of the ethics of the restoration of antiques. It can perhaps best be summed up in a single word, restraint. Anything which is overdone will look obvious. If it is underdone, on the other hand, it will probably pass muster. There are very few manufactured articles, including furniture, which are totally free of flaws, and it may well be that the finisher should bear this in mind whenever the client asks him to restore a piece to what is often called 'first class condition'. Exactly how this should be interpreted is up to the craftsman rather than the client. The true craftsman should be an advisor as well as a practical workman.

29

Restoring and Refinishing Minor Imperfections

FOR the craftsman who wishes to acquire antique furniture and refinish it, the initial knowledge must be concerned with the type of finish which was prevalent when the piece was originally made. It is not at all unusual to discover early Victorian occasional tables smothered with cheap modern varnish or even a polyurethaned Queen Anne chair. Some antique furniture dealers have their stock items quickly refinished or touched up purely for the sake of attracting the less informed buyer when trade is slack. It is simple to detect such pieces, for any carved sections will have the edges sharpened up or, alternatively, rubbed with steel wool to create a fake patina, while the flat surfaces will betray evidence of the scraper and, occasionally, the blowtorch.

The antique which looks a little too perfect is always suspect. One of the clues is the surface finish. Practically all finishes had a shellac base up to the beginning of the Victorian period, because varnishes and cellulose finishes were not invented until later. The varnish which largely supplanted shellac had the virtue of being a waterproof sealant. Recently-varnished furniture will often appear to be in its 'original' condition, whereas shellac will often have white opaque marks caused by dampness. It is not waterproof and it quickly turns white if it is left wet or stands in a humid atmosphere. Of all the finishes varnish remains the most durable apart from the essentially modern nitrocellulose lacquer. Yet it is rare to find antique furniture with its original varnish finish. In the space of a hundred years or so it has probably been stripped and refinished if not once then several times, and it is quite possible that progressively inferior materials have been used for each separate operation.

In some cases one coat of varnish will have been applied on top of another. This certainly poses a major problem as 'clean sweep' finishing is concerned, because there are very few truly effective methods of removing all evidence of varnish. If common paint remover is applied, it will simply cause a sort of wrinkling and look like old skin which will subsequently reset in hard ridges. Lacquer, on the other hand, will usually dissolve in its own thinners, while shellac will dissolve in methyl alcohol. These are the standard workshop tests which are used to determine the nature of a finish before any large-scale refinishing is embarked upon.

Deterioration is caused not only by misuse but also by the atmosphere itself. Much old furniture suffers from blushing, and looks as though steam has somehow managed to enter the polished surface and become petrified there. If polished furniture is left in a damp atmosphere for any length of time it will almost invariably develop a bloom of some kind. Bowls and vases left on finished surfaces, including even those with an expertly varnished surface, frequently develop white rings. This is easy enough to cure, because all it calls for is a gently rubbing with the finest grade of steel wool lubricated with a few drops of raw linseed oil, always working along the grain of the wood. An alternative is to use pumice powder instead of steel wool, mixing it to a creamy consistency with oil and using as a rubber a piece of soft flannel or well washed cotton wrapped round a block of wood or cork. The friction will gradually re-fuse the surface coating. Haste is not important and a frequent inspection is necessary to ensure that the grinding action is not affecting the layer immediately beneath the whiteness. Once it has vanished, the area can be repolished with wax. But if pumice is used as an abrasive, it will be necessary to remove all vestiges of the oil lubricant before applying the polish.

Many pieces of antique furniture suffer from having small areas chipped out of the finish, sometimes even removing a few wood fibres into the bargain, but in general the wood itself is unaffected. These little dents and pittings can be repaired by the use of the shellac stick, obtainable from the majority of suppliers who specialise in materials for wood finishers. The surface to be treated should be facing upwards if possible and easily accessible. The first move is to clean it out with a soft brush, and then carefully coat the interior of the chip with varnish, ensuring that it dries perfectly hard. It is very important to see that the lip of the break is well coated, but avoid any overlapping. When the inside of the little crater is well coated, it should be allowed to stand for about twenty-four hours, after which the process is repeated and this, too, is allowed to dry and harden. Over a period of several days the layers of varnish should completely fill the dent. When it is finally dry and hard it should be very gently sanded level, using a block of wood which is much wider than the imperfection. The sandpaper should be of the finest grade. When the surface is quite flush and well smoothed by the abrasive, it can be waxed. In some cases it will be adviseable to tint the varnish in order to achieve a colour match with the surrounding area, but if the chip is not very obtrusive, the application of the polish will drag colouring material over it, totally obscuring the fault.

Furniture which has been placed in a position where the sun shines directly on it, day after day, will sometimes develop a series of minute cracks over the exposed surface. While it may look very serious and damaging to those who know nothing about such things, the cause is simply that the heat of the sun has dried out the finish, which is generally shellac. That is why the Victorians used their commonsense and closed the heavy velour curtains of the parlour to protect their furniture. Crazing is quite simple to cure. All that is needed is a redissolving and resolution of the old shellac finish. Regardless of how old the finish happens to be, it can as a rule be softened with denatured alcohol or thinners, after which the near-liquid film is smoothed out with a pad soaked in thinners and left to dry and harden in exactly the same way as a new surface finish is treated.

Apart from all the other abuses which it suffers, antique furniture is more often than not bruised in some way or another. Soft woods such as pine can be quite badly dented, but hardwoods suffer less. However, no matter how deep it may be, a dent can be removed by the simple expedient of forcing water into the fibres. Once they are softened, they will swell back to their original position. Exactly how to force the moisture deep into the fibres is not difficult. All that is needed is a boiling kettle with steam steadily issuing from the spout. Alternatively, a wet cloth can be placed over the dent and a hot domestic iron pressed down on it. This is, however, not simple if the dent is in a piece of furniture with a very good surface finish because it will be necessary to removed the finish and then refinish it again once the dent has been lifted.

Although lacquer is a remarkably tough material, it will sometimes crack or craze under extremes of temperature, and this is what generally happens when a piece of furniture has been maltreated or left in an exceptionally sunny window for years on end. Like shellac, lacquer will reconstitute itself if it is treated with lacquer thinner, which should be applied with a fine brush. If the crazing is extensive and very detailed it will be necessary to carefully paint the thinner along each of the lines to ensure complete penetration. When the lacquer has softened, a gentle pressure with the heel of the hand will bring the edges together again. If there are any brush marks remaining they can be abraded with fine steel wool until they become unnoticeable, and then a coat of wax polish applied. It may sometimes be necessary to wash a lacquered surface

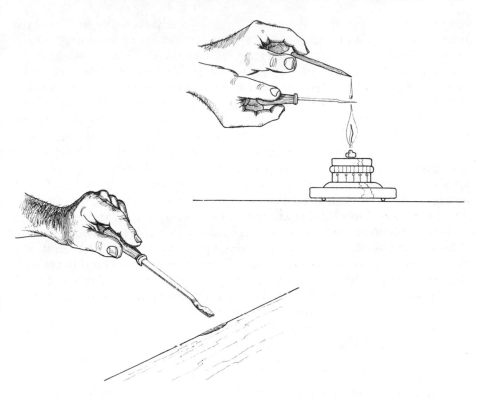

FIGURE 58. Application of hot shellac to remedy an imperfection in the surface of the wood. Shellac reacts best at a temperature which can be determined only by practice. If it is too hot, it boils and burns, if it is too cool it will react sluggishly. The answer is in working the material in the flame with the metal blade at a favourable temperature, using a slightly curved knife or tool to ease the tipping of the liquid shellac into the wood hole or dent.

with turpentine to remove earlier wax polishes before applying the thinners, which will not otherwise have any effect. One of the difficulties in working with lacquer thinners is that brushes quickly get gummed up, and so it is advisable always to have a selection of brushes suspended in a jar of thinners to ensure that they are free of lacquer and ready for immediate use. Brushes are tools and they should be treated with care.

One of the most useful tools in the surface finisher's workshop is the shellac stick, which is simply old fashioned sealing wax, obtainable not only in traditional scarlet but a variety of other colours as well. To use the shellac stick properly takes experience. The purpose is to perfectly fill in and level dents and holes, bruises, cigarette burns and other imperfections. A lamp with a clean and steady flame is an absolute necessity, also a knife with a slight curve on the blade, an emery block, and some linseed oil. The craftsman who works as a restorer will usually stock a large number of shellac sticks in all colours. He will have mastered the ability to create colour matches by mixing different colours in a molten state. The procedure for using the stick is as follows. The knife point is heated in the lamp flame and so is the shellac stick at the same time. A small drop of the molten shellac is placed on the tip of the blade. The drop is then carefully encouraged to fall straight into the hole or dent, where it will immediately start to cool and harden. It takes practice, a lot of practice, to judge exactly where it will fall and how much will be needed. It is also tricky to balance the stuff on the end of the blade. Beginners find that they have to make several attempts before they can fill the hole due to shaking hands and sheer nervous tension. The final step is to smear a film of oil over the shellac and the surrounding area and then grind level. The colour match should, ideally, be perfect, but if it is not precisely what was intended, a very minute amount of pigment can be smeared across it and the final polish applied after removing all trace of the oil.

Another method of filling deep scratches and dents is to use coloured wax. There is nothing very special about the wax for the job. In fact, children's crayons can be used, and they can also be mixed to achieve any special colour.

The hole is first cleaned out and the quantity of wax required to fill it is assessed. Some wax is melted in a spoon and poured into the hole, then allowed to cool. Any excess can be carefully shaved away, using a common table knife. The area can then be refinished with a mixture of two parts of denatured alcohol to one part of shellac, followed by a coat of shellac or varnish, after which it should be rubbed with fine steel wool and finally waxed. Such repairs can be made practically invisible if they are properly done. All that is needed is the basic skill and the right materials.

Clients often ask the craftsman finisher to do something about old light-coloured chairs which have developed a series of ugly black streaks. The reason for the streaking is generally something of a mystery even though the chairs may have been in a family for many years. The streaks have simply appeared and no matter how much elbow grease is used, they cannot be polished away. People continue to apply various kinds of polish in the vain hope that the marks will miraculously vanish. But, of course, they stay where they are. With the successive applications of polish, they are all the more securely sealed under layer after layer. The cause of the black streaking is more often than not the all-pervasive lampblack which was used by many Victorian finishers to create a sort

of imitation rosewood grain. Over the years the rest of the graining effect
has worn away, leaving only the lampblack. One of the more dubious
qualitites of lampblack is that it penetrates so deeply that it cannot be
abraded away, nor can it successfully be bleached out. When these
unsightly streaks occur, the only solution is to stain the area to a dark
colour so that they will be obliterated. An attempt at rosewood graining
may well cover the streaks if a red-mahogany stain is used in conjunction
with a surface glaze made by mixing two tablespoons of burnt umber in
a half to three-quarters of a pint of varnish. Alternatively, of course, the
affected piece of furniture can always be stained down to a tint which
approximates to the black and the streaks will then merge obligingly into
the background.

It would, of course, be possible to completely strip the black-streaked
furniture, and while the streaks may remain in a more or less vestigial
form, the surface would at least provide a 'clean palette' on which the
refinishing is done. Surface stripping is not always possible by
immersing the furniture in a tank of trisodium sulphate, a substance
much used in the pine stripping trade. It may be advisable to strip
certain pieces of furniture section by section in order to check the general
quality of the wood and the construction of the piece as the work
proceeds. In such a case it is advisable to use a fast acting caustic
solution. There is nothing very special about caustic soda as far as
surface stripping is concerned but, be warned, it is caustic, and can be as
dangerous as nitric or sulphuric acid. The important working factor is to
make a solution which is strong enough to act very quickly and not give
the water content enough time to penetrate the wood. This will cut down
the drying time. One bucketful of water should have as much as two or
three pounds of caustic soda dissolved in it for a fast acting solution. If
the water is hot, the action will be even faster. In order to create a
working medium which can easily be localised and not drip uncontroll-
ably all over the furniture, it is a good idea to mix in two cupfuls of
wallpaper paste, which assists in the application of the solution to
vertical areas. This solution is strong enough to remove two or three
coats of paint at a time, providing it is applied very hot and plentifully.
After ten minutes a softwood will start to turn brown, but in some cases
the wallpaper paste may start to dry and flake off before the paint begins
to peel. This can be counteracted by applying another layer of the
caustic solution or by dabbing some hot water on the coating. Once the
wood has been neutralised by washing down with neat table vinegar, it
can be lightened with a conventional bleach. Ordinary household bleach
should do this within an hour or two, after which the workpiece should
be completely dried out and sanded in preparation for staining or
repairing.

Mention has already been made of trisodium sulphate, which is the chemical used in the pine-stripping trade. It is used as a rule in the ratio of one lb to about six quarts of water, and it has the great advantage of needing no neutralising. It is simply washed on to a surface and left for a time, when it will effectively move paint, polish and any other deposit. As a second cousin to caustic soda, it also darkens the wood. As a mass production chemical it is probably more economic than caustic soda, because entire tankfuls can be mixed at a very low cost for dipping purposes. It is well known that it also attacks joints and may reduce some pieces of furniture to a heap of sticks and fragments.

When furniture is made in a workshop the wood may well display some irritating black marks, usually called mineral stains, and they can occur in the best and most choice pieces of timber. Nevertheless, some careless furniture makers still proceed to use the wood, and the furniture eventually reaches the market complete with its black marks, which look like small cigarette burns. The cause of the marks occurs during the growth of the tree and during the time spent in the wood stacks before manufacture when moisture somehow manages to saturate certain areas. It does not dry out completely and acts as a catalyst deep in the grain. Such marks can be removed by using a saturated solution of oxalic crystals, which is also useful for other small bleaching jobs, including the treatment of ancient oak which has turned black over the years. Restorers often use it along the edges of furniture where a light patina or highlight is required. It is, however, extremely strong stuff and it should not be left too long on the wood. A sign that it has finished its task is the deposit of white powder which appears when it dries out. This is the signal that it should be irrigated with clean water. In some cases the oxalic acid may react on the lighter wood stains by turning them pale pink, but this can be avoided if the area is first washed down with a mixture of ammonia and water in a ratio of one to three. The ammonia will provide a quick penetration medium and carry the oxalic acid straight into the wood pores and short circuit the pinking.

30

Découpage

ONTRARY to widespread belief, découpage is not simply a
matter of sticking scraps of coloured paper on to wood and
covering with varnish. It is a technique which provides many
opportunities for refinement and adaptation and in the hands
of a true artist it can provide a finish which cannot be created by the use
of any other single technique. It was the forerunner of what is now
known as decalcomania, an American late eighteenth century technique,
by the use of which it was possible to transfer pictures from paper on to
furniture, porcelain and glass, using a photographic process. Modern
découpage probably started in the eighteenth century in France. Its
origins were not French, however, because it was earlier used in Italy on
intricately patterned lacquer furniture which reached France from
Japan and China, when it was known as *lacca contrafatta*. From the
earliest times the practitioner of the craft was called a *découpeur*, although
the term is seldom used nowadays. Some commentators believe that
découpage does not require anything more than a facility for selecting
pictures and applying them in a satisfying conjunction. This is far from
the truth. It does call for skill. The fact that there is a lot of inferior and
amateurish work about endorses the fact. But much the same can be said
about practically any surface finish. One finds good work, one naturally
shudders at bad work. It is all in the hands of the craftsman while the
final judgement is in the eyes of the client.

The weakness of découpage as a surface finish is that it is somehow
associated with the dilettante. Obviously, low standard work looks ugly
and shabby, and yet in the eighteenth century the art was lifted to a very
high level, using mainly cuttings from hand-coloured engravings. At a
time when Chinese lacquer was not in very plentiful supply but the

demand remained very high because ownership implied high status, an entirely new form was developed. Known as *arte povero* and *lacche povero*, literally, the poor man's lacquer, it consisted of conventional découpage mass produced in small factories. In Italy it was enhanced by the use of gesso, which meant that inferior woods could be used. But it was in France that *l'art scriban* became all the rage. Far from simply affixing ordinary coloured engravings to wood and then covering them with varnish, it employed paper cutouts in the form of lace-like designs and offset them with coloured engravings of flowers and insects. There were, too, the portraits of François Boucher (1703–1770), the most representative French painter of eighteenth century *art galant*, Antoine Watteau (1684–1721) and, most notably, Jean Baptiste Pillement (1728–1808), who imitated the Chinese style.

Découpage, while then a minor art as far as the furniture decorator was concerned, nevertheless had its natural influences. In Germany the simple decorative style of the Bidermeier school of the 1820s to the 1860s utilised embossed papers, and it was this which strongly influenced the English *nouveaux riches* school. The number of famous people who practised découpage is impressive. It includes Marie Antoinette, Beau Brummel and Lord Byron. Some idea of the size of the obsession can be drawn from the fact that when a craftswoman called Mary Delany died in 1787 she left over one thousand original flower designs cut from tissue paper and water-coloured, ready for use.

It is difficult to place découpage in the American scene with any great precision. The German Biedermeier school continued to cast its influence well into the 1900s and onwards, and it would seem that a nation of mixed cultures paid greater attention to the craft than did the English. There was, for instance, a major exhibition of the work of Caroline Duer in 1957 at the Addison Gallery in Andover, Mass, but for at least a quarter of a century prior to that there had been a flourishing découpage industry, the centre figures of which were Maybelle Manning, who studied the technique in France, and her son, Hiram. Others involved included Dorothy Harrower, Patricia Nimmocks, Frances Wing and Marie Mitchell. The fact that women have up to the present been leading practitioners in this particular branch of surface finishing and decoration should not deter male craftsmen.

It should perhaps be said that there is something of a mental block to découpage on the part of many craftsmen, and this may be due to the fact that the motifs which are applied to the wood are 'ready-made' and the work of some other artist. The finished product may even be thought of as 'secondhand' and something for which the craftsman can claim only a minor credit for affixing and varnishing. The doubts and the misgivings are not unfamiliar and can be found in the field of art. When Max Ernst, who led the Surrealists, and his school in the Twenties and

Thirties started to exhibit collages, the public initially sniffed at them, declaring that they were nothing more than paste-ups and artistic scrapings. The now firmly established forms, known as montage and collage, are in the same group, the only difference being the application and final treatment. Yet there is no real argument about the merits of it except a purely aesthetic one.

The word 'découpage' has never changed, but it remains a stumbling block for many people because they do not know exactly what it means. The meaning is that pictures are cut out of books, magazines and other publications and stuck on furniture, the edges are chamfered to get rid of the sharply cut look, some restrained sanding is used, and the surface is then heavily and protectively varnished. In another meaning, it is also applied design. The word 'design' has to be treated with care, because it is not possible to immediately rush into découpage and make a success of it simply by chopping bits out of magazines and sticking them on the wood. The proportions of the design have a very important role to play, for too big and oppressive a design will overpower the object to which the design is affixed, while too minute a design will become trivial and may go unnoticed. What is needed is design organisation since time spent on arranging and rearranging maybe thrice that required for fixing and varnishing.

While specially printed and coloured découpage sheets are available and produced on the very desirable thin paper, the secret of découpage lies in its uniqueness. This means that the beginner may well start by using designs from mass-produced sheets, but he should quickly gravitate to the designs which he finds for himself in magazines, greetings cards, catalogues, playing cards, picture postcards, gift wrapping paper, wallpaper and the old and often spine-broken books of engravings which turn up in the bargain boxes of secondhand booksellers. Other materials include gold and silver foil, though this should be used with restraint because it can look tawdry. When he is selecting printed material the craftsman should know whether the print quality is good or bad and whether it will last or fade. Some colour supplements are suitable, and even if they are heavily printed on both sides, the desired picture can be sealed with an acrylic sealer such as is used to protect charcoal and pencil drawings to prevent any print-through. The test is to find out whether the printing ink is aniline, which runs and cannot be used. This is done very simply by soaking the section in water. Other non-aniline printing inks are 'fast' and can be used for découpage. In an age of fine art printing, many desirable items will appear on thick art paper, which can be thinned down by about fifty per cent by coating the reverse side with white vinegar and then rubbing it gently with the fingertips until the fibres come away. An entire layer can be removed very quickly by this means, after which the print should be

FIGURE 59. Decoupage composition is not done haphazardly, but should be carefully planned and only gradually built up. Patterns or repeat patterns, can be created; practically any subject can be portrayed and it is also possible to combine such media as cutouts and painted sections.

sprayed with charcoal-and-pencil sealer, and then dried. An alternative method is to spray with sealer, allow it to dry and then place the paper in warm water for up to fifteen minutes. It can then he laid flat and rubbed with the fingertips to remove a layer of the paper fibres.

We will assume for the present that the craftsman intends applying the cutouts to furniture. It may be necessary to colour the printed material. Old engravings, for instance, can often be improved by colouring. Oil-based colour pencils are used to tint and render engravings, and the process should start by putting in the lighter tints, using very sharp pencils, and then gradually working in the more dense colours. When the colouring is completed, it should be sprayed with acrylic sealer. Two or three coats should be put on to make sure that all the dyes are locked behind a shield against the time when varnishing is done. Some craftsmen do not favour this particular sealer, but make their own, consisting of three parts white shellac mixed with one part denatured alcohol. This provides a very thin fluid which is brushed on to the paper. Only one or two coats are required for a perfect seal.

The treatment of the wood is as important as any other surface finish. In the case of plain and bare wood, it is necessary to decide beforehand whether a painted base is required. If so, the wood will need to be sanded and cleaned in the usual way, after which it can be treated with a spirit-based stain or painted. If the latter, it is advisable first to apply three or four coats of shellac. Another possibility is gesso. A very inferior and bruised and chipped surface can be made completely smooth, using a branded gesso which, when polished with a piece of damp silk, will yield a surface like fine porcelain, providing a very attractive background for the cut paper designs.

There are many different schools of thought when it comes to a consideration of how the printed design should be cut. Some claim that straight-ended nail scissors are best, others use scalpels, while others adopt curved nail scissors. Regardless of which tool is used, there is one basic rule about the system of cutting. It is not advisable to cut directly round the whole of the design in the initial stages. Instead, some rough-cutting should be done to remove the excess paper, gradually working inwards towards the edge of the design. Many designs have interior areas which must to be removed so that the base finish will show through. By the time several of these have been cut out, the paper area will probably become fragile. The solution to this is to leave temporary 'bridges' to hold the sections together until the final stages. All the cutting must be very precise and any ragged edges must be cleaned up, otherwise they will show as feathering when the paper is fixed to the wood.

Assuming that the cutting is completed and the placing of the cut pieces has been settled, the next stage is to bond them in place on the wood. One of the great points of contention in découpage is the choice of an adhesive. It is governed by the need for it to be water-soluble when it is used but non water-soluble when it is dry. It must also possess the quality of not drying too swiftly, and it should not affect the printing ink. Several branded paper adhesives are available from specialist-suppliers and one based on petroleum such as 'Cow Gum' would be suitable. When it is applied, all that is needed is a film rather than a thick coating, which may trap air bubbles. One of the occupational nuisances of découpage is the air bubble, which shows itself only after the paper has been applied to the surface. It can as a rule be dispelled by piercing the paper with a very fine needle and expelling the air by pressure, though this is something to be avoided, because the hole will often be at a strategic point of the design and may have to be disguised with a touch of pigment. Various thicknesses of paper react differently to the type of adhesive used. In general, it is best to use a thin glue on a thin paper, and it can be brushed on or else applied with the fingertips. Most craftsmen use their fingers and keep a damp rag or a sponge handy to clean their fingertips.

The sequence of working depends very much on the craftsman. In general, any of the flourishes and general ornamentation which may surround the main design should be added last of all, because the design should grow outwards from the centre. The scheme of the design should be such as to avoid any overlaps of the separate segments, because this will create a double thickness of the paper and can, when the varnishing is done, create a build up.

The final stage, when the adhesive has set and the design is completely in place, is the varnishing. A number of variations are possible. The accepted découpage varnish is either glosssy or matt, or dull, and it must, above all, be waterproof. A conventional copal varnish has to be thinned down by something like forty per cent, using an appropriate thinners, such as turpentine. On the other hand, the polyurethane varnish is ideal, although it should be pointed out that it is not easy to rub down with abrasives due to its toughness when dry.

The varnish, whether copal or polyurethane, is applied with an oxhair varnish brush which does not suffer from any shedding of the bristles. If it is a new brush, bought specially for the job, then it should be well washed in varnish thinners so that all the warehouse and shop dust is wrung and stubbed out of it. Dust is the dire enemy of découpage, and so the room in which the varnishing is done must be as dust-free as possible. The technique of applying the varnish is that the brush should be charged to about three-quarters of its bristle length and then pressed on the side of the container to dispel air bubbles and surplus varnish. It is applied first in one direction and then the other to create a perfectly even film. If the work is done against the natural light, it will be possible to examine the film as it grows on the surface and ensure that any dry patches are equally covered. Each coat is rubbed down with a superfine sandpaper and then thoroughly cleaned, using a pad soaked with denatured alcohol, which evaporates very rapidly. Abrading is not required for a matt surface.

It is debatable just how many coats of varnish should be applied. Some purists believe that there should be as many as thirty, but this is excessive. A lot must depend on the nature of the workpiece. Furniture, for instance, has to be durable, and may even benefit from thirty coats, but a purely decorative article, such as a section of wall panelling, will require only ten or fifteen, bearing in mind that it will from time to time be dusted or wiped with a damp cloth. The final finish is beeswax polish.

Some designs may benefit from an antique effect. This is done by using an alternative to clear varnish. The formula for an ageing effect is as follows: mix into clear varnish a very small amount of linseed oil, turpentine and some raw umber to impart a slightly brown tint. A standard tint can be made by using three parts of turpentine and umber to one part of varnish. Obviously, a greater richness of tone and a suggestion of age can be created by adding more raw umber, but it should not be overdone, otherwise the design may be almost totally obscured by a brown cloudiness. An overall browness can be applied by brushing in the way previously described. The alternative is to wipe it over with a cotton pad, depositing the umber tint more prominently around the lines of the cutout. Only one preliminary coat of umber tint varnish should be applied, followed by the clear varnish.

Of all surface finishes, découpage is able to offer many opportunities. It calls for both imagination and deftness in addition to creating pieces of otherwise mundane furniture which has its own unique qualities and visual appeal.

31

Materials

THE wood finisher has to be familiar with the properties of a wide range of materials. He should know what they are used for, their qualities, and he should certainly be aware of any health hazards. It is unlikely that the amateur or even the professional will want to keep a stock of all these materials in his workshop, because many of them may well deteriorate if they are on the shelf for lengthy periods. The following is a list of the more common materials, some with alternative names, together with notes on their properties.

Acetic Acid 6% is dilute acetic acid, supplied in liquid form. It is non-toxic, and can be obtained from the chemist. It is used in some furniture revivers or fresheners. If unobtainable, white vinegar can be used as a substitute.

American Rock Potash is crude caustic potash, supplied in either flakes or lumps. It is poisonous and harmful to the skin. Obtainable from the chemist or ironmonger, it is used for turning oak deep brown, but a follow-up treatment with chloride of lime will turn oak a grey colour. It should be handled only when wearing rubber gloves. Any splashes on the skin should immediately be well washed with clean water. If splashed in the eyes, seek medical attention without delay.

Ammonia is known as ammonia 80/80. It is in fluid form and toxic, and turns the skin yellow on contact. Supplied by the chemist, it gives off dangerous fumes which affect the eyes. Used as a rule for stripping wood and fuming, or darkening, oak. It can be added to a water stain to improve the depth of colouring by penetrating the fibres.

Aniline Dyes are aniline black, blue, Bismark brown, eosin, nigrosine and other colours, supplied in powder form. While not harmful to the skin apart from staining, these dyes are nevertheless toxic. Obtained from polish supply houses and some ironmongers, they are used for making stains and can be added to a neutral polish as colour. Skin stains can be removed by applying methylated spirit or a dilute domestic bleach.

Benzine is distilled from petroleum and is highly flammable.

Benzoline is coal tar naphtha and a poisonous liquid which is not, however, harmful to the skin. Obtainable from ironmongers, it is flammable and the vapour should not be inhaled. A mask should be worn when handling it. The main use is for dispelling oil and grease in varnishing.

Berlin Black is a pigment and supplied by some ironmongers as a paste. It is non-toxic and harmless to the skin, and it dries to a dull finish.

Bichromate is bichromate of potash, and is supplied by the chemist in the form of orange/red crystals or a fine powder. Although toxic, it is not especially harmful to the skin. It is used in a solution, and the trade finisher generally makes up a concentrated solution and dilutes as required. Used as a rule for darkening mahogany and similar woods.

Borax is supplied by the chemist in crystal or powder form. It is non-toxic and harmless to the skin, and is used as an ingredient of some water-based varnishes and strippers.

Brunswick Black is obtainable from trade suppliers in paste form. It is not harmful to the skin, nor is it toxic. It was used originally for black lettering, but can be thinned with turpentine to make a substantial brown wood stain.

Burnt Sienna, otherwise brown umber, is supplied in powder form and is non-toxic and harmless to the skin. It is obtained from art materials shops and is mixed with glue size for water staining.

Butter of Antimony, otherwise solution of ammonious chloride, is supplied in liquid form is toxic and harmful to the skin. Obtainable from the chemist, it is used in certain furniture revivers.

Carbon Tetrachloride is supplied by the chemist in fluid form, and it gives off a vapour which is toxic if inhaled. It is also poisonous if absorbed through the skin. It should be used only in the open air and rubber gloves must be worn. Its most general use is for removing the grease from teak and similar woods.

Carborundum Powder, otherwise silicon carbide, it is non-toxic. Supplied in different grades by trade houses, it is used for abrasive purposes.

Caustic Potash, otherwise potassium hydroxide, is supplied in powder or granule form, it is toxic and harmful to the skin. Obtainable from some ironmongers, it dissolves in water and can generate heat. It is used for stripping finishes and removing old polish. Rubber gloves and goggles must be worn and any splashes on the face or clothing avoided. If splashes do occur, medical attention should be immediately sought.

China Clay, otherwise known as kaolin, is obtainable from the chemist or trade supplier in the form of a white powder. It is non-toxic and harmless to the skin; its main use is in making heavy paste wood filler.

Chloride of Lime, otherwise known as chlorinated lime, is a white powder which is non-toxic and harmless to the skin. It is used to create a weathered finish in oak, when it imparts a distinctive grey hue.

Copal is a pale yellow to red-brown resin, and is non-toxic and harmless to the skin. It is used in the manufacture of varnish and obtainable from trade suppliers.

Copperas Blue/Green/White, otherwise copper sulphate, ferrous sulphate and zinc sulphate, is supplied by chemists and trade houses in crystal form. It is toxic but harmless to the skin providing the area is washed immediately. The principal use for green copperas is to colour oak a grey-blue and to reduce the red of mahogany.

Dragon's Blood is supplied in broken chunks by chemists and trade houses; it is non-toxic and harmless to the skin. It is used for imparting colour to polish.

Driers, otherwise known as Japan drier, or terebine, is a pale yellow fluid; it is toxic but harmless to the skin. It is obtainable from paint suppliers and some ironmongers. Used sometimes as a substitute for pure turpentine, although it is, in fact, considered to be inferior.

Flake White is also known as lead carbonate, and is obtainable from polish supply houses in powder form. It is toxic, but not harmful to the skin. It is mixed with Scotch glue for use on lighter coloured woods, and can be an ingredient with white polish to lighten the wood.

Glue Size is supplied by ironmongers and paint suppliers in powder form. It is non-toxic and harmless to the skin. It is useful as a filler on open-pored woods and in the manufacture of artificial wood.

Gold Size is supplied by paint stores and some ironmongers in liquid form. It is non-toxic and harmless to the skin. It is used as a base for the application of gold leaf and can also be utilised in making paste fillers.

Gum Benzoin is supplied by polish houses in lump form. It is non-toxic and harmless to the skin, and is used in making glaze.

Hydrogen Peroxide is supplied by chemists, and is toxic and can also blister delicate skin. It is used for bleaching wood and should be stored in a sealed bottle in a dark place.

Linseed Oil, obtainable from paint stores and ironmongers, is brown when raw and dark brown when boiled. It is non-toxic and harmless to the skin. The boiled variety is used as a drying oil in various preparations, notably in french polishing.

Mastic, otherwise known as gum mastic, is supplied in yellow to light brown 'tears' trade houses and some chemists. It is non-toxic and harmless to the skin. Basically a gum, it is used for making varnish.

Methylated Spirits, otherwise known as mineralised methylated spirits, is highly volatile and should not be used near naked flames. Obtainable from chemists and specialist suppliers to the finishing trade, it is toxic but harmless to the skin. It is used to make french polish when quick drying time is required, and in spirit-based stains.

Mineral Oil, otherwise known as light liquid paraffin, is an oily fluid, obtainable from the chemist. It is non-toxic and harmless to the skin. It can be used as a superfine lubricant in french polishing.

Nitric Acid is a colourless fluid which is toxic but harmless to the skin. Sometimes used to remove dark marks from wood.

Oxalic acid is supplied in crystal form, and is toxic but harmless to the skin providing the area is immediately washed. Obtainable from the chemist, it is diluted in warm water and used for wood bleaching and the removal of stains.

Pearl Ash, otherwise known as crude potassium carbonate, is obtainable from trade supply houses, and is used for stripping old polish, paint and varnish. It is non-toxic and harmless to the skin.

Permanganate of Potash, otherwise known as potassium permanganate, is supplied by the chemist in the form of purple-black crystals. A strong concentration is toxic, but merely stains the skin. It is used mainly for making a variety of stains.

Pumice Powder is a pale grey powder in a number of grades, from coarse to superfine. It is non-toxic and harmless to the skin, and is obtainable from trade supply houses and some chemists. It is used mainly as an abrasive in french polishing.

Pyrogallic Acid, otherwise known as pyrogallol, is supplied in white flakes. It is non-toxic and harmless to the skin, and is obtainable from the chemist. It can be used in the fuming of oak and when mixed with ammonia appears to accelerate the process.

Resin, otherwise known as colophony, is a yellow powder which is non-toxic and harmless to the skin. It is obtainable from trade supply houses, and is used to harden wax polish, but it will also make a stopping when mixed with wax.

Sanderac is supplied in yellow 'tears' by trade supply houses, and is non-toxic and harmless to the skin. It is used mainly in the making of varnish.

Shellac is supplied in a variety of forms, including white, orange, button, garnet, and is available in flake or granule form from trade supply houses. It is non-toxic and harmless to the skin. It forms the main ingredient in french polishing.

Silex, otherwise known as silicon oxide, is a powder, and is non-toxic and harmless to the skin. Available from trade supply houses, it is used for making a paste filler.

Soda, Washing, otherwise known as sodium carbonate, is supplied in crystal form by the chemist, hardware stores and grocers. In solution, it is used to break down greasy deposits and strip off old polish.

Spirit Black/Chrysoidine/Green/Mahogany/Walnut are supplied by the trade materials houses in powder form, and are non-toxic and harmless to the skin. They are spirit-soluble colours for making spirit stains and varnish, also tinted french polish.

Tripoli Powder, otherwise known as rottenstone, is a fine powder available in various grades, and it is non-toxic and harmless to the skin. Obtainable from jeweller's supply houses, it is used for imparting a sheen to french polish.

Turpentine, otherwise known as turpentine oil, is a clear liquid, is obtainable from ironmongers, chemists and trade supply houses. It is non-toxic and harmless to the skin. Only the pure unadulterated product should be used in the making of wax polish and oil stain.

Vandyke Brown is brown powder which is non-toxic and harmless to the skin, and is available from artist's materials suppliers. It is used as a colour for water stain.

Vandyke Crystals are brown crystals or a powder and is non-toxic and harmless to the skin. Available from trade supply houses and some ironmongers, and used in the making of wood stains.

Waxes: Beeswax, **Yellow or White** is obtainable from trade supply houses and chemists, and is non-toxic and harmless to the skin. It is supplied in lumps, and is used for polish making. The white variety is superior for fine quality work. **Carnauba** is yellowish and supplied in lumps by trade supply houses. It is non-toxic and harmless to the skin. **Paraffin** is supplied in the form of blocks and is non-toxic and harmless to the skin. It is obtainable from some chemists and the trade supply houses, and is used for polishes where a light surface finish is required.

White Mineral Oil, sometimes known as light liquid paraffin, it is clear fluid, and it is non-toxic and harmless to the skin. Its main use is as a lubricant in french polishing.

White Spirit is a clear fluid, and it is non-toxic and harmless to the skin. Obtainable from the chemist and from trade supply houses, it is used for making stains and degreasing wood.

32

Formulary

THE question of whether to 'go metric' was considered very early in the writing of this book, and it was resisted for the reason that the craft of wood finishing is almost as ancient as joinery and as such is not subject to violent change. There is the inevitable counter-argument that the majority of modern books on technical subjects are done in metric. Yet in the most practical and traditional terms, workshops and their craftsmen in the English-speaking world happily persist in thinking and working in the old imperial measures. The practised wood finisher more often than not uses a rule of thumb which transcends both metric and imperial, and relies upon instinct. But for the sake of those who believe in total precision, the quantities expressed in imperial terms can be readily converted to metric by the application of the following table.

		1 dram	=	1.7718 g
16 drams	=	1 ounce	=	28.35 g
437.5 grains	=	1 ounce (oz)	=	28.35 g
16 ounces	=	1 pound (lb)	=	0.4536 kg
14 pounds (lb)	=	1 stone	=	6.3503 kg
		1 fluid ounce	=	0.0284 litre
20 fluid ounces	=	1 pint	=	0.568 litre
2 pints	=	1 quart	=	1.136 litres
4 quarts	=	1 gallon	=	4.546 litres
		1 inch	=	25.40 millimetres
12 inches	=	1 foot	=	0.3048 metre
3 feet	=	1 yard	=	0.9144 metre

Stripping Compounds

The following are suitable for stripping furniture and woodwork generally. All of them should be treated with respect and handled with rubber gloves while wearing protective clothing. Any splashes on the bare skin should be washed with clean water without delay. It is necessary to wear protective goggles to protect the eyes while mixing and applying these and all other similar compounds.

1. Dissolve 1¼ lbs caustic soda in 5 pints of water, stirring constantly. Add 1¾ pints of mineral oil and 1¼ lbs of well sieved sawdust. When the oil is stirred briskly into the water, it should form an emulsion. The sawdust is mixed in to form a stiffish paste. This compound is then pasted on to the wood surface and allowed to stand until the paint or varnish or shellac becomes soft enough to be scraped off without scratching the wood. The stripped surface must be washed with vinegar and water to neutralise it before any form of surface finish is applied.

2. Dissolve 8 lbs of caustic soda in a gallon of water. Add 8 lbs of common whiting and 4 lbs of starch. This offers a much better binding quality than the compound above, and will adhere more closely to the surface. It will also have a keener bite, and the paint or other material will probably begin to peel within half an hour, aided by a gentle and encouraging scraping. The surface should then be washed with water and vinegar as a neutraliser.

3. Mix together 5 quarts of benzole and 2½ pints of acetone, then add ½ pint carbon bisulphide and 2 ounces of paraffin wax. This is suitable for the more delicate surfaces and is widely used in the antiques restoration trade in Germany and France but less so in other countries. It has the virtue of spreading into hidden recesses and generally lifting the paint or wax away like a skin; particularly useful for the restoration of carved figures where a lot of detail has to be stripped cleanly.

4. Mix ½ lb of common starch with a small amount of water; dissolve 4 tablespoons of caustic soda in 3 pints of water and add it to the starch. This is a rather crude stripper and it may turn some woods brown, but the colour can be rectified at a later stage by bleaching. It should in any case be well washed with domestic vinegar to neutralise the action of the caustic soda. The stripper is useful even for delicate work on prized furniture, and can be regarded as a general utility material in the workshop.

Water Stains

Seasoned Oak for use on English Oak

Dissolve 4 ounces of walnut aniline crystals in one gallon of hot water, apply and allow to completely dry, then sand smooth. Now dissolve in one gallon of hot water 6½ drams nigrosine and 1½ drams scarlet aniline. No filler will be required, and a suitable finish is provided by orange shellac followed by a finish of wax or matt varnish.

To render oak a golden colour, for use on almost any wood

Dissolve 3 ounces of loutre aniline and one ounce of naphthol yellow aniline in 2 gallons of hot water, then brush on several coats, depending on the depth of colour required. Now sand smooth. Use a filler for any of the coarse grain woods and colour it with Vandyke brown mixed with oil and a small quantity of asphaltum varnish. The best varnish should be an orange shellac, followed by varnish and, preferably, a glossy finish.

Fumed oak for use on all varieties of oak, except Japanese

Mix in one gallon of hot water ½ ounce of bichromate of potash and ½ ounce of carbonate of potash. Brush on generously and, when dry, sand smooth. Now mix together in a dry form the following: 2 drams acid brown aniline, 2 ounces walnut aniline, 1 ounce nigrosine black, 1 dram naphthol yellow, 22 drams sulphur brown. Take 4 ounces of the dry mixture and stir thoroughly into a gallon of warm water. Brush on, allow to dry and then sandpaper smooth. The final finish should consist of a mixture of 2 ounces of boiled linseed oil, one ounce of japan drier and 6 ounces of benzine. This mixture should be thoroughly rubbed into the surface with a cotton rag and, when dry, painted with orange shellac. When dry, apply a dull varnish.

Common brown stain for use on all woods

Mix, in one gallon of hot water, one dram of bichromate of potash and 8 drams of naphtha yellow aniline, and then apply to the wood. When dry, sandpaper smooth. Now mix into 2 quarts of hot water 28 drams of walnut aniline and 3 drams of mahogany brown aniline. This is brushed on in a generous quantity and, when dry, followed by a coat of shellac. The filler is silica coloured with Vandyke brown well mixed with oil. The final finish is thinned shellac, preferably in a proportion of 50% white and 50% orange.

Malachite stain for use on oak and chestnut

Mix in one gallon of hot water, ¼ ounce of methylene blue and one ounce of green aniline. Brush on generously and, when dry, sandpaper the surface. A second coat is then applied. The filler is silica mixed with 6 ounces of nigrosine and one ounce of chrome green. The finish should be thinned shellac, the dry surface being rubbed dull for the best effect.

Red mahogany for use on mahogany and birch

Mix as dry powders the following: 8 ounces mahogany red aniline, 8 ounces of bichromate of potash, 2 drams naphthol yellow, and stir 6 ounces into one gallon of hot water. After brushing on to the wood, allow to dry and then sandpaper smooth followed by a coat of orange shellac. The fillers should consist of silica powder mixed with Vandyke brown and nigrosine with a quantity of rose pink, all mixed in oil. The finish is shellac followed by a coat of gloss varnish.

Grey for use on the finer woods

Dissolve one ounce tannic acid in one gallon of hot water. Brush on in generous quantities, allow to dry and then sand smooth. Now dissolve the following in one gallon of hot water: 15 grains nigrosine black, ½ dram orange aniline, ½ ounce sulphate of iron, 2 ounces of sulphate of soda, and apply to surface, then allow to dry. The surface may be varnished, but looks better if waxed.

Fumed oak for use on oak, pine, maple and similar woods

Dissolve 4 ounces of tannic acid in one gallon of hot water, and brush on, then allow to dry before sanding. The next coat should consist of 4 ounces of bichromate of potash and one ounce of potash carbonate dissolved in one gallon of hot water. When this is applied, the wood should darken dramatically.

Oak for use on oak and chestnut

Dissolve 6 ounces of permanganate of potash in one gallon of hot water, and brush on to the wood. Now make a second coat consisting of iron acetate in a weak solution. When thoroughly dry apply an oil solution consisting of 2 ounces of raw linseed oil, one ounce of japan drier and 5 ounces of benzine. The correct method is to apply one coat by rubbing it on with a coarse cloth, followed by a second coat which is brushed on. The final finish should be shellac, followed by a thorough waxing.

Spirit Aniline Stains

Mahogany

Mix 4 ounces of Bismarck brown, spirit soluble, with one gallon of denatured alcohol. Resist the temptation to add more Bismarck brown, because this can create an overpowering stain which will go muddy when the finishing coat of shellac is applied. If more body colour is required, add only a small quantity of nigrosine black.

English oak

Mix into 1 gallon of denatured alcohol the following: 2 drams malachite green aniline, spirit soluble; 8 drams auramine, spirit soluble, aniline; 4 ounces nigrosine, spirit soluble. After it has been brushed on and allowed to dry, paint with thinned orange shellac, just enough to lock in the colour. The filler colour consists of equal parts Vandyke brown and black mixed with oil. The final finish can be shellac or varnish.

Oil Stains

Oil stains are useful because they are so easily applied and can be manipulated for a considerable time, enabling the craftsman a margin in which to work round joints and awkward cracks and crevices. Yet despite their oil base, they are not as deeply penetrating as may be imagined, although their surface appearance is very satisfying.

Light oak

Ingredients: 8 ounces nigrosine black, oil soluble; 4 ounces yellow auramine; 1 ounce walnut aniline; 1 quart hot turpentine; 1 gallon asphaltum. The best way of mixing the ingredients together is to use an electrically heated and thermostatically controlled double boiler on a low heat, adding the nigrosine yellow and walnut last of all. When well mixed, this should be stirred into the varnish and then, when cold, applied to the surface. Follow with a filler, working both with and against the grain to assist total penetration, and rubbing in with a pad of coarse clean hessian. If a neutral colour filler is used, it will take on the strong colour and this makes it unnecessary to add colour as it will adapt of its own accord. When dry, the surface can be finished with thin shellac. The choice of a high or dull sheen is optional.

Jacobean oak for use on oak and ash

Ingredients: 2 ounces walnut aniline, oil soluble; 1 ounce orange, oil soluble; 8 ounces nigrosine black, oil soluble; 1 pint hot turpentine; ½ pint boiled linseed oil; 3 quarts naphtha. Heat the turpentine in a double boiler and stir in the walnut, followed by the nigrosine and orange. The oil can now be added, followed at once by the naphtha. Brush the stain on to the wood until the required depth of colour is reached, and then finish with orange shellac and a well waxed surface.

Oak of weathered appearance for use on oak & other wood

Ingredients: 4 drams scarlet aniline, oil soluble; 3 ounces nigrosine black, oil soluble; ½ ounce walnut brown aniline, oil soluble; 1 pint hot turpentine; 1 pint benzole; 1 gallon benzine. Mix the ingredients with the turpentine, using a double boiler except the benzole and naphtha, which are added when the turpentine is cold. Brush on to the wood and, when completely dry, apply a coat of thinned orange shellac, applying it quickly and smoothly, taking care not to disturb any undercoat colour. A recommended finish is either dull varnish or shellac, followed by waxing.

Antwerp oak suitable for ash, chestnut and oak

Ingredients: 4 ounces black nigrosine, oil soluble; 6 drams auramine, oil soluble; 5 ounces scarlet, aniline, oil soluble; 1 pint boiled linseed oil; 1 pint turpentine; 1 gallon benzine. Heat the turpentine in a double boiler, and dissolve the colours, one by one, but not all together. The oil is then stirred in, allowed to cool and the benzine is then added. It should be brushed on and allowed to dry, followed by a coat of white shellac, and sanded smooth when dry. The recommended filler is silica coloured with oil-based black. The finish is white shellac followed by a coat of varnish, which should be rubbed down to reduce the sheen. Alternatively, a flat varnish can be used.

Oil Pigment Stains

These are the general utility stains which are made by mixing certain tinting pigments with benzole, linseed oil or turpentine. It cannot be claimed that they are of exceptional quality, but they can be used for mass production staining or general domestic use in cases where the furniture is of no particular value but is in need of renovation. As far as woods are concerned, this type of stain reacts best on softwoods, when only one or two coats may be needed. Hardwoods call for several coats. Whereas other stains may fade over the years due to strong sunlight and other factors, this range will firmly hold their original colour for an indefinite period. However, they are limited in colour range in the autumnal shades such as burnt umber, Prussian blue, green and associated hues. It is advisable to give all softwood surfaces a single coat of very thin shellac before application of any of the oil pigment stains to ensure an even distribution of colour and avoid the possibility of patchiness. This is unnecessary on hardwoods. An alternative to a shellac base for the stain can be made by mixing together 25% of boiled linseed oil and 75% turpentine, and applying it with a brush. It should take about thirty minutes to dry. When the oil pigment is applied, it should be left on the wood for up to twenty or thirty minutes, care should be taken to avoid any excess. While it is not always possible to create lighter tints with this range, a certain amount of effect can be achieved by brushing it on and then almost immediately wiping it off with a cloth, creating a progressive stain. A final surface finish can be either shellac or varnish. Softwoods will require a coat of fillers, applied in the usual way, but this does not apply to hardwoods.

Multi-purpose stain

Ingredients: 1 lb pigment dissolved in oil; 10 ounces japan drier; 6 pints boiled linseed oil; 12 ounces turpentine; 12 ounces benzole. This should make one gallon of all-purpose stain.

Dark oak

Ingredients: 1 lb raw sienna; ½ lb burnt sienna; ½ lb burnt umber, ½ pint japan drier; 1 quart turpentine; 1 quart benzole; 3 pints boiled linseed oil. This should make one gallon of stain.

Light oak

1½ lbs raw sicnna; ½ lb raw umber; 8 ounces japan drier; 1 quart turpentine; 1 quart benzole; 3 pints boiled linseed oil. This should make 1 gallon of stain.

Black oak

1 lb Vandyke brown; 1 lb black; ½ pint japan drier; 1 quart turpentine; 1 quart benzole; 3 pints boiled linseed oil. This should make one gallon of stain.

Grey stain

1¾ lbs raw umber; ¼ lb black; 1 ounce Prussian blue; ½ pint japan drier; 1 quart turpentine; 1 quart benzole. This should make one gallon of stain.

Walnut

1 lb Vandyke brown; 1 lb burnt umber; 1 ounce rose pink; 1 quart turpentine; 1 quart benzole; 3 pints boiled linseed oil. This makes one gallon of stain.

Red mahogany

1¾ lbs burnt sienna; ¼ lb rose pink; 1 quart turpentine; 1 quart benzole; 3 pints boiled linseed oil. This makes 1½ gallons of stain.

Brown mahogany

12 ounces burnt sienna; 4 ounces rose pink; 4 ounces Vandyke brown; 4 ounces burnt umber; ½ pint japan drier; 1 quart turpentine; 1 quart benzole; 3 pints boiled linseed oil. This make 1½ gallons of stain. These quantities can be adjusted pro-rata if a smaller amount is required.

Varnish-Based Stains

There is nothing very mysterious or particularly difficult about varnish stains. Basically, all they consist of is varnish with an added pigment, using transparent colours. The major advantage of using them is that they both colour and coat the wood in one single operation. They should not be confused with branded polyurethane stains. It is debatable whether varnish offers a longer life than the more recently introduced polyurethane. Given the right materials and a studied application, it would seem that varnish does have a certain superiority. The varnish stains remain very useful because they can be applied to inferior woods with practically no prior preparation of the surface apart from any necessary degreasing and sanding and yet will still provide a perfectly satisfactory and enduring coating. There is, moreover, some element of experiment possible, because if the colour content is intensified, an enamelled appearance will result. The preferred colour pigments include green, Prussian blue, burnt umber, burnt sienna, pink, ultramarine, black and orange, all of which comprise an inspiring colour range. Each of the following will yield one gallon of stain.

Oak – dark
7½ pints varnish; 1 lb raw umber; 4 ounces burnt umber; ¼ ounce black; ½ pint turpentine.

Oak – light
7½ pints varnish; 1 lb raw sienna; ½ pint turpentine.

Mahogany – red
7 pints varnish; 1 lb burnt sienna; 3 ounces pink; ½ pint turpentine.

Mahogany – brown
7½ pints varnish; 1 lb Vandyke brown; 4 ounces burnt umber; ¼ pint turpentine.

Walnut
7½ pints varnish; 1 lb Vandyke brown; ½ pint turpentine.

Wax Finishes

Although there are many branded products available, the craftsman finisher who wants to extend his basic skills will generally make his own wax compounds. It is possible to add any colour to the following if required.

1. Ingredients: 1 lb white/yellow beeswax; ½ pint turpentine; 1 tablespoon ammonia. The wax should be broken up into very small pieces or, preferably, shaved with a sharp knife, and then placed in a double boiler to melt down to a liquid. Now add ammonia and turpentine, taking care not to inhale the ammonia fumes. Store in a closed vessel.

2. Ingredients: 1 lb carnauba wax; 1 lb ceresine wax; 1 pint turpentine. The wax should be well shredded and melted in a double boiler, and the turpentine then added. Store in a closed vessel.

3. This is probably the best of all the wax polishes. If properly made and stored, it will last for a long period. Ingredients: ½ lb carnauba wax; 1 lb ceresine wax; 2 lb paraffin wax. Shred all the waxes very finely and melt them down in a double boiler. Now add about 2 pints of turpentine, and pour into a vessel, then allow it to cool and set.

Polishes for Woodwork

There are on the market many different types of polish for furniture and woodwork in general, some of them wax based, many in the form of creamy substances, and others in aerosol packs designed for spraying on to the wood. At least one such polish offers a universal application 'for all wood', but its effectiveness is governed more by the addition of silicones than the composition of the basic polish itself. No self-respecting craftsman will attempt to freshen up furniture either for himself or for his clients by the use of any of these preparations. He will prefer the very traditional polishes which have to be made in the workshop, their selection being governed by the wood to be treated. The following formulae have been in use in the craft furniture and restoration trades for more than a century and are regarded as superior in performance.

1. Ingredients: 1 ounce paraffin oil; ½ ounce butter of antimony; 1 ounce denatured alcohol; 3 ounces water. Mix all the ingredients together very thoroughly, and then add a quantity of carbonate of magnesia, sprinkling in until the mixture starts to fizz and bubble in a somewhat alarming manner. The uproar will gradually subside. When it finishes this means that the mixture is neutralised. Now make up to one pint with water and add two tablespoons of carbonate of magnesia, and store in a well sealed jar or bottle.

2. Ingredients: 1 pint raw linseed oil; 2 ounces spirits of camphor; 4 ounces vinegar; 1 ounce butter of antimony; ½ ounce ammonia. Mix together all the ingredients and then bottle, always agitating the polish immediately before use.

3. Ingredients: 1 pint vinegar; 1 pint denatured alcohol; 1 pint paraffin oil. This polish takes a little time to work on the surface, and it should be wiped on and left for thirty to forty minutes before polishing with a soft cloth.

4. Ingredients: ½ ounce butter of antimony; 1 quart cider vinegar (available from grocers and health food stores); 6 pints turpentine; 1 quart denatured alcohol; 3 quarts raw linseed oil. When mixed this should be kept in earthenware or glass containers, not metal ones, because it is corrosive. To be effective, it should be rubbed briskly into the wood.

33

A Check-list of Six Basic
Methods

THE essence of proficient wood finishing is the knowledge of what has to be done at each successive stage. While it is not always possible to be completely dogmatic about this, there are, nevertheless, six basic methods which may be helpful to the beginner until they are carried out by instinct. The outline material which follows is an attempt to systemise the basic finishes, commencing from a point where the wood is cleaned, sanded and ready for treatment. The more experienced craftsman will know at once that each of these systems is capable of certain variation. Similar checklists can be devised to cover almost any system of woodfinishing, and it will be helpful for teachers and others to compile their own once they have mastered the separate techniques and gained a knowledge of the properties of the materials and the woods themselves.

Filler
1. Decide which type of filler should be used, either glue size or superfine plaster.
2. Cover surface with two coats of thinned shellac and allow to thoroughly dry.
3. If plaster is used, place dry in tray next to workpiece. If colour is required, thoroughly mix in quantity of powdered pigment.
4. If glue size is used, apply to surface. If colour is required, use water-based pigment and thoroughly mix with size.
5. If plaster is used, damp a cloth and make pad, then use to pick up a quantity.
6. Rub vigorously on wood until thick paste forms.

7. Use clean, coarse sacking to rub off surplus.
8. If surface is streaked, wipe with cloth soaked in raw linseed oil.

Shellacking bare wood

1. Use a mixture of one part white shellac of the 4 lb cut and three parts of methylated spirit, and apply plentifully.
2. When dry, rub down, but not too vigorously. Remove all dust.
3. If staining is required, apply at this stage.
4. Apply mixture of one part shellac and one part methylated spirit.
5. When dry, rub down but not too vigorously. Remove all dust.
6. Paint on shellac in consistency of 1, above.
7. Wax polish.

French polishing

1. Fill the pores of the wood if it is open-grained.
2. Clean the surface and apply any required water or spirit stain. If water stain, sand smooth.
3. Ensure that room temperature is approximately 70 degrees Fahrenheit.
4. Apply first coat of polish, using a figure-of-eight action with the rubber.
5. Use wedge-shaped rubber to ensure that corners are fully covered with polish.
6. When first coat is dry and hard, use fine sandpaper to rub down, then clean with tack rag.
7. Apply second coat of polish and rub down as in 6, then clean.
8. Continue until required degree of brilliance and lustre is reached.
9. If final result required is a dull sheen, rub down with fine steel wool.

Varnishing hardwoods

1. Apply the stain to the clean wood and allow it to dry.
2. Apply three coats of varnish and allow to dry.
3. Rub down with a fine abrasive to a dull sheen.

Lacquering hardwoods

1. Apply the stain to the clean wood and allow it to dry.
2. Apply the sealer.
3. Rub down with extra fine sandpaper. Remove all dust.
4. Apply up to four coats of gloss lacquer.
5. Dull down by rubbing with pumice or a fine abrasive.

Gilding

1. Apply four coats of white shellac and allow to dry.
2. Apply japan size or home-made size to surface.

3. Test surface for tackiness at intervals up to three hours. Start gilding when surface is faintly tacky.
4. Lay out gold leaf on palette and cut to sizes required.
5. Charge brush or gilder's tip with static electricity and lift leaf into place on workpiece.
6. When suitable area is covered, flatten out ridges and ripples with silk pad.
7. Burnish leafed area smooth.
8. Rub surface with bronze metallic powder or wipe over with turpentine.
9. Apply one coat of orange shellac.

34

Technical Note on Shaker Finishes

ONE of the Shaker declarations was 'There is great beauty in harmony', and this precluded the excessive use of surface ornamentation. The Elders of the sect regularly warned against such accessories as carvings, turning, inlays and veneers, and one, Giles Avery (1815–1890), stated that the habit of non-Shaker cabinet-makers of 'dressing . . . furniture of pine or white wood with the veneering of bay wood, mahogany or rose wood' a deception. Yet despite what may at first appear to be a dull and even unadventurous approach, the sect did have some affection for colour. Bed frames were often painted bottle green, carpets were striped, while 'comfortables should be of a modest colour'. Curtains were white, blue, green, but not striped or chequered. There was something quietly simple about it.

The idea that Shaker furniture makers, who were the leaders in the chair manufacturing industry, had no sense of ornament and colour and were repressed by their religious ideals is quite erroneous. While other countries copied each other, often to the point of extinction of the original motive, the Shaker craftsman worked within his own school of design and finish, using colours very sparingly but making ample use of oils, varnishes and stains of water-based umber and sienna. The term 'Shaker red' has often been used, but the basic colours were, in fact, ochre-red or terracotta, but there were other variations, including a surprisingly bright red. Other colours were a mixture of red and yellow, apricot-orange and yellow. The evolution of applied stains ranged from the mere traces used in the early part of the Shaker movement to a more solid covering in the latter stages. A receipt book of 1849 details several formulae. Here are some of them, printed as found:

Red Stain

Take 1½ oz. Brazeil dust, put in 1 pt of Alcohol – warm it a little in a water Bath, or on a Stove – say ½ hour, then put in, say, about One teaspoon full of Bookbinder's acid, which will turn it to a beautiful red. . . .

Lacker

Take 1 Gall. Linseed Oil; 1 lb Literage (probably litharge); ¾ lb Red Lead, ground fine. Boil slowly until it is so thick, it will not strike thro writing paper, which will take most of a day to accomplish. Stir it often, and add when partly cool One Gall. Spts. Turpentine, and bottle for use.

White with blue shade

To 100 lbs White Lead or Zink, add 1 oz. Prussian Blue and 1 oz. Lampblack. Take the Lead and stir in Black and Blue, until you get the shade you desire.

To Colour blue on wood

Pulverize 1 oz. best spanish Float Indigo, put it into 7 ozs. Sulphuric Acid in a glass vessel – let it stand 2 days. When used put a quantity sufficient into pure water and add Pearlast till the shade suits.

To Colour Pink or Red on Wood

Put one lb of chipped Nicaraqua Wood to 1 Gall. pure water, boil 10 minutes in a brass vessel; then brush or dip the article in it and after, brush it over with the following mixture, viz. to 1 oz. Muriatic acid add 1 oz. Grained Tin, leave out the stopper of the bottle till the Tin is dissolved. When wood is dry – varnish.

Author's note

The Shakers were also bookbinders, and 'Brazil dust' was in all probability a powder-pigment used for staining leather. 'Bookbinder's acid' was a reagent which reacted on the pigment in much the same way that certain substances will convert vegetable dyes.

Literage, or litharge, is monoxide of lead (PbO), and it is obtained now, as then, by oxidising lead at a high temperature. Two forms of the monoxide are known. The first is known as massicot, and it is obtained at moderately high temperatures. The second form, known commonly as litharge, is obtained by fusing massicot and then permitting the molten mass to solidify. In a furnace made of bone ash and pearl ash, the oxidation would lead to the lead being oxidised, giving the name litharge, or 'silver stone', which can be extracted by blowing it off with bellows or by suction. Litharge is a yellowish powder which is nowadays used in the manufacture of glass and glazed earthenware, and in the wood finishing trade in the preparation of quick-drying oils and varnishes. It is also the source of the preparation of lead nitrate and the basic acetate used for pharmaceutical purposes. The Shakers used it to impart body and substance to their version of lacquer.

Float Indigo was most probably obtained from the juices of the *Isatis tinctoria*, known until recent times in England as the woad plant, and used by the Shakers for the dyeing of woven .cloth.

Regarding 'Grained Tin', it is reasonable to suppose that the Shakers had access to veins of the oxide – either tinstone or cassiterite (SnO_2). One of the compounds of tin is a pink salt, $SnCl_42NH_4Cl$, which is used as a mordant in dyeing. A mordant is a substance, chiefly the weakly basic hydroxides of aluminium, chromium, and iron, which combine with, and fix, a dyestuff on the material – in this case wood – in cases where the material cannot be dyed direct. Clearly, the 'Nicaraqua' wood to which the receipt refers was a local timber which gave off a substance when boiled and which reacted to the 'Grained Tin' by turning pink or red. The word 'Grained' in this sense in all probability referred to the oxide when turned into a compound. It formed the basis of the 'Shaker red', to which the text refers with some variations, such as 'ochre-red' and terracotta and the much brighter hue of a more pure nature.

Although the Shakers are generally regarded as simple country folk, they did have a knowledge of chemistry which was used to good effect.

35

Inventory of Furniture Collections

for the study of Surface Finish

O NE of the major difficulties in understanding exactly what a standard surface finish should look like is the lack of specimens and precisely where the most superior examples may be seen. It is not simply a matter of examining coloured photographs, good though they may seem, because they rarely suggest the reality. Surface finish cannot be communicated by photography. Both amateur and professional alike should cultivate the habit of closely examining as many different types of finish as possible, and the methods of decorating furniture should also be examined by looking at the best historical examples. Museums throughout the world are fortunate in being able to provide specimens for first-hand study, and it is here that the student should make a start, because such pieces are as a general rule maintained in first class order by the aristocrats of wood finishing and they are also well provenanced. Many of the craftsmen of the past mentioned in chapter one and elsewhere in this book made furniture which appears in the collections outlined here. Some are pleasingly exhibited in authentic room settings, like creatures in their natural habitat, while others are isolated as exhibits. If it is wished to make a closer and more detailed examination, then a letter should be sent to the director of the museum in question, requesting permission to do this. Agreement is not as a rule withheld from the true craftsman when the purpose is explained.

An effort has been made to mention collections which are easy of access, but there is always room for further exploration, most notably in Britain, for instance, by consulting *The National Trust Guide*, compiled by Robin Fedden and Rosemary Joekes (Cape, 1973 and subsequent editions), while other specimens can be found by referring to *The*

Libraries, Museums and Art Galleries Year Book (Clarke). More specific traces can be found in *The Bibliography of Museum and Art Gallery Publications and Audio-Visual Aids in Great Britain and Ireland*, edited by Michael Roulstone (Cambridge, Chadwyck-Healey, 1980).

As far as the student is concerned there is a radical difference between Britain and the United States. In Britain practically every conceivable type of finish and style in furniture can be seen under one massive roof at the Victoria and Albert Museum, London. The Ionides Collection, for instance, contains two or three impeccable and fine Italian walnut chests, partly gilded and partly made to display the wood finish. There are in the museum innumerable individual pieces in addition to a series of period rooms. In America, on the other hand, the selection for study is scattered across the Continent, although some institutions, such as the Smithsonian in Washington, contain sizeable collections, but none of them are on a par with the Victoria and Albert.

It is almost impossible within the scope of a relatively few pages to provide details of every single piece of interest in Britain, but the following are worth a note. The Adam style can be found at Kedleston Hall, Derbyshire, Saltram House, Plymouth, and at Kenwood, Hampstead, also Osterley Park House, Middlesex. Adam's work can be seen, too, at Corsham Court, Chippenham in addition to Harewood House, Leeds and Newby Hall, Ripon.

Various examples of the English style through the centuries are displayed at the Geffrye Museum, Shoreditch, London, while the Arts and Crafts Movement can be found at Arlington Mill, Bibury, Gloucestershire, Newarke Houses Museum, Leicester and the William Morris Gallery, Walthamstow, London.

Chippendale seems to occur in most collections, and any recommendations as far as surface finish are concerned must be based on excellence. The Lady Lever Gallery at Port Sunlight, Cheshire has fine examples, and so do the following: Badmington House, Gloucestershire, Blair House, Perthshire, Nostell Priory and Temple Newsam House, Leeds.

Art Nouveau is elusive as far as furniture is concerned, but in London the Bethnal Green Museum is suggested for its small selection. Larger collections are found in the Museum of Modern Art, New York, and, in France, at the Musée de l'Ecole de Nancy, Nancy, and Musée des Arts Décoratifs, Paris. In Brussels, Belgium, there are two collections, the Galerie L'Ecuyer, and Galeries l'Art.

The so-called Chinese Chippendale style occurs in many of the major collections, perhaps indiscriminately when it is exhibited in conjunction with formal Chippendale, but in the following locations the pieces are of exceptional quality: Kedleston Hall, Derbyshire; Badminton House, Gloucestershire, Scone Palace, Perthshire, Nostell Priory and Temple

Newsam House, Leeds, Yorkshire.

Georgian furniture can be found at Chatsworth, Derbyshire, and at Marble Hill, Twickenham, Middlesex, also at Wilton House in Wiltshire and Holkham Hall in Norfolk, and there are several very fine examples at the Lady Lever Art Gallery, Port Sunlight in Cheshire.

Apart from specimens in the Victoria and Albert Museum, London, there are practically no noteworthy examples of the Glasgow School in England, and it is necessary to go to the National Museum of Antiquities in Edinburgh or, in Glasgow, the natural home of the style, the Art Gallery and Museum, the School of Art and the University Art Collections.

Heppelwhite styles of finish are found at the Minories Art Gallery, Colchester, the Museum of Art at Hove, Temple Newsam House, Leeds and at the Geffrye Museum, London.

The Arts and Crafts Movement was mentioned earlier, but to examine the work of the man at the centre of it, William Morris, the reader should go to the City Museum and Art Gallery, Birmingham, Bradford City Art Gallery, Kelmscott Manor at Lechlade, Gloucestershire, the William Morris Gallery at Walthamstow, London, and Warwick Manor, Wolverhampton.

The distinctive Queen Anne style can be seen at Dyrham Park, Gloucestershire, The Vyne, Sherborne St John, Hampshire, where there is also some Chinese Chippendale, Blenheim Palace, Oxfordshire, and, in Hampton Court Palace, Middlesex.

Flamboyant finishes of the Regency period focus, naturally enough, upon the surrealistic Royal Pavilion, Brighton, although there are other locations, including Buscot Park, Farringdon, Berkshire; Belvoir Castle, Grantham, Lincolnshire; and Normanby Hall, Scunthorpe, Lincs.

When it comes to Stuart and Commonwealth examples Britain is, surprisingly, not as well served, although some can be seen at the Ashmolean Museum, Oxford, the National Museum of Wales, Cardiff, and Aston Hall, Birmingham.

One of the glories of modern Britain is the selection of great houses which have been opened to the public and are largely in their original condition or act as repositories for furniture. They include Hardwick Hall, Derbyshire, Badminton in Gloucestershire, Hatfield House, Hertfordshire, Knole in Kent, Burghley House, Lincolnshire, Montacute House, Somerset and Arbury Hall, Warwickshire.

The dark-toned and occasionally gilded and polychromed Gothic style can be seen at Windsor Castle, Windsor, but there are two outstanding sites abroad, including the Musée des Arts Décoratifs, Paris, and Lyndhurst at Tarrytown, New York.

Any student of furniture design and the history of the trade and its patronage will know that its products have a tendency to travel to the extent that early French examples can be found, in Britain, at Waddesdon Manor, Aylesbury, also specimens of Louis XV and Régence. In France it can be found in its gilded splendour at the Musée des Arts Décoratifs, Paris. Directoire is exhibited principally at the Musée Nationale du Château Fontainebleau, Fontainebleau, the Louvre and Musée Marmottan in Paris, and at Rueil-Malmaison in the Musée Nationale du Château de Malmaison.

There is in France an exceptional collection of Empire furniture, which features many different types of surface finish. It can be seen at the Musée National du Palais de Compeigne, Compeigne, the Musée National du Château de Fontainebleau, Fontainebleau, and in Paris at the Hotel Beauvais, Musée des Arts Décoratifs and Musée Marmottan. Louis XV and XVI are covered in Britain by specimens exhibited at Waddesdon Manor, Aylesbury, and the Wallace Collection, London, in Paris at the Louvre and the Château de Versailles, and in New York at the Metropolitan Museum of Art. While French Régence occurs in many national collections, the Residenzmuseum, Munich, has in its possession some quite exceptional pieces.

German baroque and rococo is widespread, as follows: in Austria the Tiroler Volkskunstmuseum, Innsbruck; in Germany the Museum für Kunsthandwerk at Frankfurt, the Museum fur KunstdGewerbe at Hamburg and, at Munich, the Bayerisches Nationalmuseum. There is also a good collection at the Amsterdam Rijksmuseum.

French furniture has frequently invaded Britain, but German rococo is less frequent in collections, although there are some very striking examples in Holyrood Palace, Edinburgh and at Luton Hoo, Bedfordshire. The Schonbrünn Palace, Vienna and the Osterreichisches Museum for Angedandte Kunst possess specimens in excellent condition. The main centres are, naturally enough, in Germany itself, and the following should be borne in mind: Museum für Künsthandwerk at Frankfurt am Main, the Residenz at Munich and at Nymphenburg the Amalienburg Pavillion Bayerisches Nationalmuseum, also the Germanisches Nationalmuseum, Nuremburg, and Sans Souci and the Neves Palais at Potsdam. There is also a collection at the Residenz, Wurzburg. In Holland the Amsterdam Rijksmuseum offers specimens for examination.

Many of the most striking surface finishes have their origins in Italy, and something can be learned by examining extant specimens. There are examples on show in Britain at the Courtauld Institute Galleries, in Holland at the Rijksmuseum, Amsterdam, and at the New York Metropolitan Museum of Art. In Italy, however, the collections are of paramount importance, notably the following: Villa Farraganiana, Albisola, the Palazzi Rosso, Bianco, Spinola, Reale and Durazzo-Pallavicini, Genoa. At Turin the principal collections are on show at the

Museo Civico, Palazzo Reale and the Pallazzini di Stupinigi. In addition, furniture of the Renaissance can be seen in Florence at the Museo Horne, Museo Nazionale (Bargello), Museo Davanzati and Museo Vecchio. The stronger and perhaps more striking Venetian style with its ornate colouring and glitter can be seen in Venice at the Ca'Rezzonico and Civiso Museo Forrer.

The richness of Russian furniture can be seen in a few collections outside the Soviet Union, most notably in Britain at Luton Hoo, Luton, Bedfordshire, and the Ross Collection at Hillwood in Washington, D.C., USA. In Leningrad the major collections can be found in the Museum Palaces of Lomonosor, Pavlosk, Petrodvorets and Pushkin, also the State Hermitage Museum and the State Russian Museum. In Moscow the places to visit are Arkhangel'skoe, Kushovo, Ostankino and the State Historical Museum.

Spanish furniture from many different periods is deposited in Barcelona at the Museo de Arteo Decorativas, the Museo Naçional de Artes Decorativas and the Museo di S. Cruz, Toledo.

American Colonian styles are well worth studying, and can be seen in Britain at the American Museum, Claverton Manor, Bath, where there are examples of early styles. The principal American collections are found at the Museum of Fine Arts, Boston, the Winterthur Museum, Delaware and Old Sturbridge Village, Sturbridge, Mass. The Colonial collections are at the Metropolitan Museum of Art, New York, and the Museum of Art, Philadelphia, but examples are included at Boston and Delaware, as above.

The American Chippendale styles are deposited at Colonial Williamsburg, Williamsburg, the Museum of Art, Philadelphia, Metropolitan Museum of Art, New York and the Museum of Fine Arts, Boston, while Early and Later Federal is found in the same locations in addition to the Smithsonian Institutions, Washington D.C. Examples of machine-made furniture are also to be seen.

Shaker Furniture is somewhat specialised and occasionally difficult to find in museum collections, but the major one is at Shaker Heights, Ohio, where it is looked after by the Shaker Historical Society. Specimens elsewhere are at the Boston Museum of Fine Arts, Winterthur Museum, Delaware and the Philadelphia Museum of Art.

The wide proliferation of lacquered furniture means that the student is generally within easy reach of specimens. The Victoria and Albert Museum, London, has a selection of cabinets and other objects, many of great age but in perfect condition, and the National Museum, Copenhagen, Denmark, possesses specimens, also the Musée Guimet, Paris, the Rijksmuseum, Amsterdam, and, in America, the Cleveland Museum of Art and the Metropolitan Museum of Art, New York.

Flamboyant ormolu can be found, in Britain, at Waddesdon Manor,

Aylesbury, Harewood House, Leeds and the Wallace Collection, London. In France there are specimens in Paris at the Musée des Arts Décoratifs, and the Rijksmuseum, Amsterdam, and the Metropolitan Museum of Art, New York.

Boulle can be seen in London in the Wallace Collection, and in France it is present on specimens in the collection of the Musée des Arts Décoratifs and the Louvre.

KEY PERIODS

English

Late Gothic	1475–1509
Tudor Renaissance	1509–1603
Stuart	1603–1688
William and Mary	1688–1727
Georgian	1765–1810

French

Louis XIV	1643–1715
Regence and Louis XV	1715–1774
Louis XVI	1774–1789
Directoire, Consulate and First Empire	1795–1815

American

William and Mary	1690–1725
Queen Anne	1725–1780
Townsend-Goddard	1737–1858
Chippendale	1755–1790
Early Federal	1790–1815
Late Federal	1810–1825
Greek Revival	1825–1840
Gothic Revival and Rococo	1840–1860
Arts and Crafts	1876–1918

A Brief Glossary of Terms

ABRASIVES describes a number of materials, such as sandpaper, employing the use of glass, flint, garnet, aluminous oxide and certain other materials in various grades. Used for reducing surfaces and smoothing wood and other substances.

ACETATE consists of types of alcohol and acetic acid, comprising nitro-cellulose solvents, used in the plastic coating of wood.

ACID DYES refers to aniline colours which react to acid.

ACID STAINS are water soluble.

AGEING is a term used in one of two senses, the first being the action which occurs when varnish and oil are stored together for a certain time, after which they can be mixed to a smooth consistency. The second use of the word is in the antiques trade to the process of deliberately distressing a piece of furniture or a wooden object in such a way as to make it appear old, although the wood itself may be contemporary.

ANILINE is used to denote a substance which is derived from coal tar, as in many modern wood stains and dyes.

BEAUMONTAGE consists of shellac in the form of a stick or lump, available in many different colours and similar to sealing wax. Used by wood finishers to fill bruises and dents in wood.

BLEACH refers to any material capable of lightening the surface of the wood, including chloride of lime in solution, a two-stage bleach or the domestic variety used more commonly for lavatory cleaning.

BLEACHING LACQUER is a misnomer but still in general use in the trade. It refers to a lacquer which is used to seal the surface and acts as a barrier to a filler which may darken the surface.

BLUSH is a slang term referring to an imperfection of a lacquered surface which is caused as a rule by application of pumice or some other abrasive too soon after the lacquer has been applied.

BLOOM refers to the white cloudiness which materialises on a lacquered surface, caused as a rule by humidity or atmospheric dampness or, when the lacquer is applied, when it is carried into the wood by the velocity of the air from the spraygun nozzle.

BURNING-IN is the phrase used to describe the application of beaumontage by heating the material and applying it with the knife.

CARNAUBA WAX, also known as Brazilian wax, melts at 185 degrees Fahrenheit. It is the hardest of all the polishing waxes.

CLEAR FLAT varnish which dries dull without any gloss or sheen; is applied in the usual way.

CLEAR GLOSS is a varnish which dries to a mirror finish.

COLOUR-IN-JAPAN means that a colour is mixed with japan drier.

COLOUR-IN-OIL means that the colour is mixed with linseed oil.

CRACKLE FINISH is created by applying a base coat of lacquer followed by a top coat which contracts and crackles. It is usually done in two contrasting colours, suggesting an Oriental lacquer finish.

DECALOMANIA is a method of taking printed designs from a special paper base and transferring them to wood.

DEWAXED SHELLAC is used in the making of french polish. It is also known as bleached shellac.

DRYING OILS can be applied to a surface to effect drying in about 48 hours, and they are used as a shield from dust and dampness.

EARTH PIGMENTS includes the principal colours which are derived from the earth, such as ochre, umber, sienna and Vandyke brown.

ENAMEL includes the paint-like fluids which are brushed on to a surface and do not bear brush marks. Although true enamel dries to an exceptional hardness, the use of the term has in recent years become ambiguous so that nowadays it means very little. Even quite ordinary paints are now and then referred to by some manufacturers as enamels.

FILLERS is a material made from china clay, silica, powdered mica and whiting, and is used to fill the wood pores prior to the application of lacquer, shellac or varnish.

FRENCH POLISH is liquified shellac applied to wood for a finish.

GLAZING is a method of applying transparent pigments to painted surfaces to create a blended effect.

GRAINING is a technique used to imitate the grain of wood, using various paints and pigments and using such tools as combs and brushes.

HIGHLIGHTING is a technique used in antiques restoration and the reproduction furniture trade in which some areas are lightened to provide a contrast with other darker areas.

JAPAN DRIER is a varnish gum to which salts have been added to accelerate the drying time.

LACQUER contains nitrocellulose with certain solvents and gum resins.

LACQUER ENAMEL is a coloured lacquer.

LEAFING is a trade term which means the process of applying gold, silver or bronze leaf to the surface of the wood. It also applies to cheaper methods, such as the application of metal particles in liquid suspension to impart a gold leaf effect.

LINSEED OIL is one of the staple materials used in wood finishing. It is made from the oil discharged from crushed flax seed. Available in two varieties, one being raw linseed oil, and the second consisting of the oil heated by the manufacturer and with the addition of driers, and known as boiled linseed oil. The second is more generally used in the wood finishing trade.

MARBLING is a novelty process in which the colours are floated on water and then transferred to the surface of the wood by dipping. Also applies to a marble effect which is executed with a worn feather.

MINERAL SPIRITS is derived from petroleum and it is used for dissolving paint, varnish and other materials.

NAPHTHA is distilled from petroleum and is used for the cleaning of painted, varnished and enamelled surfaces.

NEUTRAL OIL is sometimes erroneously referred to as mineral oil. It is a thin substance, used as a medium with pumice stone or powder when dulling down varnished surfaces by rubbing.

OIL COLOURS are the pigments which are used for touching up and are generally used with boiled linseed oil.

OIL SOLUBLES refers to any substance which can be dissolved in oil. In the wood finishing trade they refer to a range of colours called oil-yellow, oil-red, and so on.

OIL STAINS mean the penetrating tints which are used to colour wood. In some finishing workshops the term 'pigment oil-stain' is used to define the use of a pigment which is used in conjunction with a binder and linseed oil.

PASTE FILLER consists of silica or similar dense material mixed with turpentine and used to fill the pores of the wood before other treatment, such as shellacking or varnishing.

PATINA is the appearance on furniture of signs of wear, such as the naturally created highlights and a generally mellow appearance.

PEARL ESSENCE is the incorporation of minute fish scales in a lacquer to produce pearl lacquer.

PLYWOOD SEALER is a special lacquer-type material for use on plywood.

POLISHING VARNISH is a material designed specifically to produce a very high sheen when rubbed with pumice powder or some other abrasive.

POWDER STAINS describes the range of colours available in powder form for mixing with water, oil or spirit.

ROTTENSTONE is an ultra-fine material used for polishing, but it is not an especially effective abrasive.

RUBBING OIL is a mineral oil which is used in conjunction with pumice powder for rubbing down lacquered and varnished surfaces.

SPIRIT STAINS are pigments which can be dissolved in methylated spirit.

VARNISH STAIN is the name of a material used for a rapid finish on inferior woodwork, and is used mainly to protect it from dampness.

WATER STAINS are pigments which can be dissolved in water.

Suppliers of Materials

This is by no means an exhaustive list of suppliers, but is included for the craftsman who wishes to obtain specialist materials. The more common materials are available from ironmongers, builder's supply merchants and painter's and decorator's suppliers.

Berger, Jenson and Nicholson Ltd
Freshwater Road
Dagenham
Essex
Will deal with written applications for advice on paints suitable for graining and colour combing. No telephone enquiries.

John Boddy and Son (Timber) Ltd
Riverside Sawmills
Boroughbridge
North Yorkshire YO5 9LJ
tel: 09012 2370
Specialist suppliers of English oak and other British hardwoods. A useful source when a piece has to be matched in.

Clam-Brummer Ltd
Maxwell Road
Borehamwood
Herts
tel: 953 2992
Manufacturers of filler in matching colours for all types of wood.

Colourways
70 Alderman's Hill
London N13
Stock various undercoats, transparent oil glaze and gold, silver and bronze leaf.

Construction and Engineering
   Company Ltd
Faraway House

Pygons Hill Lane
Lydiate
Merseyside L31 4AE
Supply patent stripping compound and stripping installations, including tanks and chemicals.

Crown Decorative Advisory Bureau
Hollins Road
Darwen BB3 0BG
Lancashire
tel: 0254 74951
Advice on paints suitable for graining and colour combing.

English Abrasives Ltd
PO Box 85
Marsh Lane
London N17 0XA
tel: 808 4545
Manufacturers of all types of sandpaper and other abrasives.

Fellowship of Makers and Restorers
   of Historical Instruments
7 Pickwick Road
Dulwich Village
London SE21 7JN
Reference source for information on the restoration of old musical instruments, including surface finishes. No telephone enquiries.

Fiddes and Son Ltd
Trade Street
Cardiff
tel: 0222 23047

Suppliers of polishes, fillers, stains, polyurethanes and spirits.

Henry Flack and Son Ltd
Borough Works
Elmers End
Beckenham
Kent
tel: 650 9171
Manufacturers of french polish, cellulose, spirit, varnishes, stains and wax polishes.

Furniglas Ltd
Birchwood Industrial Estate
Great North Road
Hatfield
Herts AL9 5JU
tel: Hatfield 65358
Manufacturers of polyurethane stain and french polish.

Gedge and Company (Clerkenwell) Ltd
see
John Myland Ltd
Stock rottenstone, pumice and a large range of stains.

General Woodwork Supplies Ltd
76 Stoke Newington High Street
London N16
tel: 254 4543
All branded materials, including stains, varnishes and polishes.

F A Heller and Company Ltd
24 The Pavements
London SW4 0JA
Stock many types of brushes.

House of Harbru
Common Lane Industrial Estate
Wath-on-Dearne
Rotherham
S. Yorks
tel: 0709 874887

Manufacturers and suppliers of specialist cleaning, polishing and restoring aids, including: french polishes, varnishes, fillers and dyes, waxes, pumice and bleaches.

ICI
PO Box 15
Newton Works
Hyde
Cheshire
tel: 061 368 8321
Advice on paints suitable for graining and colour combing.

Langlo Products Ltd
PO Box 32
Langlo Works
Asheridge Road
Chesham
Bucks
tel: 02405 784866
Manufacturers of polishers, strippers, preservatives and stains.

A Leete and Company Ltd
129 London Road
London SE21
tel: 928 5283
Specialists in all types of varnishes, stains and brushes, also pumice and other abrasives.

Liberon Waxes Ltd
7 Park Street
Lydd
Kent
tel: Lydd 20107
Suppliers of a complete range of finishing products including strippers, bleaches, fillers, waxes, varnishes, french polishes, brushes and steelwool.

John Myland Ltd
80 Norwood High Street
London SE27 9NN
tel: 670 9161
All materials for every type of surface finishing, including dyes, lacquers and specialist brushes.

The Orton Trust
Stoa House, High Street
Brigstock, Kettering
Northamptonshire
tel: 053673 253
The disused church of Orton is used for weekend courses in carving, restoration and finishing.

E Parson and Sons Ltd
Blackfriars Road
Nailsea, Bristol BS19 2BU
Stock wood dyes, varnishes, stains and french polish.

E Ploton (Sundries) Ltd
273 Archway Road
London N6 5AA
Stock a large range of pigments, gold, silver and bronze leaf, and metallic powders.

J H Radcliffe and Company Ltd
135A Linaker Street, Southport
Merseyside, PR8 5DR
Stock transparent oil glaze, special-use brushes, graining combs, metal leaf and specialised oil glaze.

Rentokil Advice Centre
Freepost: East Grinstead
West Sussex, RH19 2BR
Advice on how to deal with the infestation of furniture.

Rustins Ltd
Drayton Works, Waterloo Road

London NW2
tel: 450 4666
Manufacturers of the complete range of finishing materials, including two-stage bleach, methylated spirit and stains.

Simpsons Paints Ltd
122–124 Broadley Street
London NW8
Stock transparent oil glaze, metal leaf and pigments.

Sterling Roncraft
Chapeltown
Sheffield S30 4YP
tel: 0742 467171
Proprietary restorers, revivers and liquid waxes for restoration work.

Turnbridge Manufacturing Co.
72 Longley Road, Tooting
London SW17
tel: 672 6581
Manufacturers of the Joy range of products: stains, polishes, preservatives and scratch remover.

Wilcot Company Ltd
Fishponds
Bristol BS16 2BQ
tel: 0272 653256
Manufacturers of stripping compounds.

Paul Winner Marketing
  Communications Ltd
Strode House
44–50 Osnaburgh Street
London NW1 3DN
Provides an advisory service regarding a range of french polish, stains and high-grade specialist polyurethanes, also woodwork adhesive and hardset finish, which is heat-resistant and solvent proof.

Index